of the Great Reset

Questions

Martin Liedtke

BewleyBooks

The Holy Grail of the Great Reset - Questions
First published in 2021 by
© BewleyBooks.com

All rights reserved.
© Martin Liedtke 2021

The right of Martin Liedtke to be identified as author
of this work has been asserted in accordance with Section 77
of the Copyright, Design and Patents Act 1988

This book is sold subject to the condition that it shall not, by way of trade or otherwise, be lent, resold, hired out or otherwise circulated without the publisher's prior consent in any form of binding or cover other than that in which is it published and without a similar condition including this condition being imposed on the subsequent purchaser.

Cover Design by: Angie Alaya
Cover Photography by: Melanie Helen (Melage)

Digital ISBN: 978-1-909426-49-8
Paperback ISBN: 978-1-909426-57-3

PUBLISHER'S NOTE

The chapters presented in this book are transcripts from Martin Liedtke's YouTube channel. For the titles to each chapter, please see the references in the Appendix section of the book.

Please also note that a publisher's role is to remain impartial and may not necessarily agree with an author's views, descriptions or observations or uphold all of the content explored. However, BewleyBooks works on the premise that all avenues of education should be sought and explored, and the reader should be able to learn whatever interests them and, from that learning, make their own informed decisions along their life's journey.

www.BewleyBooks.com

DEDICATION

I dedicate this book to my son, Laurence, for being my rock through hard times.

IMPORTANT INFORMATION

Digital purchases: This book will be updated continually. If you spot an amendment that needs to be made, please notify us and we will endeavour to alter it. For this reason, Amazon and other digital book platforms offer a service to their readers to 'push' the new version of the updated book. To update your digital book, please send a request to the company you bought your digital content from and ask them to 'push' or 'update' your version of the book. You may need to ask the company if you need to delete the old version from your digital reading device. Updates are announced in the BB+ newsletter available for free from BewleyBooksPlus.com.

While creating Martin's first book, *The Holy Grail of Our Flat Earth*, Martin's channel was hacked and he lost most of his videos. His publisher, BewleyBooks, also had much of the work stolen by hackers and viruses were sent through downloadable files. Thankfully, both author and publisher worked through and managed to produce a book that offered a reasonable amount of content. This, *The Holy Grail of the Great Reset*, is Martin's second book which was, again, not without problems from outside enemies. Many hackers have attempted to stop the information getting out to Martin's supporters, his loyal followers and the general public. We believe the people (and bots) who tried to ruin this work did not reckon on the persistence on our side and also a protection from a higher source. In the end, both author and publisher have managed to push through the hurdles in order to give to you an idea as to humanity's alternative history.

PRAISE FOR THE HOLY GRAIL OF OUR FLAT EARTH

A completely different perspective on this place we call Earth. We live in a reset bubble. Our history is what we are told. The dates we live by are false, how this place works is a lie. This book allows you to comprehend how and why such a trick has been played over and over again on humanity. After you read it, then you will never think about things the same way again. Martin's YouTube channel contains hours of backup evidence, and this book is a good introduction to how this plane really works and how if you manipulate history, you control the populace.
Gillypoof

A reminder that we live in a wonderful plane, where the mystery of life and living is an oft kept secret. Excellent introduction to the occult and filled with lesser thought questions. Definitely one for the soul.
Cassie

Fabulous xxx *Mrs C. Ballard*

Love this book and all the questions it awoke within me. *Sweetlise*

L'ho divorato. Grande Martin. *Pachinko32*

Very well written book. Eye-opening material to get your brain thinking. Our past is different from what we've been told, and the information in this book is fantastic. *PacificNorthwest360*

Martin (FEB) truly is awakening humanity and so full of positivism, one can't not love him or his dedication. Very well written. TONS of Epic information. Has changed the way I see everything. It means so much to me. Martin has truly opened my eyes. I recommend this book to anyone and everyone. Sit back, fasten your seatbelt and hold on for the ride of your life! Much love. *Michelle G*

Very well researched and written. Start here if you seriously want to know WHY many people, who are not stupid or particularly religious, have decided that the scientific evidence to support a spinning space pear of a planet that has as sun zillions of miles away and yet we still get night time etc. All the answers are here, and this guy earned his spot as the sharpest mind on this topic as this is the manhole cover to the rabbit hole where the Earth being a flat plane is the ladder. This is your chance for an adventure with so much compelling content that you appreciate – as it gives you a break from your brain exploding over and over with these well-researched opinions. This is the start of the adventure. Just thank Martin for having the guts to write this. *Darren Cox*

This book answers many questions we didn't even know to ask. It is very informative and the author, Martin Liedtke, is a genuine researcher who asks the questions that have needed to be asked.   *Marcia in Michigan*

The Holy Grail of the Great Reset

Questions

Martin Liedtke

BewleyBooks

CONTENTS

ACKNOWLEDGEMENTS
FORWARD
QUESTION THE NARRATIVE
HIGH SCHOOL LIFE

PREFACE
QUESTIONING THE NARRATIVE
THE GLOBE LIE
OPENING MINDS WITH QUESTIONS
ME, AS A FLAT EARTHER
A SPIRITUAL AWAKENING?
TIME TO REVAMP THE SYSTEM?

INTRODUCTION 1
WHERE DO I BEGIN? 1
What's it all about? 2
They can never stop the truth 5
Our Souls Know 7
Protesting People 8
PIECING TOGETHER THE PAST 9
The law of entropy 10
My intentions 11
Timescales? 13
A New Dawn? 14
The level of the lie 17
SO, WHAT'S IN IT FOR ME? 17
What do you want? 18

1. IS HISTORY A LIE? 21

How ancient is ancient? 26
Are Ancient Civilisations recent? 27
ANCIENT TECHNOLOGY? 30
India and Arabia 31
The Americas 33
Europe 34
Inner Science 36
POSSIBLE RESET DATE? 37
The Greenland Theory 38
The Power of Rome 40
The Great Fire of London 43
The Last Crusade 46
HISTORY IS A LIE 47
Castles and Chandeliers 49
Cowboys and Indians 52
The Streets of San Francisco 54
MEDIA IS A LIE 57
SPACE IS A LIE 60
THE RESET GENERATION 62

2. ARE THE ANSWERS IN ARCHITECTURE? 64

Nature and buildings 65
Asian East 69
The Americas 71
Puma Punka and Easter Island 72
Africa 74
BUILT BY GIANTS? 75
Castles and Star Forts 78
Empty Cities 85
The Mental Asylums 86
The vanished expositions 87
Brunel 90
Train Stations 91
Ports and Palaces 93
ANCIENT CLUES 96
Qibla compass 99
Electricity conductors 101
Advanced energy? 103

    Magnetic Water *110*
    Resonance *115*
    Evidence of advanced high cultures? *116*
   ARE WE GOING BACKWARDS? 119
    Entropy – nature's way *120*
    Destruction – humankind's way *121*
    Re-writing history *124*

3. ART OF THE APOCALYPSE 128

    The Sutton Hoo Hoard – 0004 .... *130*
    Hieronymus Bosch – i500s *132*
    Giovanni Battista Piranesi – i700s *134*
    Camille Flammarion - i800s *136*
    Gallica Books *141*
    Decoding music *141*
    Artistic clues *142*

4. WHAT DO THE MAPS REVEAL? 146

    Buddhist Maps - i000s *147*
    Mappa Mundi – i200s *149*
    The Piri Reis Map – i500s *150*
    The Azimuthal Maps *151*
    The theatre of the sky and earth *152*
    Arab Maps *153*
    A cataclysm? *153*

5. HOW OLD IS PHOTOGRAPHY? 156

    Photography of the i800s *156*
    Three-Legged Horse sand Vanilla Skies *158*
    Egypt *160*
   TIME LIFE MAGAZINE 166
    People *166*
    Buildings *168*
    Vehicles – Air, Sea and Land *170*
   WHAT'S THE TRUE AGE OF PHOTOGRAPHY? ...171
    Link to Freemasonry *172*
   A VERY PECULIAR DISCOVERY 176
   JUST FOR LAUGHS 177

6. WHO ARE THE MAJOR PLAYERS? 181

- NOSTRADAMUS A FLAT EARTHER? 182
  - *The Bible Code* 185
  - *Remote viewing* 186
  - *Greenhouse Effect* 187
  - *Timeline Tweaking* 188
  - *Controlled thinking* 189
- KING HENRY VIII 190
  - *Agincourt and the Somme* 193
- SABBATAI THE 17TH CENTURY ANTI-CHRIST 195
  - *Shabbatean Movement* 197
  - *Christopher Wren* 198
  - *The Carnegies' & The Astors'* 199
  - *Rothschilds* 200
  - *Mad King George III* 200
  - *New World Order?* 201
  - *Aliens?* 201
- THE TALE OF THREE COUSINS 202
  - *Prince of Wales, King George V* 203
  - *Kaiser Wilhelm* 205
  - *Tsar Nicholas II of Russia* 209
- MY LOCAL AREA 213
- HOW DO THEY RESET HISTORY? 214

7. WHAT PART DOES SATAN PLAY? 219

- BETWIX THE DEVIL AND THE DEEP BLUE SEA 219
- SATANIST DATES AND BRITISH DISASTERS 228
  - *Aberfan Disaster* 229
  - *The Hillsborough Crush* 229
  - *Lockerbie Disaster* 230
  - *Dunblane School Massacre* 230
- THE VATICAN ARCHIVES 231
  - *What's hidden in the archives?* 234
  - *Hitler and the Vatican* 236

8. WHY ARE WE ALWAYS AT WAR? 238

- DID THE JESUITS PLAY BOTH SIDES? 238
- SEVEN YEARS WAR 243
  - *Lisbon* 244
  - *Plagues* 246
  - *Strange phenomena* 247

The Ice Age	248
A species in amnesia	251
Indus Valley	251
LEST WE FORGET	255
The Peterloo Massacre	256
The Dresden War Crime	260
FLAGS & NATIONALISM – IS IT ALL TO DIVIDE US?	266
BOMBING ALL OVER THE WORLD	266
LOCAL 'COLD WAR' HOAX BUNKERS	269
LSD in Wales	270

9. ARE WE HUMAN GUINEA PIGS? 272

IN-HUMAN ABILITIES?	273
WAS THE BUBONIC PLAGUE A HOAX?	274
ALCHEMY	278
Hearts of Gold	283
Wigs	289
RITUAL MAGIC AND CHANGES IN CONSCIOUSNESS	293
Himmler's Castle	294
Blood Flag	295
Essenes	297
5G - FASCES RESETS TO BEDLAM	298
Renaissance of Resonance	301
Mental Illness Linked to Technology?	304
DAMAGING OUR ESSENCE	308
Memory in Water	315
YOUR CHILDREN'S FUTURE	317

10. THE GREAT RESETS 319

HISTORY, BUT NOT AS WE KNOW IT	321
UNESCO	323
Stories of gentle giants?	324
Why destroy history?	326
The Phoenician Death Cult	327
Other evidence of a Great Reset	328
HISTORY REPEATING ITSELF	329
Technology from another era?	330
Clues to our past in films?	332
Reverse-engineered technology?	334
Polar Flipping	340

    Fashions and products we buy *341*

11. IS THERE AN ANSWER? 343

OUR AWAKENING 343
    Brave Truthers *345*
    Martin's Mindset *346*
    Spread the Healing *347*
RESET SCENARIOS 348
STATION OF CREATION 349
SO, WHAT'S THE TRUTH? 350

APPENDIX 357

ARE YOU AWAKENING YOUR DIVINITY? 357
    Body aches and pains *358*
    Feelings of deep inner sadness. *358*
    Crying for no apparent reason. *359*
    Sudden change of career *359*
    Withdrawal from family *359*
    Unusual sleep patterns *360*
    Intense dreams *360*
    Physical disorientation *361*
    Increased self-talk *361*
    Feelings of loneliness *362*
    Loss of passion *362*
    A deep longing to go home *363*
ARE YOU READY? 363
WAKE UP PEOPLE! 364

REFERENCES & LINKS 365

VIDEOS TRANSCRIBED: 366

ABOUT THE AUTHOR 377

FROM THE PUBLISHER 381

ACKNOWLEDGEMENTS

There are a lot of people in this world I am grateful for, without their persistence and patience, it would not have been possible to produce this book. However, there are a few dedicated people who have been with me all the way through this work and I would like to offer them my special thanks.

Lee FEB, for his priceless contribution.

Igor from St Petersburg in Russia, has been a great supporter. I want to thank him for being there. Effing awesome.

Serge, from Russia, who's sent me some brilliant info for Flat Earth British Think Tank.

UAP for loads of support and loads of intelligent information. Impressed.

Mel who has not only been a great support to me over the years but has also provided this book's cover photograph. Cheers Mel.

The translation team spend their valuable time deciphering the ancient manuscripts to find out what's in them and Matt Ferguson, from Vermont, in Americaland, has been ultra busy. So I want to give a special thanks to Matt and his lovely wife, thanks guys.

Angie Alaya of pro-covers, for the beautiful cover image that she has created. Thanks Angie, you're a star!

Kaye Bewley, my publisher, who worked hard at translating my chatty style into something more readable, and then putting it all into a book. Cheers, much appreciated.

Martin Liedtke, 2021

FORWARD

QUESTION THE NARRATIVE
Do you ever get that feeling that things aren't quite right and there may be people hiding information from us? Manipulating the story of who we are and what our true past is?

Just look at the year we had in Z020, it is enough to make even the most docile human question the reality that we are given by the mainstream and those in positions of power. If you're one of those people who question the narrative we are given, then let me assure you, you are in the right place and this book is definitely for you.

Martin Liedtke is a thorough and tireless researcher into the historical narrative and the nature of our reality. He delves deep into hidden history with his research uncovering historical anomalies to show how the story we are given of our past is clearly not true. With a passion for truth, Martin is prepared to go where the research takes him, a place most researchers of history won't go for fear of upsetting the mainstream and the accepted narrative.

Researching topics including the mud flood Theory, star forts, ancient technology (Antiquitech) and historical resets, Martin shows us that our past was much more fantastic than the history books tell us, or should we say His-Story books? His research also helps to tell the true story of who we are and what can be achieved when we work together without the restrictions of the powers that want to be.

Hang on tight this will be quite a ride.

Cambell Purvis 'Autodidactic' 2021

HIGH SCHOOL LIFE

Few of us have a bad memory of the times when we were in high school. Many consider their life in college to have been the best part, but in my opinion, high school was better because there was more fun and less workload. Our bodies underwent a series of changes during those years, the boys turned into young men, while the girls blossomed into beautiful women.

At that point, we were already immersed in memories enough to remind teachers when they told us that learning math and physics would save our lives. The other subjects, sooner or later, would have prepared us for the future by providing us with a robust cultural background.

High school was a stronghold for the mind in which to take refuge whenever we needed it.

This happiness also depended on the absolute

confidence we had in the truthfulness of what we were taught. In those joyous times, we were too distracted by living to doubt what the glossy and shimmering textbooks contained.

But what if we had discovered that much of what was taught and studied was the fruit of imagination? Things would never be the same inside our little world.

With this book, *The Holy Grail of the Great Reset,* Martin Liedtke proceeds to a 'controlled demolition' of our deepest convictions, dating back to times even before high school: that history went exactly as it did in the glossy books we were handed.

In fact, what we know of the ancient Romans we can count on an oral tradition handed down through our ancestors. Are we sure that the story behind ancient temples, obelisks, statues and amphitheatres is the one told by academic texts? After all, what we see in the field is just a bunch of more or less well-preserved buildings.

At High School, we were dazzled by certain sublime masterpieces of classical art, wondering which modern artists would be able to reproduce them. Nonetheless, the timeline is debatable. Would ancient tales such as the Greek and Latin classics, such as the *Iliad* or the *Odyssey*, or the narration of the life and death of Jesus Christ, have survived oblivion for two or three thousand years? Or, are these events that have occurred in more recent periods and someone has cunningly dismissed over time?

A recent survey states that most American adults see the value of higher education in preparing them for progress in their existence. The percentage is expected to increase in the future. Maybe we will want to return to High School to ask the questions that have not been answered in a long time or, perhaps return simply because of the regret of that carefree life. Who can say?

By reading Martin's book, our granite certainties should begin to crumble like a sandcastle, overwhelmed in the high tide. Our historical knowledge needs to be reviewed from A to Z.

Anyway, have a pleasant reading!

Albino Galuppini 2021

PREFACE

I'll give a little bit of info here about my work, what I'm doing and where I'm going with it. You may already know that I produce a video channel called FLAT EARTH BRITISH and that I'm a hard-core Flat Earther. In my mind, enough people are chipping away at NASA, so in between my research, I do what is known as 'Flat Earth Activism'.

Recently, I joined with many other Flat Earthers, which is a hell of a buzz for me and brilliant for team building. The thing is, because of the research I've been doing and the online communities I've gotten involved in, I've been bringing together a big Flat Earth Think Tank which you can check out on my website www.martinliedtke.com

As a result of the things I've unearthed, I wanted to put it together in a format that people could keep. When my publisher, BewleyBooks, offered to put my work into words on the page, I thought our Creator had a hand in getting this noise out to more people, and I thankfully accepted the new challenge.

My first book revealed the secrets to the Flat Earth

and how the Controllers have deceived us. This second book asks many questions about what has happened over the centuries, right up to when marketing was used as a tool to sway people's minds. You might know of men like Edward Bernays and his work into marketing and how it can sway our decisions.

Marketing is the work that operates in the world you see around you through messages about fashions, moods, music, mobiles, and the various products we buy, as well as all the popular trends we are encouraged to follow. You'd think that something like the Hippy Movement came from the imagination of the people, but it didn't. It was a movement led by government agents. You might remember that Timothy Leary told everyone to 'tune in and drop out!' Well, if you follow that advice, you'll find out first-hand how the demonic system encourages you to give up on life and rely on the State. This book is all about this sort of stuff and more.

QUESTIONING THE NARRATIVE
The Holy Grail of the Great Reset asks lots of questions, and while it gives you some answers, mostly, it encourages you to arrive at the current situation with your own thoughts. It's a book that dares to ask how much different government agencies and conglomerate companies have to do with the mess we've gotten into. As far as I know, they bring in many paradigms that people are influenced by, paradigms like fear, such as the Cold War, which never even existed.

Then there's the question of the evolutionary bullshit (I do use a few swear words in this book, so be warned). I say it is bullshit, because you can see that a monkey is still a monkey, and we haven't changed very much over the past few hundred thousand years or so. They also say that our distant relatives were the Neander-nots. Come again?

There's also the Big Bang Theory. Now, what can I say about that? It tells us we've come from nothing and produced all that you see around you today, and we'll go to nothing. I ask you, how is that possible? It is a theory, and that's all it is. It even has 'theory' in the title, which everyone seems to ignore.

We're taught that this universe (which none of us has ever seen), has come from a tiny spec of unreality. Something out of nothing. This is based on the works by Richard Dawkins-type scientists. When I look into that man's eyes, all I see is the devil. People like him can be thought of as profoundly evil when they permeate the lie of evolution and the Big Bang.

Why is the Big Bang such a big deal? Our scientists say everything coalesced and, out of that, consciousness arrived. In my opinion, consciousness was there at the start. Consciousness is eternal. It never goes anywhere. Our spirits, inside our bodies, do not die.

Whatever has happened to us, we seem to be trapped inside a body that seems like a really, really bad sixth-sense deprivation tank. When you look at what a snake can sense with just its tongue or an ant with its pheromones, it just doesn't make any sense that we can use only five senses. Other animals and insects can sense so much more than we can. Why is that?

Regarding the government agencies and corporate giants, social engineering, and the Tavistock Institute, is it possible they have planted people in the Flat Earth movement to eff with us? Have a little think about the people that get up every day, and their main job of the day is to go online and debate their globe viewpoint. It is bullshit they can never prove, so they argue with the Flat Earthers. There's something deeply wrong with these people.

If you don't believe that the Tavistock Institute and social engineering is a real thing, well, I'm afraid they've done a good job on you and you're fast asleep – which is how they want you to be. This isn't a conspiracy, it is not a theory either; this is a reality. Go and visit my online community, the Flat Earth Think Tank, and there you'll see all of the books on social engineering available for you to read. It goes deeper than you can possibly imagine.

Understanding this one small aspect (social engineering) will help you understand a lot of what is going on in the world today. It appears this Institute has no good intention for humanity. I'm not a scaremonger; I'm just telling you the truth as I see it. We all need to wake up to the games that are being played out around us and, if the current 'pandemic' has any good in it or positive points about it, it's only because it's woken up a heck of a lot more people than

I ever could have and I'm grateful for that.

As I said, in this book you'll see that I ask a lot of questions, hence the sub-title. There's a lot of information available, not just online, but in libraries and especially in the ancient books, but how much of that is truth? In the online Flat Earth Think Tank, you'll find lots of links to the old books I reference throughout this one. I put them there so that, even if you lose this book, or if this information gets banned, you'll still get access to them. Visit that website to find out more about this subject and join us in our efforts to help humanity wake up.

THE GLOBE LIE
This book goes over the subjects I've explored in my many videos and in the Reference section at the end you'll see those that have been transcribed (not word for word).

The Holy Grail of the Great Reset is my attempt to figure out the resets humanity has faced not once but many times. Yes, it does seem to have happened time and again. One of the biggest clues to the lies we are being fed is the lie about the shape of our earth.

The false story about our earth (which I refer to as the globe lie) can help us figure out how these resets keep happening and, more importantly, why they are happening. This book is only the beginning; its purpose is to offer a gentle nudge to wake sleeping people up.

To answer the question of why I think our earth is not what we have been told it is, you only have to look at the water. Water always finds a level. The supposed ball that we sit upon is 70% water. If there was a curve, the water would find its level on that ball. Think about a wet tennis ball you throw for your dog. If we were sitting on a spinning ball, the water would just fly off in the same way it does from that tennis ball.

To find out how much of what I say about the flat earth is true, you only have to look at the horizon. From my hometown in Cardiff, Wales, I can see buildings twenty-five miles away, a distance which should be well below the horizon line.

The only thing that limits you is the strength of the optics that you use.

OPENING MINDS WITH QUESTIONS
Though I enjoy doing this work, and I enjoy debating with people who have their minds open, I am getting tired of repeating myself to people who won't open their minds to the possibility of any of it being true. The evidence is there. If only these so-called scientists and academics, who are just trying to justify their income, wouldn't just agree with the narrative that's already there, then we could begin to question everything. Isn't that what science is supposed to be about? They should have the confidence to not only search for the truth but debate other possibilities and validate their findings publicly.

In this book, I'm asking my own questions. I'm asking questions about the historical timeline and how this has happened, how humanity has allowed it to happen and, more importantly, what we can do to stop it from happening again. It's a summary of the work I've done in my videos. Not too much detail, as I don't want to overwhelm you if you're not awake. If you're interested in finding out more, you can always check them out here.

- Martin Liedtke
- The Celtic Tartarian Channel
- The Tartarian Chronicles
- Flat Earth British Think Tank
- Martin Liedtke's Nectar

I think it's awesome that we can come together and figure all these things out for ourselves. If you are just beginning to question what's going on around you, then this book will give you an idea of what's going on so you can start to ask questions of your own and open your mind up to other possibilities.

As this book has been transcribed from my videos, don't have a go at me or my publisher about the grammar. It's me. Raw. In fact, don't worry about anything that these 'up their own arses' type people tell you is right or wrong in the way I've presented this book of my thoughts and the research that the Flat Earth Think Tank has dug up. The education system is not all it's cracked up to be. Most of it is bullshit. There are good teachers out there, but they're few and far between as they're all into this Common Purpose-type Agenda now. All that's needed is for you to open your mind and it will all fall into place.

ME, AS A FLAT EARTHER
A lot has been happening in my life with the Flat Earth British's channel, and I'm getting busier every day. I'm pleased to have found one little corner in Britain, in Glastonbury, where all the people are Flat Earthers, and it's wonderful because I can see our community growing from this.

Anyway, some of the things you'll read in this book may not agree with your way of thinking. That's ok. Don't hate me for it. I have a few 'haters' on my channels, but I don't hate them. There's no need for that in this life. We all have more than enough to deal with. To the people who think I'm off my rocker, I say:

> *"My name is Martin and that's only one letter away from Martian!"*

It's my way of helping them on their way but, I guarantee you, if you stick with me through this book or visit me on my social media channels, you might just find yourself learning something new - not only about yourself but about the world we live in.

A SPIRITUAL AWAKENING?
In my experience as a Flat Earther, I've learned that there's always someone who's going to eff you over.

When I was younger, I was a bit foolish, but I've learned that I'm a high-end empath and, because of that, I felt a lot of pain from the world and tried to correct it. I soon learned it was all part of growing up and it is part of the spiritual awakening pathway that I've been on.

Now, as a Flat Earther, I'm reinventing myself. I've completely turned my life around and have a clear vision in that I know what's going to be happening, and I'm going to focus on making it all come into reality.

This shit can't go on.

I look at what's going on in the world. All our money poured into NASA and CERN and, yet, half the world is starving. Years ago, I came across George Orwell's books, and I took the time to find out about the man. It looks to me more and more like we are living the scenarios he predicted in a fictional story. The point where he says, in *1984*, about the 2+2 = 5, he's using terminology that is being used today. Our memory is messed with, so our minds can be controlled. The lie that has been pulled over our eyes is a big one.

All history is retold for the mindset of today.

I find that all the good people on this earth are desperately trying to get together because of the division that is being made between us through ego. I suppose when people present on YouTube, they get a bit swelly-heady, and you can pick up on that when they do their presentations, but I try not to be like that. I realise I have to be true to myself and not bull-shit myself. I'm as God made me. I'm not trying to be anything other than me. I have some incredible abilities and, just like anyone else, I can do anything I want, if I want. But some people think I'm a bit weird. Why? Perhaps because I say to them:

I'm on a mission from God.

I believe this is the time for humanity to see the world for what it is and it's good to know that we're all having a spiritual awaking. In the last chapter of this book, I've written about recognizing the pathway to a spiritual awakening and the twelve signs that show you are awakening the divinity with you. To me, these things give you a clear sign that you are awakening. Thankfully, it's not only the Flat Earthers who are going through this, it's the Globers too. Some people reveal the mythical history we have. While some still say we are on a planet, the good thing is, I can see many are sitting on the fence. They are hedging their bets. I understand some won't go the whole hog, only because they feel foolish.

To me, this awakening is worldwide.
Plane-wide.

Grenville flat fire in London, UK, woke many people up to what our governments and big businesses are capable of. Though the 'powers that should not be' didn't mean for people to go this route, the covid plandemic has done a lot of good to the world of awakening too. People are beginning to see it all now.

It's plain to me that our Controllers do nasty things just to play humanity against itself. Man against man. Brother against brother. The sad thing is people are still falling for it. Why? Because it's on the television. It's on the radio. It's in the newspapers. It annoys me why many people won't wake up to the lies they are being fed.

I know this is a reality. I'm not being intellectually dishonest. I'm not spreading false models. The truth is, we don't know what the Elite, the 1%, the Controllers, are hiding. We will never know if we continue along the road we are going. We will only know if this turns over to a new day where we can begin to get the answers we need and those answers are locked away in the Vatican Archives, or wherever their vaults are nowadays.

TIME TO REVAMP THE SYSTEM?
Before I go on about this work, I have to talk about the systems we have on this plane. Some people say we have to keep the education system the way it is but, I question how it can carry on. The system we have is broken. If we were to change it, we could consider bringing mysticism schools to the masses. Schools that teach the following subjects:

- 9-10am - Teaching of the ages

- 10-11am - Sacred geometry
- 11-12noon - Appreciation hour
- 1-3pm - Horticulture/food growing
- 3-4pm - What's really going on with nature

No doctrines. No bullshit. No lies. But there would be a few cuss words.

Yet, with these options available, what do you think people would choose? Most, who are not awake, would opt for more academic lies and brainwashing because they want their piece of paper to stick in a frame on the wall.

People say we have to carry on with the banking system, and they can't seem to see how we could possibly carry on without it. But there are so many different ways of living available to us, they still can't see it.

This book aims to get you asking questions about what's going on. With it in your hand, I urge you into action. I hope that you will open your eyes and see the light that's shining in them.

What are the stars but lights?

Some of the things I say in my vlogs and my books help people, and I'm glad about that. I only carry on with this work to do my bit to help humanity open its eyes to another possibility. To another way that this life can be lived. But you know what? It has to start with you.

The important thing is, I've got these ideas and these questions out to you. You have it in your hands. Now all you need to do is just sit back and enjoy having your mind opened.

Oi Peace & love!

Martin Liedtke, 2021

INTRODUCTION

WHERE DO I BEGIN?
The Holy Grail of the Great Reset is my second book and I've enjoyed doing it. I'm just going to be myself in this book. You'll find some subjects that might not make much sense to you but, bear with it, what you've got to do is take in the overall message.

Piecing together the past has never been so exciting. I find lots of good stuff and it's all very interesting. I have had a tremendous lot of help from a Flat Earth Think Tank, which has grown over the years I've been doing this. In my videos, I normally have a little chat first, then I go through all the information that I've received.

What's going on here is that I am essentially a lovely person who bears no harm on anybody, but when I'm faced with globe-believers who pretend that they're on a spinning ball and shout over me as I'm trying to explain something that's going to blast the globe presentation out of the water with a Howitzer, it gets me down a bit.

I have my haters, which I call knobs because they can't seem to see beyond the end of their noses. Mostly, I'm not bothered by the haters and respond to them when the mood takes me.

In this book, I won't be getting myself messed up with any of the haters too deeply but, you'll learn that my development has been televised for everyone's pleasure. All the bad bits, nutty bits, the crying bits, they are all in the videos. It's all good as I don't need to hide anymore, I've never been the hiding type anyway.

I must mention that, in this book (and the previous one), you'll notice I refer to the year as beginning with the letter 'i' or 'z' rather than a number 1 or 2. For instance: i889 instead of 1889, or Z009 instead of 2009. Why do I do this? Because the evidence presented to us tells us the year we are living in is untrue, so why should I acknowledge it? Quotes and dates of books remain unaltered.

What's it all about?
This book, *The Holy Grail of the Great Reset*, explores the questions that keep being raised about the resetting of our history. It asks whether the buildings we see around us today come from a different age, an ancient age and whether water is a source of lost technology that can provide free energy and how wars have been created to keep humanity busy.

In my first book *The Holy Grail of Our Flat Earth*, I explored the evidence that keeps being thrown up, the stuff that shows us the flat plane we live on. This book, my second, continues that exploration, but it digs a bit deeper into the history being kept from us - and why. I ask how a Reset of humanity can keep it in the dark and how it can hide the truth of our potential.

When I first got involved in the Flat Earth community, I began to explore all the ways and methods and means used to hide knowledge from us. How a few lucky people have used that knowledge to improve their lot above and beyond the rest of humanity – leaving us behind.

We're left to wallow in the mud of our own ignorance.

What follows is a summary of comparisons collected from around the world where I try to open closed minds and try to reveal some secrets from our past. Much of that is done by looking at the buildings around us and figuring out how they reveal the secrets that have been deliberately hidden from us. Once you begin to see this, you can't ever forget it. It's like being told not to imagine an elephant. Go on, try it, now I've told you not to. You can't, can you!

My last book closed with an exploration of Amsterdam. Amsterdam offers clues as to how the Controllers reset our history and how that knowledge was used to create cities with power and energy beyond our current imagination. In Amsterdam and other cities around the world, we are left with the ruins of Star Fort systems and Roman Amphitheatres, all of these give clues of a hidden energy system. The biggest clue as to human abilities throughout this hidden history is in the amazing architecture that remains all over the world. They are finely decorated, beautiful and ornate and, after you've read this book, just like I told you not to imagine the elephant above, you won't be able to not to see them anymore.

We are told that most of the big buildings we see about us today were constructed in the Victorian era, the i800s, but photography reveals this to be a lie. You usually find that styles of buildings are very similar in structure throughout the world, particularly in America and Europe. The strange thing is, at some time before or during the early i900s, many of these buildings were destroyed very quickly. Sometimes stone and metal were burned to dust in a day. No trace of them was left behind, except the evidence of them is shown in the old photographs from the i800s. Another thing I revealed in my first book was the lack of roads that should have led up to these fantastic buildings.

In *The Holy Grail of Our Flat Earth*, I revealed how churches, cathedrals and places of religious worship are always built on or near water. I briefly explored the element of water being used as an energy source. Here, in *The Holy Grail of the Great Reset*, I ask questions about the results you get. I question how, if, and when humans were capable of creating such structures.

The huge water flows as well as controlled mud floods hold a big key as to what has happened to previous civilisations. You'll find that water is very important, especially for the use of energy.

I also explored how water was used for far more than drinking and washing in. It has always been all about the water. The Coliseum in Rome, for example, was not really for Gladiators to kill one another in. No. It was a highly advanced reservoir or water storage area – a water tank if you like. If these huge water tanks were used to begin the floods, these would have been a very effective weapon for the depopulation of the area.

The architecture of the buildings, where the water was kept, linked into the sound waves. The style of the architecture was made specifically for their resonance. Those sound waves were captured by fantastic machinery but, sadly, we've now lost that technology. However, the clues are still there, especially in the churches.

While I'm aware that none of us knows how any of this works, we don't know where the water comes from, we don't know how the earth works, this is a good thing. Why? Because it means it's all open for debate.

They can never stop the truth
So, what is it that makes you believe that something is up? The fact that evil people have shown everything that has ever been given to you. There are now so many people coming over to this way of thinking, it's like a tsunami - and it's going to get bigger. There's nothing that can stop this information coming out now – unless they are ruthless enough to end it for all

of us in another Great Reset.

People tell me that they look at the moon, the stars, the sun, the eclipses etc., but I must say, the answers are not in the sky. We can't get up there, so it's a waste of effing time. Don't even go there. The sky is pretty, I grant you that. The little white lights up there are stunning, I know, but the circumstances do not exist for us to live up there.

Consider this, what's the highest thing these NASA scientists have got? Bar their pretending rockets, which do not go up there, let's say they have the V2 Bomber. That flies at 74,000 feet, but it has wings like a football pitch to hold it up there because the air is so pathetically thin and cold and hot – all at the same time.

Space is a no-no. Think about it. How can it be boiling and freezing all at the same time? How does that work? We're told all the atoms and particles are spaced out individually and layered and basically, they come together at different times. How? Because, we're told, they have a memory. They're clever waves and I'm nuts. It's all nuts.

What about the atmosphere? It's being kept away from the apparent vacuum. There's no barrier between them yet, we're told, they exist - but a vacuum has a sucking nature. Have you seen how a petrol can squashes when there's no air? So, why doesn't it suck our atmosphere away when there's no barrier between them?

These scientists hope that the people like you and me won't ever sit down and think about this. You won't have the time to sit and work it all out. Wars have been created to keep us away from thinking about this. World War One, World War Two, World War Three – well, yes, it's sort of World War Three right now, isn't it. There might not be any bombs going off or bullets being fired, but it's more of a psychological warfare, a war for our minds and emotions.

These wars are designed to trap the human consciousness and mind into more pressing matters, like surviving. Why? So you don't think about the environment you are living in. You only have to look around you right now to know this is the truth.

Our Souls Know
I don't have to go too deep with some people. It's a soul thing. God gave us our best tool: Intuition. So, our souls know.

Everything presented to us has been made up by evil people who don't give an eff for us.

If you have any doubts about the despotic state that's around you and the powers and how they control and enslave the masses, take a look at my YouTube channel. It's constantly under attack. Subs being taken away, material Copyrighted when it shouldn't be. Yet, I say nothing wrong. I show how people are being divided and I try to get them together without fighting. I try to bring people together with love. So, where's the problem with that? There's more violence on the streets than there is on my video channel.

Protesting People
Major protests are happening around the world. Nearly every day, something is going on somewhere on this beautiful plane that we're living on. The mainstream media presents these people as 'anti-capitalist individuals' or 'far right' or 'far left' groups. But they're just ordinary people, like you and me, and they are just sick of the shit that's been shovelled on them.

Many of the protests are demonstrations against what is seen as a 'global government' or a 'new world order' – and they cite apocalyptic speeches from Presidents, Prime Ministers and the like. Trump's speech mentioned something like "Whether the West has the will to survive", which tells me that Western civilisation is in trouble.

In these riots, demonstrations and protests, many thousands, even millions, of people all over the world have been saying no to all of this. But do our governments listen? Not to the people. Governments the world over are listening to big business conglomerates who are whispering in their ears.

Except, they're not whispering anymore.

They're openly stating what they want to happen. Even Klaus Schwab, the Leader of the Economic Forum, has published a book about *The Great Reset* and what the Elite want to happen in the world – according to their plans.

> *"You will own nothing, and you will be happy" The World Economic Forum*

Most of the demonstrations are peaceful. Women, men, children, grandmas and grand-dads with their dogs all take a walk with their homemade banners along the streets of their home counties and they say they don't want what is happening. Good on them. Even the police (in beautiful, brave Italy, at least) have been shown to join them.

What are we to make of it all? Is it a government operation to incite the masses into what is seemingly a good thing – that people are waking up? Or is it something more sinister? Is it to get us to fight each other so that they can bring in their police state? The questions you have to ask are:

- Who organises these marches?
- Where do they get the funds from?
- How do they shut down the streets for these demos?

Because it ain't cheap!

PIECING TOGETHER THE PAST
In this book, I try to make sense of the past outside of the given historical narrative. As Martin of Flat Earth

British, I have all good intentions to make some sense of the historical timeline but, for all those good intentions on my vlog, you need to bear with me at times. There's no production company in my house, it's just me, a bloke in his home, juggling his thoughts, trying to present a narrative to those who will hear me out.

There's an awful lot to cover and I try to lay it all out in some order. I do swear, I try not to, but there's always going to be some words that slip through now and again. I'm not apologising, because that's me. I've got friends who watch over me and, while that gives me a nervous kind of energy, it's a good thing. You can always contact me through my email and I'm always happy to hear from you.

The law of entropy
When you look closely at the evolution theme, the scientists tell us it exists, but Tom Campbell (a scientist I respect), wrote a book called *My Big Toe,* which showed me how the law of entropy would cancel out the law of evolution.

I mention in this book how entropy tackles buildings. To me, entropy would run at a similar rate as in the decay of matter, as in the evolutionary process of the coalition of the universe – and they would cancel each other out. That means, if you go with the accepted narrative of the physics model we have from today's science, the universe ceases to exist.

Crazy stuff, so I won't go too much into that. If you

want to know more about it, I urge you to get Tom's book for more detail on the subject. Though I have brought that up as a point in some of my vlogs, to my knowledge, it has never been brought into anyone's consciousness.

The thing is, I do see this whole thing, this Great Reset, as a war. The reason I'm writing about this is that we've had all this hidden from us and I aim to find out and break up the historical timeline. More and more, every day, I'm finding out what has happened, and I'm presenting it to you as best I can with the tools I've got. I am getting somewhere with it, but I need to present my information multiple times over through different methods so people can understand it.

With the information that has been put together in the Flat Earth Think Tank, it can be proved that there has been a cover-up. It can also be proved that it's all a high-end psychological operation to keep us asleep. Never mind the scientific quibble, as that could go on forever and we could be chasing tails with silly arguments, so try not to get tangled up in this.

In this book, I dig to try to find out when and where it all happened. The clues are out there, you just have to know where to look, you have to use your discerning mind and you have to ask the right questions.

My intentions
In the following chapters I run through some ideas that have been brought to my attention by other

people. I have some good positive plans and, as I'm the type of person who likes something to look forward to, I do get excited when I get the bit between my teeth. I love the buzz of creating something that's of interest to others. What I've noticed is that when I'm on YouTube, people who are on the outside looking in, think, "Who are they? They're really interesting!" and then they join, making the group bigger and bigger. That's one of the aims of my video channels, to show people that I'm a normal person with everyday problems of my own. I might moan for a bit, but I usually rise above all the shit that happens.

Another one of my aims is to open up the debate about what we've been discovering, which is all very intriguing. I also aim to take the hate away from the people who are hating the Jews. Why? All this hating on a race, any race, is hateful, and that's not what Flat Earthers are about. It's not what I'm about.

There are people at the top permeating hate and I'm getting a bit concerned about the hate that's going on. What I'm doing is digging myself in so I can find out what certain people are really telling us and whether it's the truth. More often than not, we find people jump straight to the Jews and the Zionists and blame all the worlds ails on them solely. Well, when I discovered this, I found out that's not so. I thought if I got it out there and told people what's accurate, then they couldn't keep pointing the finger at people who are victims of their country, the same way we British are victims of our country. The thing is…

*...we're not to blame for our shit
government and they're not to blame for
their shit government. We're all just
people in our houses trying to live a decent
life.*

When you look around you, you have to admit this has to be the stupidest reset generation of all time. This is the final frontier. There is one good thing about the current Great Reset, it's that it is revealing the truth about the world and who runs it. Anything that you find and anything that you think about, let me know and I'll make sure everyone else knows about it. There are no secrets here.

Timescales?

People keep asking me for the timescale of the Great Reset. I don't do that sort of thing. The reason is that *it can be averted*. That's the way I see it. It can be stopped with knowledge and understanding and the consciousness of people. If we tell everyone about the weapons on every corner that can fry our arses – we won't allow it. Surely?

There is a lot of bullshit in the world, but we have to expose the truth. We have to show everyone what is happening - then let them decide for themselves. One way of showing people what is going on in the world is to show them photographs and to show them exactly what they're missing in those photographs.

The secrets that have been deliberately hidden from us are revealed through the many photographs available from the conception of photography in what we believe to be 1800s. In this book, we will be exploring the lie that photography portrays to us and how it inadvertently reveals the truth.

Please note that I didn't want the photographs in this book because I intend to invite you to explore the Flat Earth Think Tank on a deeper level. There are thousands of pictures on the Flat Earth Think Tank site, and this book would only hold a few of them so, if they were here, you would do yourself an injustice.

A New Dawn?
A new dawn, or new day, is needed for all. Why? Because what we're going through today basically sucks. Do you want the whole world to slip into Communism? Or a new way of Neo-Socialism? Or is it that you are happy with this effing Demon-ocracy? Are you delighted to be living in this Satanic Masonic Hellfire system that we exist under?

I know I'm a bit of a carnage head, but I try to do my best to help humanity build back better (for want of a better phrase). All I want to do is spread peace and love and help you to see humanity can not only survive but thrive on its own without all this evil shit going on around us.

If you are reading this book and have come across this type of information for the first time, then I praise you for your bravery in wanting to find out more. It takes a lot of courage to ask questions. You have to kick that ego into touch before admitting you don't know everything and, to be thought of as weak as a result is quite frightening. But if you don't ask questions, then you don't progress. You don't learn. You don't, and won't, know the truth.

This book aims to help you begin to ask those questions. It aims to give you the courage not to be afraid. It reveals to you the suffering that humanity has gone through over the ages and how we shouldn't be fearful of what we face in the future.

If you are ever flagging or having a bad day, I'm here to make it all go away - I mean to blow it away. I like creating a magical world of discoveries. I like smashing paradigms, and I love bringing down Babylon. It sounds like an excellent plan to me.

The key is, as it has been all along, numbers. The more people wake up to what is happening, the better. For myself, it is woefully frustrating. All the effort involved in putting this together to see that everyone seems to be asleep and believing the lying narrative, irritates me. It's insanity.

This is why I keep pounding away at this work. It's about waking people up or, as I like to say, Red Pilling them. It's heart-breaking when I hear of people who are close to their family members who just won't wake up. They either don't want to know, or they want to stay happy in their ignorance. They talk about what they've seen or heard on the news and they are worrying about it.

THE HOLY GRAIL OF THE GREAT RESET

ERRR! It's not real!

The local newspaper might tell you that there was a cat up in the tree of Mrs Jones' rose garden down the road and that the firemen, Ivan, who she'd known as a little kid, was called out to get her little kitty down. That might be real news, but the rest of it? It's all fake. It's all put out there just to make you frightened. To keep you down in your fear. Everyone seems to be locked into it. As soon as those tellies were made, that was it. Hypnotisation of the masses began in earnest.

We all have bad days, I know that, but don't fall for it. Anything negative is them picking away at your psyche. What I recommend you do is go out in the garden, take a look at bumblebees busily buzzing around and beautiful butterflies flitting from flower to flower, walk among the weeds, get those feet out of those shoes and stand them on the soft green grass.

If ever a doubt comes in, just ask yourself:

"Hang on a minute, are you a doubt? Eff off then!"

Then it goes away. It has to. That's the power you have.

The lockdowns that the world has been put through during Z020 and Z021 have got everybody down. We're all anxious and depressed and suicidal. To combat this, you have to begin to go outside and connect with nature. Nature is one thing that will bring you back to being a spiritual human being.

The level of the lie
I do have a lot to say on this subject, if you watch my videos on YouTube or wherever I'm allowed to upload them these days, you'll see that I have a machine gun mouth that never runs out of bullets.

The Great Reset that we're being told about is happening today and has happened before. There is a playbook on this type of thing. You know the saying 'history repeats itself', which is the best truth you can ever get into your head. However, there are a lot of good things happening in the arena of the Flat Earth and the paradigm is changing daily. It effing rocks and I'm glad I'm a part of it.

SO, WHAT'S IN IT FOR ME?

What do you think the people from the Matrix (or consumer society, or the Globers) are thinking about the Flat Earthers? To respond to any such question, a Flat Earther must be better and there are tools that we can use, good food and natural health and all the knowledge you need can give you a happy and meaningful life.

I saw a video by CuriousLife, who makes videos about predictive programming and shows you what they do in the cinemas. Pretty cool stuff. I had some thoughts about one of his videos, where one shows you President Bush telling you about the *War on Terror* – and, after it, you have to ask if that's what it's all about. For example, this is how the average mindset thinks:

"Flat Earth, what's in it for me?"

Unfortunately, with all the materialism and stuff, that's their first thought. Before Flat Earth, I realised the bullshit of evolution and I know everything that I know now, except that I wasn't aware the earth wasn't a ball. I wasn't aware of the food and water and electromagnetics that were being used against me, but now I am. When you look at food, you don't want to be living on MacDonald's burgers, nor do you want to be knocking back the booze. I've had the odd Jack Daniels or a German beer in my life, but I don't drink now.

You don't want to be living on government-approved drugs either. Pharmaceuticals. And you want to keep away from chemtrails too. For the past couple of years, those skies have been streaked with dirty great marks in a grid pattern. You can deny it all you want, but I can tell the difference between a natural cloud, a trail behind an aeroplane, a contrail and a chemtrail. Plus, after so much endless research into the subject, I get a feeling that there is something going on.

What do you want?
Do you this to continue? Do you want people who you haven't given authority to, to carry on effing up your life? We're treated like mushrooms – shit is shovelled upon us while we're kept in the dark.

Never consent. If everyone knew what had really happened, nobody would consent. Nobody would play. If everyone knew what had happened since birth, the straw man, the lies, the history, the flat earth, they would find it unbelievable. At times, I can't believe it myself. Sometimes, I slap myself. I say to myself in frustration, "Ah, how could I not have seen?" It's like this magic spell has been put over everyone. Something you can't see. It's really weird.

So, that's what I'm going to do. I'm going to de-magic it. Ok? I'm just going to lift the spell of hypnosis so everyone wakes up.

1. IS HISTORY A LIE?

If another Great Reset did happen, then in my mind, Rome is important. The millennia is too long. I've been around fifty years and I've seen the city change so much you can't recognise it. So, how has the world not changed so much in 2,000 years?

There's no way the Coliseum has been there for that long. What about floods, earthquakes, volcanoes, severe weather conditions? What about all the wars? Two thousand years and it is still bloody standing there. Didn't they take it apart and put it back together again? No. The timeframe has been chopped. I'll give you some idea about how it's been done. Granted, I'm not certain about how they did it, but I have a general idea.

The timeline is basically bullshit, it's not to be believed. It's all part of the puzzle and must be brought together so we can all see the bigger picture. If putting this together takes the heat off of the hating, I think it'll be worth the work. It will heal up problems and rifts not only between families but nations of people across the plane.

If you want to take this Great Reset or the Flat Earth

seriously, you've got to wake up to the borders. They are the imaginary lines on the map. The flags are there to make people nationalistic, so we can be provoked to protect our own people against other people behind another flag, so they can take us to war to fight and kill each other.

What do humans do better than anything else? Kill one another. You have to believe that. The funny thing is, I've never actually spoken to anyone who wants a war. It's rubbish. All people want to do is get on with one another. We don't want to be divided. We don't want any race problems, white/black problems, religious problems, gender problems, physical/mental health differences. The trouble is we're being incited to do this to each other - to keep us divided and hating each other.

The people who are forcing the divisions between us are paid way too much by the wrong people. They probably watch me and try to make me feel bad about what I'm doing, but I don't. I just live my life and get on with it.

In the movie, *The Matrix*, they say that the older you are, the harder it is to wake up. I think that might be the case. If you have fifty years solid indoctrination, it will be difficult to see another way. It's going to be much harder to prize yourself out of the hypnosis. The official historical timeline is something you would probably see on Wiki or some rubbish platform like that. You are shown a reality that has been given to us.

Think of the historical event of the War of the Roses. We will be told this took place over a hundred years between the House of Lancaster and the House of York in Britain. When I look at Tudors, King Henry VIII and Elizabeth I, I see the insane dynasty that was the Plantagenets. I'm sure that they've been handed to us. Why? There is a problem.

It was the Age of Religious Discord, basically, the middle of the i600s through to i700s. This is because it was introduced by the Plantagenets. People were so busy with so many wars during this time all over Europe.

- The Spanish War
- The Seven Year War
- The French Revolution
- The Napoleonic Wars
- The Franco/German War
- World War 1
- World War 2
- The Cold War (which never existed)
- The Balkan War

When you go back, and you look at the international situation over a period of time, especially the British timeline, you get to the modern-day and you've got the following:

- The Battle of Britain
- The Troubles in Ireland

- The Celtic Tiger
- The Good Friday Agreement

In the period of 1660, when the people went against the Papacy (which to me was opting out of the Jesuit operation), you have to ask, what happened there? All in that one narrow band of time, you have the following:

- The Papal Laws
- The Revolution
- The Battle of the Boyne
- The Unions Act of 1707
- The Battle of Culloden (when the English ended the Scottish way of life)
- The Rebellion of 1798
- The Act of 1800
- The Catholic Emancipation
- The Irish Potato Famine (there was no shortage of food, it was kept under lock and key so people would die)
- The Irish War of Independence

It goes on and on and on, but go back before this period, to the mid-1600s, and take a look there. You'll see the information gets very sketchy. If you go back to Henry VIII, you'll see the following:

- The Scottish Reformation
- The Tudor Conquest of Ireland

There seems to be only this little bit happening in that period of time. Yet, if you go back a bit further, to the Magna Carter of the 1200s, you'll find nothing but the following:

- Norman Invasion
- Norman Conquest

After the Romans left Britain, there was a spike in raids, then it was the Norman Conquest. Unfortunately, if you see this as a whole picture laid out before you, you'll see that where nothing really happens in a THOUSAND YEARS.

A THOUSAND YEARS where there was no information, whatsoever.

All I can conclude is that the Dark Ages never happened. It's called the Dark Ages because the information that came out of that period is limited - because it didn't happen. Yet, you get up to the modern-day and you get people hacking the hell out of each other. I think the date for the reset model is around the time of the 1300s to the 1600s. Also, it seems that before these dates everyone knew the world was flat.

When you check out the Ming's in China, the Romans in Europe, and then the Norman invasions of Britain, they all seem to subscribe to the same point of view.

How ancient is ancient?
The evidence that's coming out is mind-blowing. Some of the things I've heard have really got me thinking. And the thoughts about this ancient civilisation being more recent, I believe there is a reality in it. Effing giant trees is one thing, but this is something else.

The only answer I can come up with is that the old buildings that have been deliberately destroyed, like the Expositions all over the world, would have provided evidence of what went on before - we're humans with amnesia and our gifts are being hidden from us. It is something that happened not too long ago - in the recent past. When? I don't know. A few hundred years, maybe?

We are led to believe that the entire human race evolved from what they call Ethiopia, the Nubian Desert. Apparently, civilisation took rise there, went up North, followed the Nile, settled in Egypt and the central Middle East etc. Then they burst out into Europe, then into Eastern Asia and then the Americas. However, not across the Atlantic, instead, they were said to have travelled across the Bearing Straights because the Innuits in Canada look like the Innuits in Russia. Well, to me, the Russians look pretty similar to the Americans.

What happened before BC? Before Christ. Richard Dawkins says that we've been around for a long time because we come from a monkey's bum. He and the mainstream media would have you believe this tiny fraction of history, the size of the tip of my nose, is how long humanity has been around. All the epochs of time would be represented as the length of my arm - from the tip of my nose all the way along my arm to my fingertips. How long has humanity been around? What is more realistic? A millimetre from the end of my nose?

Just reverse whatever you're told by academia or the schooling system. We are told that the stars are light-years away. Light years? Juggle that one in your mind for a bit. All that means to me is that we are supposed to add a zero. It doesn't mean anything else. It doesn't mean that the stars are 'light' years away from this plane. Some move, some don't.

I know we are shown these glyphs of people in carriages, with horse and cart, but is it conceivable that the people of those times had more? Or, are the historians choosing to show us only a glimpse of what was really going on?

Are Ancient Civilisations recent?
Are ancient civilisations way more recent than we are told? Serge, a brilliant Russian YouTuber, has unearthed some brain-mashingly good stuff on ancient civilisations. There is definitely something in his theories and his examples are superb. This is based on something real and tangible.

There are some sublime pieces of artwork that comes from the late i700s, which show an ancient civilisation. Those paintings depict a specific type of architecture.

If you are familiar with St. Petersburg, look at the Winter Palace and the Hermitage.

Serge proposes that the Winter Palace and the Hermitage have been inherited from recent history. Not hundreds of years, nor thousands of years, as we are told is the case of the Egyptians and the Greeks where some of the ancient civilisations were way, way back in antiquity, another epoch even.

Personally, I don't believe ancient Rome was 2,000 years ago. When I visited the Coliseum and the Parthenon, they didn't look that old. All of these ancient civilisations seem to have been taken out by a volcano. Santorini, apparently, caused the biblical plagues. Yet, the buildings look as though they were constructed yesterday.

A cataclysm seems to have happened in the past and all these structures have been covered in silt. The buildings have been excavated and the stone that has been unearthed are not possible to make today as they are effing huge megalithic blocks. Phenomenally big. Everything else you see is built on top of them. No matter what building from antiquity you look at, they are all built on older stone. A case in point is Baalbek in Lebanon. If you look closely at any of these ancient buildings, you will always see them built on older foundations.

Think back to the photographs that were taken in 1890 of, say, the pyramids and of the Sphinx in Egypt. The Sphinx was buried up to its neck in sand and the pyramids were quite well covered. In fact, the whole

Giza plateau is buried under the sand. Now, keep that image in your head and apply it across all of the plane – Americas as well.

Historians and archaeologists have excavated certain areas and told people that such and such was built by a particular person in a certain timeframe. For instance, in the case of St. Petersburg, it was Peter the Great who, incidentally, lived in a log cabin. Does that sound reasonable? Does it make sense that he would build such unbelievable stone structures with such splendour and eloquence and yet, live in a log cabin?

You will see the same structures in the States as well. Washington has the same architecture as the Louvre in Paris, and the Kremlin in Russia. Another intriguing thing to note is that all these cities were built on swamps. It shows up everywhere, in every country you look.

Saint Petersburg is an anomaly. Why would you move the Russian capital from Moscow to St. Petersburg (which was renamed Leningrad and then back to St. Petersburg again), then move it back to Moscow? When I found out that they moved it from the flat level ground of Moscow to a swamp that was St. Petersburg, I thought it had something to do with the naval presence at Kronstadt.

Think of the expositions that were presented across the world in the 1800s. They were in London, Paris, Chicago, San Francisco and they had these really ornate cities made of hard granite, marble and stone. In the centre of all these metropolises were these beautiful structures, like the Crystal Palace in London. The puzzling thing is, they were all demolished. Every single one of them. None of them are left standing today. I'm under the impression that these buildings, and many more like them, may have been there already, before the civilisation depicted in the photographs of the 1800s.

As far as I can make out when you look at the buildings, the technology mentioned in stories and the photographic evidence, everything seems to have happened since the Victorian era or the Napoleonic Wars. Is this a stretch of the imagination?

ANCIENT TECHNOLOGY?

The level of civilisation we are looking at really strikes a chord. Like a memory, if you like. It's strange. So, what could have happened? Where did the people go? How did this ancient technology disappear?

I think it's something to do with the electric universe hypothesis. I believe that there has been a large amount of electro-static charge gathered in the air and that this caused discharges, like a pulse of energy that blasts shit away. In the electric universe theory (if you are a globe believer), they reckon this has happened on the surface of Mars and it is this that has ripped out the biggest crater on any planet in the supposed solar system. Bigger than the Grand Canyon.

There are references to said events of cataclysms despite a deluge, I don't know if we are talking diluvian, pre-diluvian, or pre-ice age in this timing. It's pretty hard to work out, but I'm sure we will all be enlightened at some point.

People are really interested in ancient civilisations and I think it's because they are intrigued because they know they are not being told the truth. We are beginning to work out the timeline for ourselves and we are beginning to understand that we were not travelling around on horses, or on foot, for 2,000 years - and then bang, we got all this technology. Where did all this technology come from?

India and Arabia
Did ancient civilisations have the capability to build UFO technology? This kind of technology is mentioned in the Indian Vedas, where they made a thing called the 'bell'. There is photographic evidence that it existed. Apparently, it disappeared and then reappeared in 1952, in Pennsylvania. Who knows if any of this is true?

I tend to believe the stories from the ancient Indian Sanskrit epics, the poetry of *The Mahābhārata*. The whole story in *The Bhagavad Gita* describes battles that have spaceships or flying ships. How would they have known how to describe them if they hadn't seen them? Did they have sci-fi writers in those days? The thing is, they've described specifications for these flying ships, and they are said to run on mercury, which makes it spin and elevates them.

A few years ago, social media channels were reporting that the reason for the Gulf War was because one of these Indian spaceships, or flying ships, had been found in a cave in Afghanistan. It's from that, we have all this tech that we see today. This technology had weapons that were akin to our nuclear weapons.

This ancient civilisation seems to have had advanced tech. You can find examples of it in their cemetery art, it's the kind of art that we wouldn't be able to produce today. Yet, when you look at the dates on those gravestones, it's artwork from the Middle Ages. Could those dates have been altered with a chisel and hammer?

The media wants us to believe ISIS smashed up lots of ancient buildings and artefacts. In fact, I've seen evidence of some cities being blown up and demolished and yet, when you hunt for them on Google Earth, some of them are still there, intact. In complete and good condition. Why would anyone want to blow up ancient history?

In Istanbul, there's a building that is meant to be Byzantium. It's mega ancient, even older than the Coliseum in Rome. Yet, the original paint and the original gold leaf is still on it and we're still led to believe it has gone through two millennia, through all that heat of the desert. Do you believe it?

Sumerian artwork shows us an advanced civilisation. The depictions show the people wore wristwatches, they also had pinecones and strange objects that made power and, it seems, they even had electricity. I'm sure the pyramids were something to do with an energy grid, and I'm sure it was something to do with us, what we are inside.

We are led to believe these vanished civilisations existed for so long and then just up and disappeared. They are the people who built cities like the *Home of the Elamites*. It looks so modern it could have been built yesterday.

The Americas
Have you seen the stonework of the ancient buildings in South America? Some stones have joins that are so seamless you can't even fit a piece of paper between them. They look as though they've been melded, or melted, together. We haven't got any technology that would do that to our buildings today.

What could produce this kind of thing is a process called disaggregation where a series of mirrors and magnifying glasses seem to intensify the sunlight so strong that actually, it disintegrates stone. It has been found that they used that last technique for cutting stone.

The technology to lift extremely heavy stones has been used recently by a man who built Coral Castle in Florida, America. I go into this a bit later, but briefly, a little fella built an entire village made of large, or megalithic, stones – all on his own. Apparently, he put this together in the middle of the night. He said he had managed to tap into the knowledge of the ancients. So, where did he get the idea from? What has happened to his knowledge?

Europe
In comparison to the last couple of thousand years, the previous one hundred has seen a remarkable transformation. If we go with 'ancient aliens', what this leads you to think is that they got all this technology from a crashed UFO before the war.

In a German forest, apparently, a spaceship was found which the scientists basically picked apart and got all the fibre optics and the rest from it. The technology which we enjoy today, and the superior technology that humans used during World War Two, is because of that.

The disaster at Pompei, in Italy, we're told, was 2,000 years ago, but I think there's a bit of tourist attraction novelty going on there. I just don't believe that someone would sit in those positions (eating, drinking, going about their daily business, even cuddling each other) while they were waiting for the burning ash to rain down on them. Apparently, it had been raining ash for three days. The whole place was up to its windows in this hot stuff.

If the people of Pompei knew what was happening to them, would they have sat and waited for it to cover them and solidify them? I don't think so. We're told that the Port was packed, and many people couldn't get to it. The flow of heat incinerated people into a putrefaction state so that they were solidified. Those solidified people are what you see today. Yet, what puzzles me is that the heat left some of the walls with paint and artwork still intact. Surely, it couldn't have been that hot? Something is a bit inconsistent here.

Pompeii was identical to any city you would walk around today. There were shops with windows, shop signs advertising their wares, you could even buy a burger there. When you look at the artwork that remains on the walls, you can see how modern those people look. They look like Italians look today.

Everything you see is supposed to be Roman or Norman or Saxon, yet, you will always see the buildings standing on older stone. Larger stone. Megaliths. How long ago were these people supposed to have existed?

Locally, in Wales, I've found a burial site called Tinkinswood, five minutes up the road from where I live in Cardiff. When you visit there, the first thing that hits you is how the hell did they lift that 100-ton capstone into place? What you see is the capstone on the side, one stone on the back and one on top. Inside, they found about a dozen bodies in foetal positions, which are now housed in the Welsh museum. I'm aware of some techniques for lifting weights, using sand and shoring the sand out and letting the weight drop but, not for that size.

What of the ancient castles that are all over Britain? These giant megalithic castles were built so people could fight who, again? If you look into those battles around the castles that are dotted around the country, look into why they were built. Were these edifices were built for tribal warfare? What kind of weaponry did these tribal people have? I don't think the

Paganistic ancient Brits would get into these castles in the 1400s-1500s.

Inner Science
Did these ancient peoples have advanced tech? Did the man who built Coral Castle find it? Quite possibly. But, I believe all these abilities to build such things are based on human 'inner tech' or the inner science of who we are. It's done by us, by vibrational words, incantations, harmonics to activate structures that are made of crystalline. As in the pyramids, as in Stonehenge. I believe it's something more to do with who and what we are rather than the technology we can invent.

It seems to me that the 'powers that be' (whoever they are) have locked us down into a five-sensory organism – a deprivation tank kind of thing. Compare our senses to that of a snake, and you'll find an incredible difference.

We have taste, touch and smell, sight and hearing. We've also got a sixth sense which seems to do nothing. Imagine if we could see what was really out there. We only see a squeeny tiny little amount of the visible light spectrum – which, if you look at it, is vast. It's all there, but we can't perceive it.

I do not believe that ancient civilisations we're told about were a long, long time ago. I believe that the con men, the racketeers and the money-makers of the 1800s made up their silly shit about history. I'm sure they made up the dinos to confuse our timeline. The

Jurassic Coast, the south coast of England, is meant to be filled with dinosaur bones, but they could be telling us anything.

Have you ever seen the Gates of Babylon? Well, you'll see them in the Museum in Berlin. Apparently, the animals that are depicted on that frieze are dinosaurs. This is one of their weak-arsed proofs that dinos actually existed which entitles them to say: "We have pictures of people with dinosaurs, they existed together!" Hmm. Ok.

These so-called ancient civilisations had advanced tech, but there was something else going on. If we got a group of transcendental humans together, and they could resonate a hum or an Om, they would show us what's possible. I'm sure they could manipulate matter to do something. Whatever. This technology is out there.

POSSIBLE RESET DATE?
Before I go further, I want to mention a brilliant insight I've found in the film *Apocalypse Now*:

> *2014 explores the unrecognised but mighty conspiracy which has been hidden from humanity for ages. Unfortunately, to the detriment of all forms of life which have inhabited this plane earth briefly. The Roman Era, commonly referred to as Ancient Rome evidently faked its own death 715 years ago.*

Well, that makes sense. 715 years ago is a time-span I can deal with. Thinking of this, what I'd like to know is, have there been an extra thousand years added to our calendar? To figure this one out, you only have to look into the Greenland Theory.

The Greenland Theory
Go to the website www.GreenlandTheory.com, and read it. The website says that it exerts its power over 206 nations of the world through its primary proxy state, Switzerland. It goes on to say that Switzerland was formed in the i300s. Well, this falls in line with the 715 years ago.

The Greenland Theory puts forward the notion that around 1,300 years have been added to the Gregorian calendar. The Roman New Year officially begins on April 1st - April Fool's Day. The Greenland Theory website says that the i300s are known as the 'Dark Ages' because they never saw the light of day. It also says that the Roman Empire moved its capital to various places, namely:

- City of Babylon
- Rome in Italy
- Constantinople, modern city of Istanbul, Turkey
- Thule, Greenland.

Constantinople, Istanbul and Moscow were originally called Rome. Now it seems to have been moved to Greenland. Greenland is often covered in ice and snow. The capital was placed here to deceive the enemies of the day, i.e. the Persian Empire and the Ming Dynasty.

It mentions how the Roman Empire thrived and that they put the 'harshest restrictions on China and Iran' with a totalitarian fascist rule. The reason why China and Iran had these restrictions put upon them was because they were not allowed to learn about the histories of their once great empires.

The Greenland Theory mentions that the inhabitants of China built the Great Wall because of years of Roman aggression. The Romans even changed their language to pictures. They destroyed the culture's histories depicted in the Bible, which referred to ancient Egypt, Sumer, Greece, Babylon, Rome and the Vikings as coming from the same ancient lineage originating from the Minoans, Crete in Greece.

The website says that the Minoan culture had their histories altered, they were twisted and made into fables so that the fascist Roman rule, which had been in place for over a thousand years, could be hidden.

Knossos in Greece seems to be an important location. In World War Two, the Germans went to the Labyrinth of Knossos, which is depicted on the Mappa Mundi (located in Hereford, UK). This is significant because you can't get in there anymore because the Nazi's went to the Labyrinth blew up the entrance. It's obviously not the minotaur that's keeping people out.

THE HOLY GRAIL OF THE GREAT RESET

The cave system in Crete is supposed to be connected to an underground system which goes from London to Istanbul and ancient Rome and then it comes up, believe it or not, in the Mediterranean. This ancient tunnel system is underneath all of Europe.

Now, there is not one reference to ancient Carthage. I have recognised this before and I can't believe they are not important or powerful enough to be mentioned and yet, they had more territory than Rome. So, what's going on? Why have they left Carthage out?

The Power of Rome
Rome with a current reset date of 715 years ago seems to be accurate for now. The thing is, I'm a bit suspicious about the triple-barrelled name of the person who has put the information on the Greenland Theory website. The reason is that a book in my Library said the triple-barrelled names are connected to the Freemasons, authors like David Chase Taylor, JR Tolkien, GE Lawrence, HG Wells - and now we have JK Rowling. Is this something the novelists do to make them seem superior?

There are a few sayings, which I'm sure you've come across before:

When in Rome, do as the Romans do.

Rome wasn't built in a day.

All Roads lead to Rome

These sayings are allegories, or metaphors, for the power the Roman Empire held over humanity. This is the first part of the expose with proof of what I'm saying is true.

To my mind, the Reset of History was i300AD. During the last Crusade in i291, the Knights Templar brought something back with them, something they found in Jerusalem and they took it to Switzerland. Switzerland appears to be the key to the puzzle.

I originally went for a reset date of i666, mainly because of the Great Fire of London, but then I was sent the link to the Greenland Theory. This Theory is linked to other aspects that I've been researching and now the puzzle is beginning to make a bit more sense.

Bear with me on the i300 reset date. I have a theory that it was brought in on April 1st, i300. I don't know if it was a Friday, but we'll have to look it up. April 1st i300 was the first day of the Gregorian calendar. The Mappa Mundi provides a key. I know there's an underlying meaning to it that is revealing more as there appears to be a coding in it which seems to be linked to the Labyrinth of Knossos in Crete.

Jerusalem is always a meridian on the Mappa Mundi, but the date is i290, ten years before the reset. So, you have to ask what was happening at the advent of the i300s. I knew something was up because of the thousand years of bullshit to do with the Tartarians. The Philips Contemporary World History makes references to this too. So, the Mappa Mundi comes out ten years before the official reset date of 715 years ago. This fits with me and I'll tell you why.

When I was thinking about the reset date, I kept wondering why, or how, it could be 1666. There was an English Civil war and evidence of dates for that exist. Then there's Hampton Court and the Tudors and there's a lot of evidence of the Elizabethan era around 500 years ago.

Ok then, what about the crazy Plantagenets? Now, that period of time is really sketchy. The Plantagenets were before the Tudors and they were all crazy, like John and Longshanks (Edward 1) or, do you recall Braveheart from Scotland? So, the Plantagenets seem to be added to the timeline. Maybe they did exist but forget anything before the 1300s and go from that family's era. They're the ones who seem to have handed our history to us.

When you consider the saying 'Rome wasn't built in a day', you have to ask what do they mean by that? I believe it's not finished. It's still under construction and, more importantly, Rome never ended. The Roman Empire just went underground - and their Satanic behaviour went with them.

You'll know of the splinter groups, the people who make up the Illuminati, the Freemasons, the Jesuits and all of these secret societies. It all links into my research of Napoleon Bonaparte and turns out that the House of Bonaparte still covertly control France.

The Great Fire of London

The discoveries I've made tie in incredibly with what's going on in our world now. As well as the i300s, i666 may have been a reset date.

The Great Fire of London was in i666 and was a bit of a psyop. We are told that most of the buildings during that period were made of wood. A high percentage of it was, but most of it was stonemasonry. The fire missed the Tower of London, but it took out the old St Paul's Cathedral because it was attached to something they wanted to erase.

There has always been some contention about where the fire started, with the Pudding Lane Bakers often cited as the source. However, the fire completely missed Whitehall, Westminster, Temple Barr and it stopped at Fleet Street. Why? Possibly because the Bank of England was there? Everything was razed to the ground, yet those buildings stayed up.

Samuel Pepys, the famous diarist, was across the river Thames and he wrote about the lead running off the roof into the river. It is also recorded that one thousand five hundred homes and 2.8 kilometres of London were destroyed. Old depictions show London wasn't all made of wood. Fire produces its own weather force, and it's so intense that it would have been uncontrollable. Firemen of i666 didn't exist either.

Sir Christopher Wren was a high Freemason and he got the contract to rebuild London as well as the University of Oxford. He was the co-founder of the

Royal Society in 1682, and he was highly regarded by Isaac Newton. There's a story on Wiki when he was marking out the footings for the new St Paul's Cathedral, a young boy came up to Wren and gave him a stone from the old Cathedral. On the stone, it said 'resurgi' – rise from the ashes like a Phoenix.

> *Since the 18th Century, the Lodge of Antiquity No. 2, one of four founding Masonic Lodges of the Premier Grand Lodge of 1717, has claimed Christopher Wren to have been its Master of the Goose and Gridiron at St. Paul's churchyard.*

This stone showed that Wren was high in the Freemasonry society. When I looked at other events that happened that year, I came across a cult, Sabbataiism, which is practised today. This gave me an important key - that the Jews are not to blame for all the shit that's going down. Those who are known as the Crypto-Jews will kill Jews as easily as anyone else. The Jewish people are in as much danger as the rest of us are.

I explore more detail about Sabbatai Zevi later in the Chapter *Who Are The Major Players?* Briefly, though, Zevi was a man who was into Jewish mysticism and was thought to be the Messiah. He created this really strange cult of Satanic role reversal based on the religion of Philippa. Jacob Franks funded Zevi and worked together with him.

Both Franks and Zevi set up the Illuminati and it's down to these men that the events of The French Revolution, The Battle of Waterloo, The Bank of England, Karl Marx despotism and, eventually, the American Revolutionary War happened. You'll find out that Carnegie, Walberg, JP Morgan were all agents of Zevi - they were all Crypto-Jews. Is this interesting?

Zevi made up this weird doctrine based on Kabala, which is based on the ancient Jewish mysticism, the tree of life and aspects of consciousness. There are good parts to the Kabala theory, but it's been tainted by this Zevi group of people. They have a weird role-reversal thing where they will read the Lord's Prayer in reverse. They seem to like to perverse the human form and anything that is God-given.

Both Franks and Zevi gave the reins to Adam Wiese who set up the Illuminati, which was linked to the Rothschild's. Through the Rothchild's, the French Revolution originated. The British nearly had a revolution of their own, but it fell through.

If you've been a follower of this kind of alternative history, then you'll know that fake news was brought across from the Battle of Waterloo - that the British had lost. As a result, everyone sold their shares on the stock market, which made it crash and stocks became available at rock bottom prices. Having the inside information, the Rothschild's bought up those stocks until the real news came through. By then, it was too late as, from that moment on, the Rothchild's based our culture on the Satanic network.

THE HOLY GRAIL OF THE GREAT RESET

The Last Crusade
As far as I can see, Switzerland is the key. Though there are a few destinations like Ancient Rome, as in the Rome we know of in Italy, but also the Rome as in Moscow, and as in Istanbul. Rome seems to have been so vast – it seems to have been an organisation of totalitarian psychopaths who have managed to enslave the human race and use this tool of bullshit to do it.

For how long have they been in charge? That isn't known because the history books have always been altered. History is always written by the victors and Hollywood loves to permeate the myth. Anyway, the Swiss Guard are the guardians of the Vatican who are specially armed men who take no shit. The question must be asked, why is the Swiss Guard in the Vatican? Let's go to the French Foreign Legion as many know this organisation started in Switzerland.

The Swiss flag, as you know, is the cross, but it's also the Cross of the Knights of St. John. Also, we know that Switzerland never really involves itself in world wars, as a country, because it always seems to get neutrality. Why? Because it's the natural 'safe' of earth.

Switzerland is a money safe. It has mountains, the Alps, all around it which gives it complete protection (especially Zurich) from the outside world. What else have they got in Switzerland? Their 'atom smasher', the Bilderberger Group where the Elites of the world meet and the CIA are there too. I've never seen such a heavily Masonic country (except London) in all my life.

There are also the banks.

Nazi gold is directly linked to this country as well as the organised crime being rife. Switzerland is a sovereign state. I think it's safe to presume with just those links, something is afoot with this country.

As well as the Fire of London in i666, I believe one of the Great Resets was in i300. I think this is because only a decade earlier, the Knights returned from their last Crusade, from Jerusalem. Is this a coincidence? Do we believe in coincidences? The Mappa Mundi gives a huge clue as to why this is not a coincidence.

The Mappa Mundi was dated in i290 and the return of some higher Knights Templar to Switzerland was i291. Only one year later than this map was supposed to have been created. I believe something was brought back from Jerusalem and it's all connected with Friday 13th.

I'm proposing that at least one Great Reset was on 1st April i300

I'm not going with the current version of history, nor the Norman Conquest, nor the Saxons, nor the Vikings, nor any of the rest of it. The reason why is because I believe someone has added about one thousand more years to our calendar.

HISTORY IS A LIE
I can't think of anyone who has been to as many battle

sites as myself. I'm quite well-travelled and I've seen a lot but I've always had questions. Apart from not feeling right in my own environment, I've never believed the history we've been spun. I always invite people to present me with the proof that shows how all these battles were played out and where, but no one has been able to. When it really boils down to it, the evidence that is presented is really sketchy and we don't know what happened.

I have received a lot of questions from people asking about the Norman Conquest and Harold dying with an arrow shot into his eye. Have you been on the Battle of Hastings ground? Well, you won't have - because no one really knows where it is. There's a town called Hastings, but there are a couple of sites that people keep discussing.

We don't even know the story of the Battle of Hastings. There are half a dozen different versions of it and the only proof we have for the Norman Conquest is a tapestry in Bayeux in France. They tell us that the tapestry was knocked up in one wet afternoon in the Middle Ages. It's that tapestry that goes on tour - just to re-emphasise the lies we're told.

If you try to find the Battle of Hastings site, you'll see that there's nothing there. No evidence whatsoever. The only ones that you can see evidence of are the ones of WW1, where they blitzed the trenches, and also the Battle of Waterloo too. If you go to those battle sites, you can usually pick up a candle holder or some other object that they used in that era.

There is no evidence of Agincourt, either. In fact, none of the great battles of the medieval era show any evidence. Go and take a look for yourself. The only evidence we have is what the history books deem to tell us about them.

What I find interesting is that in i300, the Mappa Mundi, was taken on a tour all around Britain. It was in a big box and the communities and villagers were all told to make copies because they were told, "This is the shape of the world!" They were told, this is where you live and we'll hear no more about it. As we now know, there is more to it. Why? Because the America's were not on that map. They were lying to the people at that time.

The Norman Conquest didn't happen the way we are told it did and not in the timeline they provide. If we are being lied to about the earth's shape, then history is a given too.

Castles and Chandeliers

Germany had castles everywhere with the most unbelievable opulence and Phoenician bullshit you will ever come across in your entire life. They've got it going on for definite. Remember Germany's place in two world wars. Germany and Britain were supposed to be mortal enemies, Empire against Empire. Except they're the same effing Empire!

Germany and Britain were crawling with the Phoenician junk you see. They are the elaborate statues of angels crawling up rocks with a watery theme going on down below. They have angels blowing trumpets while standing or sitting on horses. Do you know what that trumpet sound represents? A vibration. Do you know what that vibration could and still can do? That's up for debate, but I've discussed this subject in my previous book, T*he Holy Grail of Our Flat Earth*.

Depicted in the photographs of castles there are water features with turtles swimming in the waves and statues that look almost human-like they are so perfect. All around the structures, there are some sort of aquatic creatures, like crocodiles. All of these structures are inside castles that were supposed to have been built hundreds of years ago. We see them in the photographs in the 1800s but try to imagine this in the modern-day.

Something is going on with crystal chandeliers. What are they carved out of? Could they be bone? It's all very beautiful, but crazy. I know chandeliers can be used to reflect the light streaming into a room or light from the candles but, I do think there's more going on with chandeliers.

Many chandeliers are made with crystals. Crystal has a vibration and a memory. Could these chandeliers do more when there are more of them around? The people of this era seem to have had a chronic addiction to these chandeliers, even when there was natural light flooding into the room.

Another question I have to ask is, in all the rooms in these castles, why was there a need for priceless artwork to be hung above the fireplace? Some iron fireplaces are so ornate, then they have mirrors or priceless art hung above them. Don't mirrors crack in the heat? Wouldn't the heat damage the paintings?

Above the fireplaces, you'll also find candelabras along with marble statues. Some of the fireplaces have metal plates over the front of them, blocking them from the chimney, which gives me the idea that they were not made for keeping the room heated with coal or wood.

In the castles of Germany and Britain, you will always find a lot of patriotic memorabilia depicting Britain as the most powerful maritime nation in the world. During the First World War, in the Battle of Jutland, we did have the biggest fleet on earth, but it was woefully inadequate. Britain used to have more battleships than any other nation and this was the case from the late 1700s right the way through the 1800s. You only have to think of Pirates and Nelson etc.

As I said earlier, you have to be able to imagine walking through those ornately decorated corridors or sitting in those rooms which were overstuffed with rich fabrics and colours. You can get a feel of them when you walk through the houses that have been made into museums. Places like the National Trust or English Heritage houses, or the Hermitage in Russia. You have to ask why is there any need for all of these artefacts?

There are lots of 'shiny things' in these big houses, castles and churches. Such opulence is unbelievable – particularly in that day and age. When you look at the old Victorian rooms in these big houses, everything is priceless.

I guess they would have had this kind of stuff stored away during a previous reset, or it would have all been ruined. Some of the artworks of Robert Flood will show you this is the case. The odd thing is, when you really look into the décor, it has a lot of symbolism in it. The wallpaper is covered in Fleur De Lys symbols and cherubs and it all seems to be from the Phoenician era. Nasty.

The German castles are beautiful, but they're made with the money they took from their slaves: Us.

Cowboys and Indians
At the turn of the century, from 1800s to 1900s, in my city of Cardiff in Wales (and in many other British cities at the time), there was a precession of Buffalo Bill's cavalcades. Let me step back a bit to the American Civil War, which was presented to us as follows.

You have monumental (as in Napoleonic-scale) battles where there were hundreds of thousands of men on either side and thousands of deaths on both sides. Yet, in 1866, the year after it's finished, they all decided to meet up on the battlefields and pretend to fight. They call them re-enactments, where everybody gets together in a party-type atmosphere to have fun.

Is this the same with the Wild West? Was the Wild West a real thing? Did they have gunfights like we're told they did in the OK Corral? Just like the American Civil War. I don't believe so. The powers that be don't want us to know that it was there all along and America is older than we're led to believe.

Buffalo Bill was so famous he almost became a myth. They say that William Frederick Cody, Buffalo Bill's real name, was a buffalo hunter who fought in the American Civil War. The 'Wild West' show was started by him in i872.

Just like the re-enactments, a couple of years after the Civil War, they decided to get a little show together and go on tour. It was complete with stagecoaches, horses, Indians and real-live buffalos. At that show, they would re-enact pretending to kill each other.

In i891, this show came to my lovely city of Cardiff. They also took this show to Swansea valley and the write-up for the show says that they…

> *…built the most colossal amusement enterprise that ever visited Wales. The show was a spectacle never seen before. The Arena measured 175 yards by 70 and eight buffalo grazed near the River Taff. Hoards of wild Indians and Cowboys flowed into the town. Records show that the famous frontier man arrived with three train-loads of performers, 200 horses and 250 riders.*

Wow! I would have loved to have seen that.

Buffalo Bill and Annie Oakley were said to have first visited Britain for the Queen's Golden Jubilee in 1887. They apparently, performed in front of over 125,000 people in one show in South Wales. I say apparently because, when you look at the photographs there's something wrong with the crowd. They look a bit like a 'cardboard cut-out and every single image, bar none, has grey skies.

I think this was a little psyop to show everybody that the Wild West was real and to convince everyone of what had happened. It seems odd that they would go on tour to Wales, only a couple of years after the biggest horror to happen in America.

The Streets of San Francisco
In photographs that are available of San Francisco from 1856, the population hadn't arrived in full at that time as they said they were putting together all these fantastic buildings. When you look at the photographs, the populations were not massive, however, sixty years later, the Great Fire of San Francisco and their so-called earthquake took place.

The photographs available of the Great Fire of San Francisco all look a bit 'Wild Westy' in that there's mud everywhere, no pavements and no proper stone or concrete roads. Yet, the buildings like the City Hall, looks wicked. I mean to say, how did they get all of that stone there and everything that was needed to build it – on those mud roads? They even included a nice little antiquitech tower on top and a flagpole, which, incidentally, carries a charge.

In Montgomery Street, they did have enough manpower to put some flagstones down for the people to walk on and the carriages to roll over, but the buildings are already mud-flooders and huge.

The Port area seemed very busy and some of the buildings were surrounded by soldiers and had sandbags against the steps. The American Civil War was in the 1860s, so the photographs showing San Francisco in the 1850s wouldn't have been affected by that during that period.

There was also an impressively massive building specifically for photographic production – in 1856. By that reasoning, there should be plenty of photographs available of the buildings around that time.

Dig up some photographs of this era and timeframe and you'll see the Merchants Exchange is based on a type of Greco-Romano Temple style. Why would they bring in all that stone and those huge pillars, which were already dirty in the photographs, and build those massive things – when the population is so small? Where would they get the manpower to start with?

The photographs of San Francisco of the 1850s show a mixture of old and new buildings. The odd thing is, they were all built on a fault line, so wasn't this a prime candidate for an earthquake city?

Many of the buildings you see in the photographs of San Francisco seem like old buildings with their footings covered in mud, and aerials on their rooves and in their towers, while other buildings look very ramshackle as though they were thrown up in a day. They had wooden walkways and, yet, not a tree is in sight. Not even any palm trees. They might have used them to build the city though. What I don't get is how are they able to build effing big stone structures, yet the walkways and roads are mud-covered with planks of wood. What went on there?

Just sixty years after those pictures were taken of San Francisco, photographs were taken from a balloon. Those photographs were high definition images of a city still smouldering. Apart from the devastation, which is horrendous, the scale of the buildings is puzzling. It's as though they want you to believe they had built all those skyscrapers and some huge Tartarian-styled buildings, and they built it on a grid pattern which goes out into the distance as far as the eye can see. But, further out into the distance, there are no buildings, it is just a grid pattern in the mud. It's all been cleared, charred to dust, burned to the ground, everything has gone.

Did you know that firestorms build their own energy? I go into this a bit more in a later chapter when I discuss Dresden's catastrophe. Firestorms have hurricane-strength winds and they incinerate everything in their path. They extract the oxygen from the air, which is how many millions of people die.

How is it that a big city, such as San Francisco, was depicted in photographs of devastation in i907 yet, just sixty years earlier, it was a mud flood with hardly any people in it?

The Flat Earth British Think Tank has come up with a few interesting photographs of America's cities. The photographs of New York depict buildings that are deep down in the mud, then just behind them or across the road, there are fields. There are photographs of the main streets of cities like Colorado from i871. It is supposed to denote a Wild West town, with duckboards and wooden paths on mud. Yet again, you'll see big warehouses made of red brick, and the walls look like they are old with paint on them from a long time ago. It is all evidence that points towards it having been mud-flooded.

I noticed buildings embedded into the side of steep hills, yet there are no paths, no roads, nowhere for horses to trot up to in order to either build them or get to them after they've been built. Then there is the big beautiful Uray Theatre with mud all around it and in the background, there looks to be a tiered building site on the side of a mountain. It's depicted as a Colorado mining operation. I have to ask, which came first, the mud, the rock, or the stone buildings?

As I've mentioned before, what usually happens is that the incoming civilisation usually builds on the remnants of the old civilisation's structures. Many of the photographs in the Flat Earth British Think Tank collection reveal a lot of secrets that have been hidden from us. It definitely looks like something has gone wrong somewhere.

MEDIA IS A LIE
Do you remember what Michael Jackson said before

they made him go on a long holiday? He said:

"All history is a lie"

Whereas, do you know where this little strapline comes from:

"All the world is a stage!"

Shakespeare was quoted as saying this in one of his plays, but it comes from The Illuminati.

Talking about the world being a stage, please, please, please, do not believe the media. The media's assertion that North Koreans have got a thermonuclear bomb is a lie. For a start, the missile launch practice of that country was fake. How do I know? No country worth its salt would do a rocket launch test at the end of the runway, near their well-worshipped leader. Think about it. If it blew up, it would singe his eyebrows. They do it six to eight miles away. So, you don't really go near the edge of a launch site, let alone at the end of a runway - you keep well away.

Also, when a rocket goes up, it gives off this big red glow and you would see the flashback, or the glare, in the glasses of those who were looking up. But you look at photographs of them looking up and you can't see anything. They are all working on this together. They're all one big happy family of con artists.

It's true, though, that the world is a stage. They're all actors. Anything on the news is bullshit. History is bullshit. The heliocentric earth model is bullshit. This version of reality is bullshit.

It's amazing the way all these things have fallen into place for me. I tend to collect all the data, break it down and then stretch it out over a period of time so you follow the revelations on my journey. In doing this, I want you to seriously think about it. There is something completely different to what the official narrative (pedalled by the media) tells us.

You've seen it all. You've seen the 'official narrative' and you've seen the video revelations showing you how the Twin Towers actually came down and how it was reported. You've seen the media lie about the bombing of people in the Arabian world and you've seen the footage that Julian Assange has revealed to you. You've seen how this current pandemic has been created, you may have even seen Bill Gates and his presentation to de-populate the world – he did a TED Talk about it that went viral, for effs sake. What more do you want?

People keep asking, "What's the truth?" or "Who am I to believe?" Trust your gut. Don't ignore that feeling in your heart, in your stomach, in your mind. Think about it. Give it some time. You'll get the truth.

I don't want to talk about the newspapers or the television news or the programming or anything that's going on through popular television shows, but it's all there for you to see. The way to escape the lies is to just try turning the television off for a week. Don't buy a newspaper for a week. You'll begin to see the world as it really is.

SPACE IS A LIE
I've studied planetary bodies. I've seen Saturn, Jupiter, and Venus and I've captured them on my camera. They do not look like planetary bodies. I follow a couple of sites on YouTube, late at night, that show you space. I watch with the camera and look at the moon as they show it. One of the guys often mags up on Jupiter and the odd thing I notice is that Jupiter has bands yet, they say it is made up of a giant gaseous body. To me, it just looks like it's not even actually there. It seems like it is a wisp and doesn't look like it's a solid body because it's too fuzzy and indiscriminate.

Venus, meanwhile, looks like it has concentric circles within circles within circles. In fact, I'd go as far as to say that it looks like Ezekiel's Wheels (from the Bible). I've seen some with faces in.

Don't know about you, but something was wrong the day after the eclipse. It felt all wrong to me. I followed it the whole way, all across America. In Britain, we weren't supposed to have an eclipse, but one thing that became apparent in the entire day (I was outside in the garden watching the day unfold) and the weird thing was I didn't once see the sun's face creep up. There was only one sight of the sun, then the moon that covered it up. Honestly, something was wrong with that day.

Think for a minute of the satellites that are supposedly taking photographs of the earth. Ask yourself, honestly, how do they hold their orbit when the world is supposedly spinning with the speed of a bullet while going 63,000 miles an hour around the sun at breakneck speed? How is this, when the ball is turning on its axis, hanging on an invisible hook on its invisible axis (I know), and it's basically there, spinning away, yet, the satellite stays there, and it drags along with the earth?

We're also led to believe in a Luna orbit - the space between us and the moon. This means that there's a gravitational pull on the moon and the earth. They get it perfectly synced between the two and it stays there – even while the moon, apparently, turns around the earth.

So, where does that leave said satellites? Millions upon millions of them. Unfortunately, they can't show us any of these satellites, can they? When you Google them, all you see representing them are cartoons. If you are on the pretending fake space machine, the ISS, you will see that, basically, *there are no satellites*.

If you looked at a full moon and took photographs of it, you would see the satellites dotted around there in space, in front of the moon. There should be no less than 2,300 passing the moon any time you ever looked up at it. I've watched this space thing on YouTube for over an hour. I've just sat there, in a trance, waiting to see if one of these pretending satellites would fly past - but none of them ever has.

I've asked the guy who presents on a YouTube channel if he has seen any of these satellites, and he said yes, he had. But none of his viewers has ever seen them.

THE RESET GENERATION
Napoleon had a friend called Alexandre Dumas, the author of The Three Musketeers and The Count of Monte Cristo. He was a black man, a Jesuit and was high up in the Masonic tree. I've found the story of *The Count of Monte Cristo* is an allegory for the Jesuits.

Basically, the story tells of the Count who goes from great wealth to nothing, then returns to become the richest man on earth. I believe this is the story of the Jesuit struggle and how the Illuminati and Freemasons went underground to do all their dirty deeds.

Now, apply this idea to society. If it had followed a similar pattern, was of a high culture, then was brought back from a cataclysm, we have to begin to think that our generation isn't the first step. We are the recovering step to a new civilisation.

We are a Reset Generation.

The knowledge that built all this fantastic architecture might be lost, as we don't know what has happened. In a way, it's still deep in our psyche and somehow, we've blocked the memory of it out. Because of a possible psychological amnesia, what went before us is still in our subconscious mind.

Through the fantastic architecture and buildings that you see about you today, I want to give you examples to help find out about when the cataclysm or the ice age or the mud flood happened and I want to ask: is it all rubbish? If not, how recent was the reset? Have they just made up the timeline and given us a complete fabricated history? Did the Jesuits give it to us?

Proving anything that I'm talking about, the flat earth or the great reset, means some people have to adjust their thinking. Once they get the idea that this world has been reset, and continues to be reset, and that the shape of the earth is the biggest clue to how we're all being lied to, that's when they come round to thinking about all the other lies they've been told.

In my previous book, *The Holy Grail of Our Flat Earth,* I offered proof of the earth's flatness by going through a series of videos I presented on *The Greatest Secret Never Told*. There, I mentioned the double torus, the four angels, the Cook Pines mystery, as well as the electromagnetic model of this place in which we live. When you invest the time to read my book or watch my videos, it becomes life-changing information for you. You know it's the truth because it makes so much sense. I continue on with the good work in the hope that it will wake people up to the truth.

2. ARE THE ANSWERS IN ARCHITECTURE?

When you are looking for possible eradication of our past, you need to look at old buildings and how they were constructed. There are plenty of stones that remain in the ground, stones that (thankfully) cannot be moved even with the 'advanced' technology we have today.

I keep asking how could there have been a plane-wide society if they were, apparently, in *pre-historic* times and they never had any tech to build with? What I'm talking about here is, I used to visit quarries to collect, dress and cut stones. Just for a bit of fun, I would look for a shape that I could make a face on, but I found it difficult to do that with the tools I had. What academics lead you to believe is that the people who built the fantastic buildings you see about you were working with copper chisels. From my own experience, the people during that era would not have been able to do this type of thing with those tools on that stone.

Then I asked the question about urban decay and erosion? When I look at the urban decay, I see it all around me in the cities and ask: Why is the rate of decay so quick? Decay of buildings happens over decades, rather than hundreds or even thousands of years, as we are told it does. How is it then that all ancient antiquity (for instance, the Roman Coliseum) is still there, thousands of years later?

I've looked at palaeontology, archaeology, ancient history etc. and none of it makes any sense. Yet, even though I can see it's so wrong, on so many levels, I have to stick with what academia has given us. When I do, I find that there are so many missing elements, some of them are so glaringly obvious.

Are you aware of the process of entropy? Very quickly, it's the process of decay over time. All matter is made up of atoms, the buildings and nature around us, and us too. Buildings get blasted with wind, rain and particles in the air, all of which causes erosion. Essentially, these effects make our surroundings wear away with time.

You can visit places of historical interest and you can see images of this decay in books. Some ancient buildings are supposed to have been around for 6,000 years or so, for example, the pyramids in Egypt. Except for where man has deliberately damaged them, those buildings are still standing solid, firm and strong. So, what's going on?

Nature and buildings
As you may be aware, reinforced concrete is nothing to a plant. You only have to go to your garden and see

for yourself how plants will push up through the concrete or any man-made material. Trees will ruin a property, if you have one growing too near the house, you're told to either cut it down or use an anti-systemic agent to kill the roots to make sure it doesn't grow again. Or, you're advised not to plant within so many feet of the building.

I know a fair bit about this because I've worked in horticulture and stonemasonry and in building construction too, so I've learned about what nature can do to a building. I've seen how quickly a plant can take it over. Near where I live, there is a waste piece of ground which has been left for about two or three years. It is the remnants of an old RAF barrage balloon site from World War Two where there are some absolutely huge hangers.

Over the years, nature has taken over that RAF site and now there's no sign of the buildings. Only the metal remains, and that's since the 1940s - less than a hundred years ago.

A building which you are probably familiar with is Angkor Wat. It was supposed to have been built in the 1400s, which is not a vast amount of time, but in the Middle Ages nevertheless. This makes it at least SIX HUNDRED years old.

Some people just won't open their eyes. They will go with the history that's told them and they won't question anything. That's what this book is trying to do. My aim is to help people see another way or to imagine another possibility for the way this world works.

> *All the evidence is there for people to see it
> if they really want to see it.*

Some people believe we are in the Tribulation times now and I do admit to having Apocalyptic thoughts. When you look around you, you can see that the world and its weather is responding in kind. Any hurricanes that America have, sure enough, a couple of weeks later, we in Britain always seem to have. I remember a hurricane in 1987. The weather forecasters famously reported *ideal* weather conditions for that night, they said that we would suffer perhaps a *bit* of wind. Did we heck! The so-called 'bit of wind' managed to blow down 80 MILLION trees. Meteorology is not a precise science.

When you look at some decaying buildings, you see that the inside decays first, then the concrete turns to flake on the outside. The rain, wind and weather elements get to it and eventually, the concrete disappears. But stone? No. That stays seemingly forever.

It makes me question how long do books last in paper form? Why would they leave all the books in all the old abandoned mansions you see on YouTube? There are loads of places all over the world that have been abandoned for years, yet they still have old books and furnishings in them. There are Jewish churches in Romania that, in another ten years' time there will be nothing remaining of them. Decay happens quick.

When you are told about ancient buildings, like the Roman Coliseum, you're expected to believe that it's 2,000 years old. Apparently, it's not made with stone but strong concrete. It's the same with the ancient buildings of Greece.

Imagine what it was like when people lived on streets lit by gas lamps in the Victorian era. When these Victorians went exploring, they were amazed to see these fantastic buildings so, I guess they could have been led to believe they were thousands of years old. When you compare the buildings that are supposed to be thousands of years old to the RAF hangers near to where I live, while nothing remains of the RAF base, which is less than a hundred years old, the ancient buildings still stand.

Look at Lincoln Cathedral. Before the Statue of Liberty was built, Lincoln Cathedral was the highest building in the world. It apparently took hundreds of years to build and, interestingly, was built in the same period as Angkor Wat, but that wasn't subject to entropy. The explanation given is that Lincoln Cathedral has had a constant maintenance programme.

When you look at Machu Picchu (which was rediscovered in the early part of the i900s), the top of the mountain has gone but, the stones are still there. My only guess is that an international society built these impressive buildings that still stand today, and they're not that far away in the history books.

It's mind-blowing to think like this, but you only have to look at the megalithic structures to get evidence of this. It becomes obvious that our history has been eradicated. I believe that Rome is Babylon and that it never went anywhere. If you look outside your window, you'll probably learn that the road you see out there is a Roman road. Rome has been with us for over 1000 years and yet, their buildings, their roads, their cities, haven't been overrun by nature.

We are also told that Greece is about 4,000 years old. When you look at old pictures, drawings from the Medieval Ages and photographs from the i800s, you can see how we are led to believe that. One big anomaly is that, from this same area, an astronomical device was found in the sea. That device has been found to be more advanced than the Swiss watches that we see today and yet, no one knows how old it is.

Asian East
Going back to Angkor Wat, in the Khmer civilisation in what is now known as Cambodia. We are told that this civilisation built the Atlantis microcosm on a Flat Earth plane. Historians basically rediscovered it in the i800s, in the middle of a jungle that had taken over the site.

You will see Angkor Wat is incredibly ornate, but we're being told the place is around 500 years old – not in vast antiquity. Don't you think that is really intriguing? The architecture resembles something you might see in India or Britain and America as it has the same style of arched domes and colonnades. When you see it, you begin to understand how this design has been replicated the world over.

If there is a similarity between these buildings all over the world, does it mean that we all had flying machines at one time? Does this mean we were all a 'one plane' society?

In China, there's a problem with some of the mountainsides where people have hewn houses out of the cliff face. The images of those cut-outs look ok on their own but put a human in the photograph and everything is put into perspective: they are absolutely massive, hundreds of feet high.

How have these people carved their houses in the rock face? How would they have done it? How did they get the scaffolding up there? How did they manage to work with the rock from the scaffold?

As I've mentioned, I've worked as a stonemason and it's not easy. From my own experience and what I've learned about how to do this sort of stuff in normal buildings, those ancient houses and giant statues hewn into cliff faces don't make any sense.

The houses, monasteries and great castles are built high up in the mountain tops and they look as though the people have gone to great efforts to construct them. In modern times, the Chinese will build gantry-type passes around cliff faces so that they can get around them, from this, it does appear that they can build elaborate constructions in what seems like impossible places to reach with rudimentary scaffolding. Compare that effort to the effort that went into carving the massive statues hewn out of rock faces, some of them 200ft high, it could be possible that humans could have made them.

The sad thing is, China is hiding something. When you return to the original sites where these impressive statues had first been photographed, they're not there anymore. Many of the giant statues have had their faces damaged or defaced, or destroyed altogether. Why was that done and when?

I try to look into these things, but I can't seem to get any answers. Where did they go? Why did they take them down? Why did they destroy them? What are they hiding? But, more to the point, *why* are they hiding it?

The Americas
In Central America, Costa Rica, The Dominican Republic, Belize, Guatemala and the Caribbean islands, there are some weird looking balls. They are massive, smooth, round balls, which are more like giant boulders. No one knows anything about them, but they're connected to the Olmecs. While the stone heads found in these areas look like they come from Africa.

In Guatemala, where you'll find the Olmec heads and the balls, there is evidence of a previous civilisation in stone heads found under the sea. History professors don't seem to want to know about them because these things don't fit with their made-up timelines. There is one particular statue they want to forget about and it's one that has Caucasian features. If they accepted this Caucasian-featured head in that location, in that era, the history books would have to be rewritten.

You can see that some of these Olmec heads are black gentlemen from Africa and they've got earrings similar in style to what you'll find with the old tribes of Africa. What are they doing in Guatemala? It can only mean that there was an international society and older civilisations were able to sail across the oceans. Who knows how many generations did this and how long ago?

Now, some of the statues you'll find in America look as though they've been created in the modern-day. One has the look of Crazy Horse about him, the famous Native American Indian. It's only when you compare it to the size of a human that you get impressed. It's that kind of building and craftwork that gives an example of what people were capable of.

What gets interesting is when you go over to Mexico and check out the Mayan Empire, you see that some of them were partly underwater and that canals ran through the buildings. Archaeologists have confirmed that canal systems run between the ruins.

Puma Punka and Easter Island
In Puma Punka, there was a really strange cult that was depicted in the film Apocalypto. If there's anything that strikes you about the stones in Puma Punka, it should be the way they have been made. The seamless joins, the perfect boreholes – they look as though they've been poured into a mould and sealed together. In the polygonal stones, you'll see that no mortar has

been used between them, yet they fit perfectly.

There are more intriguing aspects to these buildings, especially the mathematical equations to the angles and sizes. They are megaliths, and they are everywhere all over the countryside. What kind of mind was doing this? What were they thinking? What were they doing? What was it for?

Compare these buildings in their current state of destruction and it looks more and more as though the current generation of archaeologists and academics have tried their very best to eradicate our history completely. Academia may have tried to do a good job of covering it all up, but humanity is getting too clever for them.

The heads on Easter Island are a bit of mystery too. We're told that the people constructed them by walking them back and forth, in a rocking motion, and then buried them in the earth. But, and here's the kicker, they go down so deep and they're so heavy, there's no way any human being would be able to do this. There are no trees on the island for a start. The trees would have provided for rollers to enable the people to move the stones easily.

Once you see these impressive tall stone figures, the question you begin to ask is, why are they all facing out to sea? Some alternative history people have said there is a trade wind that rips through this part of the Southern Pacific Ocean and the previous civilisation may have had some sort of transport network, something like balloons that zipped across the jet streams.

Because Easter Island is situated in the path of the jet streams, the stone heads would probably capture the balloons as they came through - acting as breakers do on the beaches of the British Isles. This would have provided the travellers with a pit stop, a place where they could refuel and get some drinkies, a couple of coconuts and hoola hoola girls and what have you. Obviously, that's just another theory, but quite a believable one.

Do the heads on Easter Island look Polynesian? Look at the big eyebrows and big chins. Why are the rest of them underground? Was it an earthquake? A volcano blast? A flood? We know nothing and they are a mystery to us. It seems there have been a lot of statues and monuments that have been sunk or flooded all over the world and we can't seem to find the answers to what they are or who built them.

If you doubt my assertion of a more advanced civilisation that has gone before us, then check out the site that was unearthed in South-Eastern Turkey. It's called Göbekli Tepe and is a bit of an enigma. I think this whole site points towards a bit of a psyop. Why do I think that? Because there are too many reliefs on those columns that depict the dinos.

Africa
There's another weird-looking site in Libya. In Z004, there was a sandstorm and what was hidden in a sand dune was revealed. The official narrative would like to

blame the Romans and they'd even like to blame the Carthaginians. So, who built it?

Our history books record that the Carthaginian people were in Libya and that Rome took Carthage. It is very well recorded that Roman ruled Britain and a good bit of North Africa, but I think there's a lot more going on in Africa that is being kept hidden from us.

On all ancient maps of Africa, between the period of the i400s through to the i500s, castles and palaces are dotted everywhere. The Mappa Mundi shows the African landscape covered in churches and palaces, but is it now? No. The desert is slowly revealing the buildings and strange artefacts that were hidden, but my question is, why were they hidden? When did they hide them? How did they do it? And, more interestingly, why is everything so big? This is a history that has been eradicated.

It seems someone has gone to a great effort to get rid of the notion that Africa may have been inhabited by people able to build such impressive structures. To me, this is evidence that the civilisation that went before us was a plane wide civilisation.

BUILT BY GIANTS?
I've looked at the huge statues that have been carved of the Buddha in Asia, and I've hunted for evidence to see how it was all possible to carve mountains into figures. Do I believe in giants? Not really. I know there was a big fakery in the i800s, hence the giant in Cardiff in America (not the Cardiff where I live).

Some were found that were proved to be made of Plaster of Paris. One thing I do know though, is that, in antiquity, a lot of biblically big statues were hewn into the mountainsides. To make a comparison, I looked into the more recent faces carved into Mount Rushmore in America.

I followed the story of the man who envisioned Mount Rushmore. He saw the cliff face and thought he'd put the idea of President's faces carved into the rock. He basically raised funds, started it, ran out of funds, then went back a few years later to finish it. This can people become aware of the level of effort that went into doing something like that - and how many years it took.

It turns out that all over China, and the rest of the world too, are huge statues hewn out of the rock mountains. From these, you need to ask yourself, who put them there? If Mount Rushmore took that much effort and that much money over a twenty-year period, in modern times, then who the hell made these giant statues in the last civilisation that has gone?

There have been newspaper articles (which you can take with a pinch of salt) in the early i900s with headlines that read:

Giant's Skull Unearthed by WPA
Workers New Victoria

Victoria County in Texas, Texas University Anthropologists, photographed a normal-sized human head against a giant-sized head.

In old newspaper cuttings, you'll see images, drawings and photographs of men who were much, much taller than the average person. Sometimes more than twice the size of an average human being.

Who were the people who carved the monuments and statues you see all over the world? Were they just bigger people back in those days? Who knows? When I look at all these photographs of massive balls, buildings, statues and heads, I wonder how they did it. If there were people in ancient times who could build massive structures and carve beautiful huge statues out of stone, then who were they?

The buildings that the ancient civilisations constructed could be a hundred times bigger than Christ the Redeemer, but do we really know when they were built? How would they carve this stuff out of mountains? Some of them look like natural features, and yet the question remains could they be real beings from times past?

I worked on a house that was built in 1559, the top of the doorways were so low, up to the bridge of my nose, that I had to duck to get under them. I was told it was because people were smaller back then. That was 400-500 years ago, so what's going on? Is this another lie? Were our ancestors smaller? Were they bigger? How are we supposed to figure all of this out?

I have no problem with the faces that were constructed on Mount Rushmore. I can see how they managed to carve the head of Crazy Horse, but those Buddha's in China – I do have a bit of a problem with how they carved those.

My query is, how they were able to build such magnificent buildings and yet they couldn't invent stuff like cameras? I think the Elite have done a good job in dumbing us all down in the last century or so.

Castles and Star Forts
If you don't know about Star Forts then they are something for you to learn about. The simple fact that these advanced-looking buildings exist makes the Great Reset seem a reality and it makes such an unbelievable difference to your life to know that there have been Resets in the past. You must begin asking your own questions about them.

Many people are aware of Ghost Cities, and castles are everywhere, 600 in Wales alone, but not many people know about Star Forts. Star Forts are nothing like castles and there are fewer Star Forts than castles.

A lot of these castles were underwater as, when you look closely at the footings of the buildings, you can see bleach marks, or tide marks, where the water line was. Castles have also got a lot of empty space in the middle, in the area that's called the Courtyard. What were they doing? Were they pumping the water out? Where are they using that water as an energy source?

Just go to the Flat Earth Think Tank and you'll see loads of images, photographs, old drawings and illustrations of castles and Star Forts. There's a whole catalogue of information there for you to look at. Why, for instance, is a Star Fort that's so big, situated on a tiny Atlantic island? When you start to look into this, you'll find that they're all over the plane. In America-land, Fort Erie was dug out of a canal in Rochester, and in Buffalo, they were already there before the i400s.

Star Forts have been found in Cuba, Egypt, Denmark and Estonia and something stuck out in my mind about these things – the fact that no one taught us about them in school. We were taught about castles but not about Star Forts. They seem like they are for some kind of futuristic technology that civilisations were using in the past. In fact, you could describe them as the stealth bomber of castles.

They might even have been pumping stations. Many of them have towers that puff steam out, which could have taken sludgy mud out of the earth after the mud floods happened. I often wonder what kind of frequency they must have resonated at. When you look at them from above, they look as though they are formed on vibrations, like the patterns depicted in those photographs of snowflakes. They look like they're designed on some kind of somatic pattern and you'll find that no two are the same.

Whatever these Star Forts were, the fact that they're so similar in different parts of the world, point towards ONE people with the same design plans. And another thing that crossed my mind is that, you can't have countries that are supposed to be enemies sharing the same formations.

I have to ask why were they not using these Star Forts in the War? If you know anything about the First World War 1914-1918, you will know that Ypres was the main thrust of it all. There was a Cathedral in Ypres that was completely destroyed and the only memorability that remains of it are the paintings.

Bearing in mind that they dug trench lines 800 miles down to the Swiss border, the whole thing was massive and yet, there's not a word about the Star Fort that goes right up to the trench lines. Why were they digging trenches when this kind of system was available to them? Why weren't they using an old building that was not only strong but safe and already established?

Castles are nothing like Star Forts. Whereas castles have very long histories, there's a very limited record of Star Forts. We're told that there was a bit of an invasion, then there was a bit of damage and then the castle was abandoned. But, if you really look at a Star Fort, there's no way you can damage it.

People dragged stone blocks up hills so they could build giant castles. Why did they build them so high up? Were they keeping them away from something? Or was their technology better suited to high ground? Castles are built surrounded by water as well. There are some beautiful castles in Germany. The ones in Britain have giant empty forecourts that we're told were for jousting, but I think it was for something else.

Here's a thought, does moat mean 'mud' in old English? The moats were apparently built to keep enemy armies out but what about when moats froze over? It would only have taken a little lad to skate across that ice, jump in the window, creep down the alleys and open the gates. Or, you could take a boat ride.

When I look at the size of them, their position, what's surrounding them, I believe they were pumping stations that pumped water out off of the land. Then I have to ask, where would they pump the water to? Note that Holland's buildings are for pumping water, not grinding corn.

The construction dates of these buildings can't be believed. We are taught that they were built in Britain after the Norman (French) invasion, but they seem too good, too solid. Some are even too ornate to be built with the tools people were supposed to have during those times. The greatest Gothic castles are in Germany and they're so beautiful they seem as though they should be in fairy tales. In fact, Disney uses one in their logo. Do you know which one? There are some fantastic ones in Scotland, too. Ones that have magnificent turrets and are built with white stone.

I've often wondered why castles were needed in Switzerland. There's never been a war in Switzerland, yet it has loads of castles, and they are built high in the mountains on top of rocks.

Jaime II de Mallorca i300-i311 had a castle, Castillo de Beliver, in the 14th century, and it is in such good shape today because we're told that, in the i900s, it was used as a prison. Ok, that sort of makes sense but, again, it's the same shape as all the rest.

Some castles may have been defensive forts at one time, but now, they are someone's home. Windsor Castle is supposed to be the British Queen's home. It's the largest in the UK and it's supposed to have been built by the Normans. Inside, it's a fantastically massive construction with acres of land around it. Even New York City has a couple of castles that people live in. We are told that these were built in the mid-i800s. Unfortunately, even though photography was invented in the mid-i800s, there are no photographs of the construction.

Bearing in mind that there are two types of castle in America, one type is made of old grey, rustic type granite, and the other is a smaller granite stone on top which is added later. One of the castles in New York City is one of the old types - a European one, in plain sight.

We've made a big collection of Star Forts in the Flat Earth British Think Tank, you are free to visit my website and find the link to them there. When you look at them, magnify the images and look closely at what is happening. You'll be intrigued.

There are a series of paintings from i630s onwards that show the state of the place after mud floods. These paintings show you the extent of the Star Forts, how big they are, how they're constructed, where they are positioned and where in the world they are. They're everywhere. What you will find is that there are always armies throwing a lot of cannonballs at these Star Forts in order to destroy them.

There is a mystery of a Spanish-type fort in Florida in that they say it's a 'cannonball-eating' fort. The secret, we're told, is inside the walls. According to the narrative on that one, cannonballs don't do anything to a Star Fort.

When the Spanish ruled Florida in 1702, the English Fleet from Carolina approached the Castilo San Marcos, the Spanish stronghold on the Atlantic coast. The British wanted to take over the area, both for money and politics. As a result of the reluctance of the inhabitants to give up their stronghold, the British started shelling the fort. But, after nearly two months of this bombardment, the fort still stood.

Even today, it's still a mystery as to how those walls seemed to 'swallow' the cannonballs. They seemed to become embedded into the walls. It remained a mystery for the next three centuries. What usually happens is, when the cannonballs hit a castle wall, it creates long deep cracks in the stone that radiate out from the impact centre and it's this that causes the damage to the structure. However, this didn't happen with the walls of this Star Fort.

This Star Fort was built with sedimentary rock formed from compressed shells and dead marine animals. Are all these Star Forts built like this? Did they get the materials from the bottom of the ocean? If so, how? There are reports that the rock in these Star Forts wouldn't splinter, they wouldn't give way. The cannonballs that were thrown at them were like throwing a ball at a lump of cheese.

It all points to the buildings being used for something else - before people got hold of them to make them into Forts. They are very technical and something completely different to what we think they are.

When you look at the Gallica books and check out their Lead Atlases, look for Milano (1713), by Pieter van der Aa (1659-1733). He produced what seems like coded maps, they were highly detailed with incredible depictions that give many clues. On one of the maps, there is a monster Star Fort and, outside of most of these buildings, mud is everywhere. They depict the ruins of the old world with images from the Bible, set in the corners are images of the Phoenicians pouring water out of big jugs.

The maps normally show a highly concentrated built-up area inside of the Star Fort and, outside, it looks like it is perched on a hill of mud with broken trees all around it. Within those Star Forts, you see buildings that look like they are part of an advanced technological society. Hundreds of towers spike out of areas that look like aerials. There are also sculpted angels in stone on top of domed rooves. When you look at some images, there are Jesuit symbols in them too.

The old etchings you see of massive ornate and massive, magnificent buildings are standing on mud. Didn't anyone think to pave a road or a path around?

For one thing, it would have been easier to bring in the materials to build with. There are massive buildings described as hospitals, but they were probably used as 'mad houses', which is what they were called back in the Victorian era.

Futuristic buildings are depicted in images from i733, which look as though they were built only a few years ago with helter-skelter type towers, domed rooves, massive ornate arches. We haven't even got anything that futuristic in our cities today.

Empty Cities
There are photographs online of cities in China and Angola where they are filled to the brim with tall high-rise apartment blocks. The weird thing is, they're all empty. The freakiest empty castles are the white castles in Turkey. The buildings had been constructed along the lines of fairy-tale Tartarian style. They are exactly the same type you find in Angola, Africa, and China, but again, they're all empty. They look like imitation Tartarian buildings and are built as far as the eye can see. There are millions of them. Again, they are empty. It makes no sense that these were constructed for people to live in - but they're not being lived in at all. The only excuse I can think they might give is, "We ran out of money, so we had no foresight, no connection with the future's market, we could never have seen that no one would live in them."

Why was there a need for all of this? This 'empty building syndrome' can't be the same for many cities over the world. They are there, they are waiting, they are ready and there are plenty of people who would love to live in them. I suppose I could hazard a guess: they could be for the upper classes after some sort of Great Reset. They could be being prepared for when the current dystopian nightmare closes down around us.

The Mental Asylums
If there's one building that should be empty, it's the mental asylum. The way the Victorians kept people in them and the way they treated them is beyond my comprehension.

The Andaz Hotel in Liverpool Street, London, used to be called The Bethlem Royal Hospital and it is the most mysterious building at the centre of spy-gate. It's still there. It looks really old, yet modern at the same time.

It seems, in the past and, in particular, in the Victorian era, there was a lot of mental illness for some reason or another. What the hell was going on? Nothing was being built at that time, not with all those people who were off their heads. We're told that all those buildings were built during that century, yet it seems as though they were built by a previous civilisation - or people who were more capable of erecting such things.

Inside the Andaz Hotel (or the Bethlem Royal Hospital), there is a majestic Masonic temple. You need to make a note of that - the most mentalist institution on earth has a massive Masonic temple in the middle of it all. It's a temple that has been built with twelve different types of marble. It has mahogany chairs, bronze chandeliers and an organ. Bearing in mind what I've said about organs in churches, and their vibrational energies, I wonder why they've got that in there?

There's also a chequerboard floor and, if you look along the edges of that floor, there are pyramid depictions. What also impresses me is that there's a Phoenician lion door knocker and a plasma burst star that holds up the bronze chandelier. So, an opulent room. I bet it wasn't cheap.

Were the Masons messing with humanity in mental institutions? There were plenty of these buildings in the UK alone, all over the country, massive beautiful buildings were used as 'hospitals for the insane'. Insane? In my mind, the percentage of insane compared to Britain's population at that time was at odds.

The vanished expositions
In the 1800s, stone buildings were razed to the ground by freak fires that would burn out the centres of all the cities. This happened all over the world. When you look at the world's Exposition in the 1870s, you have to ask about what happened to them. There's the Crystal Palace in London, one in Paris, in Chicago, Philadelphia, and there was also one in San Francisco. Big beautiful buildings – yet they all burned down. The one in San Francisco was constructed after the earthquake, but it no longer exists. In fact, there's not one atom of any one of them in existence today. If

you can tell me how those buildings, made of stone and steel, have been demolished and wiped away, I'd love to hear from you.

What I propose is a similar theme all over the plane. In photographs from the 1800s, you'll see the big pillars that look like columns standing in big cities - but none of it exists today. What I'm proposing is that these are a remnant of a recent culture, the same people that gave us all these Neolithic structures, and some cataclysm wiped these people out. The clue lies in the silt that covers them.

I do realise that Victorian buildings have to be demolished sometimes because they're dangerous and falling down. They pose a danger but, if you think about the London skyline of the 1870s, I'm sure you wouldn't be able to tell it apart from today. The Houses of Parliament and the Tower of London and the like were there and still are, as is the Tower Bridge.

In Paris, there was a building, an archway with two massive pillars in front of it. It had the dimensions of the Taj Mahal, very clever and ornate, but it's gone. Why would they knock that building down? Even if it was burned, the stone would still be standing. The Reichstag in Germany was rebuilt when it burned down, so I'm sure they could have done the same with the building in Paris. Architects and builders have proved they can gut out old buildings and make them pretty again.

Why have all the Expositions been destroyed? They were stunning. It seems as though someone has made a concerted effort to eradicate a certain style of architecture, the style of the buildings in St. Petersburg, Moscow, or Budapest. All that solid stone and ornate marble has vanished.

Different parts of each of these buildings could easily be represented in the ones you see in Istanbul, in Russia, Paris and Germany. It's all based on an ornate, fantastically well balanced, intricately designed architectural style.

Daniel Hudson (1846-1912) was apparently responsible for the restoration of some of the old buildings, however, I would like to approach him and others involved in the restoration programmes. I'd like to ask for their expert opinion as to why every one of these buildings suffered fire damage. Could it have been for insurance purposes?

Some of the buildings are similar to the Town Hall at Bruges. There are ornate designs with massive arches, tall windows, intricate lattice – a similar theme that has not wasted away through disuse. It has been deliberately demolished.

The only thing that remains of Crystal Palace in London is a beautiful window, relocated to Kew Gardens. This window gives off a rainbow effect and the puzzling thing is, the experts don't know how it was created. What did they want to show off in these Expositions? I know that Crystal Palace was used by Victoria and Albert to promote the technology of the time. Inside was the Tesla Tech, the new technology that would have taken us into the new world, the brave new future.

One thing I find really weird is that some photographs have been taken looking down on the buildings from the skies above. I wonder how they did that. There were no aeroplanes at that time. Balloons, perhaps? If so, that must have been pretty dodgy up there with those big box cameras.

Brunel
I've been looking into Isambard Kingdom Brunel (1806-1859), the architect. One of his greatest accomplishments was the Great Eastern which was the biggest ship that ever sailed. It took a hell of a lot of people and a long time to build it. The story goes that, while many people lost their lives as they were building it, Brunel also died. He suffered a heart attack after being photographed standing in front of the chains.

The chains that were used on the Great Eastern and the propeller were massive. They were the first of their type and were copied for use in the Lusitania and the Mauritania ships. What is amazing is that because those chains were so big, it took about a year to get the Great Eastern out to sea. The sluice gates that were used for it are still in the River Thames. This is where the Great Eastern ran down into the river. Quite amazing. I would love to have seen that.

Sadly, we're told that the Great Eastern was a failure. It managed a few crossings over the Atlantic but ran into financial trouble. After this, the ship spent the last of her days on the banks of the Mersey in

Liverpool. It must have been sad to see that ship rust away in the dock and then, eventually, broken down for scrap.

Why was the greatest ship that had ever been built in the Victorian era destined for that end? Why would it be left on the banks of a river to rot? Something so impressive and a historical monument to man's achievements. Quality craftsmanship of Brunel's. Yet, as with most of those beautiful Expositions, that ship no longer exists.

Brunel often had photographs taken of him with his hand in his jacket, this is an obvious sign for a member of Freemasonry. Freemasons often get extreme funding for folly and this would answer a lot of questions for me. Brunel's father, Marc (1769-1849), was a Frenchman. The Brunel's were linked to the works of Alexandre Gustave Eiffel (1832-1923). It was Eiffel that gave America the Statue of Liberty, but he was best known for the Eiffel Tower, built for the 1889 Universal Exposition in Paris. Paris has one as well, but it's much smaller. Incidentally, the Eiffel Tower was built by Brunel too.

Train Stations
In Cardiff, there's a building that houses offices to the Queen's Street Railway Station. You might be asking, why am I suggesting this building? I have been looking into all the oldest photographs available of major cities, places like Bombay, Tokyo and Melbourne, just a random pic from colonial times. What got me thinking was that the railway stations are

all very similar in structure and style and it occurred to me; the Railway Station in Cardiff looked like a thousand other stations I had seen before. I wanted to know if one company built all these stations.

When I was a child, the offices in the Cardiff Railway Station were not used for the main station, but a secondary station, the Queen's Street Station. It was a visual delight, and there was nothing wrong with it. It wasn't decaying, it wasn't falling down, and it wasn't in need of any major works or restoration. But again, for some strange reason, they knocked it down and replaced it with a monstrosity.

If you look at the Tokyo railway station, it looks like it could be placed anywhere in Britain, in fact, it could easily be placed in London. It survived World War Two and the firestorm. What's intriguing is that it's identical to any train station that you would find in Europe - it hasn't got an oriental theme, as such. So, what's going on there? The architecture of Tokyo Central Station bugs me.

I think the railway stations are a clue to what's going on around the world.

There is a very large hotel in Mumbai, India. It's known as the Taj Mahal. A few years ago, there was a major terrorist takeover of that hotel, they've even made a film of this horrific event. The building is a monstrosity, i.e. MASSIVE. It was apparently built in the i700s, and it's similar to St. Pancreas Railway Station in London.

When you look at the entrance to Mumbai, the ancient city in India, you'll see that similar arches have been built in every city all over the world. Now, were the ancient Romans or Egyptians responsible for these arches? The Egyptians were apparently in India, they were definitely in Sumer at some point. Could it be that the ancient Romans were responsible for building in India?

Ports and Palaces
I recently visited a port near the city of Venice. It wasn't a good time of the year to go, as it stunk. I postulate that Venice wasn't always filled with water. There are dry streets in Venice that are not underwater. The thing to note is that the buildings you see are identical to those on the Grand Canal.

I think there are clues in Venice and I'd be happy for us all to dig a bit deeper into this. The construction of it was strange as what usually happens is that the water is dredged and then they begin the building process, but there are no clues as to how this was done. How old are these buildings? i600s? I'd like to know how, why and when they built Venice.

My mind points towards a cataclysm that brought a lot of water into the city. With that water, a lot of silt covered everything. Those people must have worked hard at recovering it.

In Russia, there's The Winter Palace and The Hermitage. They are impressive buildings and there's an opulence that is St Petersburg and also the Kremlin in Moscow, too. Most of Russia's architecture was built in temperatures of -16 degrees and commissioned by Peter the Great.

Bear in mind that in World War Two, when this place was called Leningrad, it didn't fall to the Germans. During the war, Leningrad's citizens survived a daily bombardment from the Germans, they suffered freezing winter conditions and ate sawdust for food. But what did they do in their spare time? They read books and repaired these buildings.

The Germans seized the Amber Room of the Hermitage - and made it disappear. It's gone off the face of the earth. Some people say that it is in some drug baron's or Diplomat's house somewhere. It's a whole room made of amber. Beyond priceless. The architecture is so sublime you can't even put into words how beautiful it was.

I asked this question before, and I'll ask it again: why did the Russians choose to move the capital from Moscow to St. Petersburg? St. Petersburg itself was built on a swamp. Incidentally, so was Washington and London - the Thames Basin was swampland. Outside, on the roof of the Hermitage, and on the roof of the Kremlin, there are colonnades so big that the people who stand next to them are like dots. I can't imagine in a million years what kind of machinery was used to build them. To give you an idea, when I worked on the Millennium Stadium, in Cardiff, I saw the biggest crane in Europe. Two of them lifted the roof sections up to fix them into place and I can honestly say that those cranes would never have been able to lift those colonnades in Russia.

Check out NewEarth on YouTube and you'll see lots of clues about the history of Russia through its buildings. Just outside of St. Petersburg, you'll see some megaliths of the palaces that have been destroyed. The stones of those buildings have been spread around the country in the hills. My theory is that all these buildings, the Hermitage and the older destroyed buildings, are from an earlier history, one that has been eradicated and erased and taken away from modern society.

Inside The Hermitage in Russia, look closely at the sculptures. They were supposed to have been made around the latter half of the i600s to the i700s. The Industrial Revolution had just got going and, yet, people were knocking out the kind of stuff that's so expensive and intricate it's beyond belief.

How could they carve those sculptures with the tools they had during that period? The part that gives it all away is the lace and the fine-thread in the material of the clothes that cover the statues. It looks like it has been 3D printed, not carved with a chisel and hammer. How on earth can they get such perfection in marble and stone with those rudimentary tools?

If you look at the edifices on the roof of the Kremlin, you'll find that it's a replicating theme. There is an overriding connection in all Western civilisation and its sculptured angels, gargoyles, and Greek Gods. These things seem to hold in their hands' items that represent the chakra system. Through those statues, you can see representations of the double-headed phoenix, you can see the clues if you keep your eyes open. You don't need a doctorate, you just need to travel the world and start asking questions yourself.

Another replicating theme you have to question is the one of Alexander the Great. Alexander was everywhere and everywhere he went, a place was dedicated to him. Alexandra Palace, Plaza, the statue in the centre of St. Petersburg, even the famous Library of Alexandria that burned down (with all the secrets of the ages held inside). We're also told that the people with blue eyes who reside on the Fertile Crescent are descendants of the armies of Alexander the Great.

The more I look into the buildings, the architecture, the structure, the size, the opulence, the fantastic marble and stone statues and the ornaments inside, the more it blows my mind.

ANCIENT CLUES
There seems to be a theme that humanity has gone bonkers with dragging big stones around on logs with ropes. Is this a reality? I think they had advanced technology, harmonics if you like, the same tech as Edward Leedskalnin had, the man who built Coral Castle in Miami, Florida.

There are strange megalithic monuments that were brought from Egypt to the UK, like Cleopatra's Needle. There's one located by the Thames, another one in Leamington Spa, there's one in Rome which, apparently, has a piece of Jesus' cross on it. You'll also see one in Central Park, New York as well.

The style of architecture looks very much like Aztec buildings – yet they smashed them up. To me, it's a Jesuit psyop to get rid of ancient history, the ancient civilisations and if you dig just a couple of feet below your feet, you'll no doubt come across some massive stones with symbols or some lost language carved into them. Many of these stones have a language carved into them that looks like a mixture between Greek and Russian, I think there's a link between the Orthodox churches.

If you look at the floors, you'll find many of them have polished marble with geometric designs etched into them in such detail and with such precision, it doesn't seem possible to do with the tools that we are led to believe they had at the time. These buildings give evidence of how previous civilisations have been reset and things, like the globe model, have been put in place to fool us all into believing we're something we're not. Those in charge of us, the Elite, have reinvented our past for their own evildoings. I would never have believed this myself if I hadn't begun to look at all the evidence that is clearly plain to see. It's all there if you're prepared to look.

In World War Two, the Germans collected up fantastic pieces of art and priceless artefacts and stashed them away somewhere. Hollywood even made a film called *The Monuments Men,* to show how the

Allies tried to get it all back. So, were the Germans collecting them because they were priceless, or because they held the secrets to our past?

As I've mentioned before, there are sculptures where the veil is made from stone, yet you can see the statue's face through it, perfectly etched, as though a lady had been dipped in milk. How was this possible with the tools they are said to have had? I believe these things were inherited from a civilisation that came before.

We have constantly been told that these old buildings were put together or commissioned by 'so and so' and 'so and so', with little evidence. They will tell us the main pyramids at Giza were built by Keops (Cheops, Kufu). Yet the only reference to Keops on the whole plateau of Giza is the plaque in front of the Sphinx, which, though it's near to it, it's not really in the same place as the three pyramids. It just appears that they looked at that plaque and said, "Oh well, he must have built that as well. End of."

These are supposed to be the people who went before us in extreme antiquity. Really? Am I mad for thinking this way? Am I mad for thinking they were not the backward people we are told they were? Just coming out of caves, scratching an existence, surviving from day to day or a warring people who just keep on effing one another up on a Biblical scale? Do you think that's what's going on?

Petra is a perfect example of an ancient civilisation. It's really strange the way they went into these deep caverns to hollow out these treasuries. The famous one that you saw in the Indiana Jones movie is a bank. But considering this thing is supposed to be in extreme antiquity, I really don't understand it. I have to question the validity of what is being told to us.

Qibla compass

Qibla, the Kaaba, also spelt Ka'bah or Kabah, sometimes referred to as al-Kaʻbah al-Musharrafah, are walls that face the direction of the Kaaba. For centuries, Muslims have built Qibla Walls. The idea behind the positioning of these walls is that when a person prays, he faces the wall and knows he is facing exactly in the direction of Mecca.

For centuries there has been a debate whether the Walls face Jordan, Petra or Jerusalem. This is interesting to flat earthers and it's this question that I ask: How is it that Muslims knew that by using a Qibla compass, from any point in the world (apart from the North Pole), they could find the exact direction of any third point? How is that humanly possible? Does Mecca have its own magnetic field? Is it only detectable by certain compasses that the Elite don't want us to know about?

I found a map on a Muslim site that made me question the narrative. We are used to seeing the world on a flat projection, from a certain angle, but the map I found that Muslims use is centred on the North Pole. From this map, you are given an idea of the continents of the world and from it, you will understand where Mecca is in relation to the rest of the world. It shows that from Alaska through to Mecca in Saudi Arabia, there's a straight line through the North Pole. It shows you that Alaska and the Qibla are almost due North.

Today, Muslims can use an Apple App to find their directions in a Google globe model. The modern App doesn't prove anything but, you might be on to something if you found in ancient books that the Muslims have written about a Qibla compass. This compass has been used for centuries to find the position of Mecca and the direction for the positioning of their Mosques. Now, through the Flat Earth Think Tank, the team have found some old Gallica books written in Arabic. Housed in these books is evidence that shows they had a Qibla compass that showed magnetic North.

I went onto a Muslim site that showed you how to find the direction of Mecca and it's mind-blowing. There is a site on YouTube that describes how to plot the direction for Mecca on a globe model. Bear that in mind for what I'm about to tell you. Something interesting cropped up, courtesy of Khalid Saukat, on Moonsighting.com, that gives you the Qibla direction for the US and Canada. The Qibla compass was able to get magnetic North during ancient times, but I don't know how this modern map can give you these numbers without this compass.

The Qibla direction is expressed in degrees, clockwise, from the North Pole. When you look at that map, from Alaska we have down into British Colombia,

Washington, Oregon and California are all on ZERO degrees.

On a globe model, this is IMPOSSIBLE.

If this model is anywhere near accurate, then when you look at the degrees expressed by other States in the US, this model should prove the earth is flat.

I wish I could read Arabic because, basically, housed in those ancient books are the exact Qibla directions from any point in the world. I have downloaded about twenty of these ancient Arabic books and they are available as links in the Flat Earth Think Tank. So, go there and have a look for yourself or, if you prefer, go and visit Gallica itself as there are direct links to those books. All you need to do is search 'Qibla' in Gallica and choose Manuscripts, they will appear.

I have a strange idea that these Qibla walls prove that some kind of ancient compass existed and that it could have shown the North Pole and could have also shown the magnetic fields of Mecca. What if this compass with two needles, one pointing North and the other pointing directly at Mecca, could show the ancient Qibla walls are definite proof that the flat earth exists?

Electricity conductors
On a Sumerian brass plate, there is a depiction of what looks like an electrical conductor. It looks like it is something to do with Tesla tech and the harnessing of the power that's locked in the ether. You'll see it in a

lot of ancient Sumerian images.

Is ancient Sumer the civilisation that they make it out to be? Well, the American military seems to think something is going on with them. As soon as the first Gulf War began, the first thing they did was go into the Baghdad Museum in Iraq and ransack it. Why would they do that?

You'll find that all these ancient sites around the world are all linked. The ancient buildings and lost civilisations show us what we were, we now need to learn to understand what we truly are. From the Sumerians, you'll find that their stories tell us that it's all to do with a certain group of gods that came from other places. Sadly, the world's historians took the tablets away that tell you of the Annunaki, that come from the planet Nibiru, and that we are supposed to be their slaves that dig up the gold. Zacharia Sitchin was supposed to tell the story about it, but he's been known to be a 'player'.

In Sumer, Iraq, which is quoted as the original black civilisation, there is a type of building called a ziggurat. Now, we are led to believe that the ziggurat is really old, thousands of years, and it has weathered the earthquakes, the floods and every other thing that can be thrown at them, yet, when you look at this style of building, the bricks are very neatly placed and really ornate, almost pyramid-like but they are so advanced in their style, they look futuristic.

I'm starting to believe that something else is going on with these buildings. Take a look at the things we are told they have found around those sites. The elongated skulls could have been bound by bandages, just like the Chinese women used to bind their feet. But, if those skulls were really that shape, where would they have come from? They're certainly not human.

If you dig into ancient archaeology, you'll find lots of references to the Flat Earth. The stories of Atlantis always refer to it and 6,000year-old bowls from Sumerian culture depict the Flat Earth in beautiful images. You'll find it in the coding in anything that comes from the supposed ancient era. Paintings, marble and stone sculptures, kitchenware, clay jugs, gold ornaments. It's all there.

Advanced energy?
Spiralling water gets energised, it is called 'living water' when it spins through a vortex path and it can be energised when put through a certain system. People knew of the health benefits pure drinking water would give you and that you can get energy from it too. Aquatec is unbelievable and mind-blowing and it's all part of our architectural heritage that has been hidden from us. Most of what has been hidden from us hinges upon the water and the energy we can get from it.

Does it ever occur to you that the Coliseum in Rome was not really a place for Gladiators to kill one another? I believe that the Coliseum is a highly advanced reservoir or a water storage area – a water tank.

Basically, in my last book, I explored the v-shaped nature of water towers. Lee Flat Earth British came up with some fantastic information on the interior of v-shaped' water towers. He brought to our attention the water storage facilities, reservoirs which are huge buildings with elaborate pathways, which seemed to have another hidden meaning behind them. They are important sites and I believe that they were intended to capture waves - sound or radio waves - as this is depicted in these structures. The stairs seem to make resonation waves as they were hollow bowls, like a parabolic antenna.

Stone steps going down for a long way were very elaborate for what they were supposed to be. It's some worldwide architectural feat, not just found in Western cultures.

Look at a dam or a ramp, you can see how they stop or divert a river arriving on one side but, what if the river arrived from all sides? You would need a v-shaped vortex path, a circular structure designed to stop a flood, similar to the ones found in ancient buildings.

Water spins in a vortex flow, so there's nothing strange when you get a v-shaped reservoir. However, Viktor Schauberger (1885-1958) discovered that spiralling water gets energised or, as he called it, 'living water' when it spins through vortex paths. Schauberger put water through a tubing and energised it in a specific way. Unfortunately, the technology is now lost to us.

The benefits of this energised water to humans was in

the drinking water, bathing water, and water used for agriculture. When you sit around it, you get energy from it, just like you do from the fountains in antiquity. For instance, the Roman Baths in Bath, UK, are thought to be an energy source. Unfortunately, the knowledge has been taken from us though, from watching the behaviour of animals and birds, they seem to know something about it.

This advanced water technology was seemingly used in amphitheatres, as discussed in my previous book, *The Holy Grail of Our Flat Earth*. Coliseums are called amphitheatres for spectators, for theatres of gruesome, bloody massacres, but are they spiral vortexes? There are plenty of these water energy machines in Italy, and there's another in Africa. There is also a double vortex in Pula in Croatia that is exactly the same shape. Were these built so that morons could batter each other to death in front of ignorant Romans? No. The Coliseum is an energising water plant and does an incredibly good job at it.

Schauberger said that it has to be an elliptical shape, like the Coliseum is the shape of an egg, to cause the double vortex flow. Schauberger tried to explain it to people, but they wouldn't allow him to get his ideas out.

There are no straight lines in the universe as they always follow a spiral path. Some are so small you can't see them. There is a reservoir in Mexico with the same spiralling effect – I believe the people knew all about how to work this stuff.

What these buildings, or aqueducts, have in common is that there is a distinctive V-shape to them, they are elliptical and they have double vortexes. There are rings that go all the way around these tunnels. Remember the etymology that we learned in my first book; the word Coliseum means 'col-lo-see-um' – which means 'circular'.

The stepping, or seating area of these so-called arenas, was probably used for workers who needed to go down and check where the water level was. The bottom of the amphitheatre itself is covered in sand, not gravel, nor muck (or mud), but sand. You could say they brought the sand in via cow and cart and that the sand was to soak up all the blood from the fighting and killing, but you'd be wrong. The sand acts as part of a filtration system and it fits perfectly with what I am attempting to describe.

The Coliseum had many tunnels, which I've personally witnessed with my own eyes. It would make sense that you would put sand in there to purify the water. Below the street level, there are big tunnels and small thin lead water pipes which brought water into Rome.

Google gave a bit of truth when it displayed a quote on the 'Roman Water System' as follows:

> *"Once in or near Rome, water from the aqueducts passed into large, covered catch-basins. Here waters were supposed to deposit their sediment. Waters from the catch-basins were distributed through*

> *free-flowing canals, lead pipes, and terra-cotta pipes to storage reservoirs and then through lead pipes (called fistulae) to users."*

BINGO. A sand filtration system.

Lead pipes did not bring about the demise or fall of the Roman Empire. They are they're still there. The amphitheatres they have constructed are large water basins - all in plain sight. In Ancient Roman times, the Roman aqueduct system took water from a reservoir via an intake valve and funnelled it along an aqueduct bridge to the city.

Photographs were taken of the contractors that took mud from near the Coliseum in the i940s. They were building the subway line. Those photographs depict not recent pipework but ancient. When you look at the depth of the tunnels they were emerging out of, the stonework gives it away.

I always wondered about the steam pipes that were found under all of these ancient structures. The ones under the Coliseum are really expansive; they are huge lead pipes that go through this vault type system.

UAP channel showed a video of the pipe steam systems in old-world America. Could these tunnels and lead pipes be some sort of steam heating system in Ancient Rome? In Chicago, they send steam to ancient radiators, which are still fully active today. The Mills System is what keeps them going. You will see more than a hundred miles of steam piping to heat the buildings in New York.

Maybe stone pipes were used to carry cold water and lead pipes to steam heat big buildings in ancient Rome? There don't appear to be any smoke deposits in the old buildings. If fireplaces were used to heat these ancient buildings, then the walls would have traces of burn marks or soot. But they don't. They have none. How were they heating king-sized buildings in ancient Rome? Pipes is how.

Where the Coliseum stands today, I shit-eth you not, stood the Roma Antiqua. It was in the same places as the Coliseum. The official story to explain the pipes away is that Emperor Nero had a private home called the Domes Orea, near the Coliseum and in the same spot, Nero built himself a giant private swimming pool.

Nero was the one who was supposed to have ordered a full-scale ship to be constructed in the middle of the city for his private pleasure. He wanted it so he could sail up and down his swimming pool. This is what they're teaching us, so they can explain away the pipeage.

You may be familiar with the explanation that the Coliseum was used for naval battles/games but that's not the truth.

> *"At times, between two gladiators, or wild animals fighting, schedules on*

> *Thursday's and Sunday's they would close the amphitheatre (amphi = two uses) to the public. It would be waterproofed within hours filled with millions of tons of water and they used to build full-scale naval battles and hold them in the water."*

Why? Because the ancient Romans want to see people kill one another and drown because it gets a bit monotonous seeing people being killed and eaten by lions. The clue here is that they tell you they were waterproofed - which is a big handy statement to make.

Now we've seen these pipes going through, they get smaller as you get down, the lower you go, the smaller they get. What we're talking about is an EM field being put through iron or copper and it makes a charge with water inside. You can attach wires to generate an EM field around a cylinder to produce resonation waves. If iron was used in the arches, would it create an EM field in the Coliseum?

What I'm saying is, if the Coliseum is capable of creating a charge, it would need metal all the way around it, so is there any evidence of this? It's difficult to say, but here's a quote I found about a Rome that had been destroyed a few times by fire. Basically, in the 6th Century, looters came in and...

> *"...over 300 tons of iron clamps were*

> *stolen. The clamps once held the travertine blocks together, yet, even without the support clamps, the structure has survived."*

Magnetic Water

Ok, what are the benefits of energised water? People knew about this in ancient times, but this technology has been robbed from humanity. But, not to worry, as Flat Earth British is giving it back to humanity with love.

> *"After centuries of being considered an 'old wives' tale', magnetism is finally coming into its own. We now know that fish are able to return to their spawning grounds by following the earth's magnetic lines, or force, in the same way that birds do. Similar results have shown up lately, in beetles, crickets, bees, grasshoppers and flies. The magnetic sense is so strong in many insects that they will rest only in definite 'magnetic positions."*

They only fly in straight magnetic lines, they won't fly everywhere. Apparently, a gardener recently found that when he scattered magnets in the garden, moths would become disorientated and left. Research available in the Soviet Union shows how the growing effects of plants are being tested with magnets. They have found an eleven-year cycle directly related to fluctuations in magnetism caused by sunspot cycles. Apparently, this increases the plant yield. Basically, South Pole energy increased below-ground tubers (root crops) and North Pole energy produced larger above-ground plants. Therefore, the health of people could be greatly improved by putting magnets in water.

We've looked at when water collects in abundance, but what happens in times of trouble? People die of thirst. Let's pretend we're in a time before orgon receptors were used in religious parades. Let's just presume that Wilhelm Reich has not been born and neither has Kate Bush, so *Cloud Busting* is not on the agenda right at this time. So how would people survive the drought? Would they have to pack up and go to a nice place up North, in Holland perhaps?

In the Netherlands, there is plenty of water around. There must be another reason as to how they're getting water in Ancient Rome. It must be another technology. There is available today a desalination process of removing salt from seawater and it's not as difficult as you might presume as there are a couple of ways of managing it. Did ancient Rome desalinate water to help out in times of drought? Well, if there is a way to do it with your pot and stove, I'm pretty sure the Romans had cracked it.

> *How to desalinate water: Fill a pot with seawater, put the lid down, heat it up. Your water will steam up and drip down the sides of the smaller pot and become*

> *freshwater. You can also do this without boiling by placing a bowl filled with salt water in direct sunlight. This will heat up the water and cause condensation to form on the plastic wrap. As condensation forms, freshwater droplets will drip from the plastic wrap into the cup.*

It does take a few hours, so you need to be patient. If there's enough fresh water in the cup, you can have a drink as it is safe and completely desalinated.

If you look at the ancient Flavian amphitheatre, you'll see that they had a 'retractable cloth roof'. It's known as the velarium. Here's the official narrative nonsense, but they do give you some clues that give the game away, again:

> *"240 mast corbels were positioned around the top of the attic. They originally supported a retractable awning, known as the velarium, that kept the sun and rain off spectators. This consisted of a canvas-covered, net-like structure made of ropes with a hole in the centre. It covered two-thirds of the arena and sloped down towards the centre to catch the wind and provide a breeze for the audience. Sailors, specially enlisted from the Roman naval headquarters at Misenum and housed in the nearby*

Castra Misenatium, were used to work the velarium.

The Colosseum's huge crowd capacity made it essential that the venue could be filled or evacuated quickly, its architects adopted solutions very similar to those used in modern stadiums to deal with the same problem. The Amphitheatre was ringed by eighty entrances at ground level, 76 of which were used by ordinary spectators."

In these two short passages, they're actually telling you that they had the technology to desalinate.

There are 'rings', similar to the amphitheatres and the Coliseum in Italy, all over Spain. Basically, they are now used as bull-fighting rings. Were they using these things to murder animals needlessly in ancient times, or were they actually water tanks for purification and magnification of water or desalination processes? The bull-fighting rings are round, they're not elliptical. In my mind, these are antiquity's desalination plants.

You can compare them to the modern ones that you see around the world. There's a desalination plant in Carlsbad, a coastal city in the North County region of San Diego County, California. It is identical to the bull-fighting rings that you find in Spain. So, the people in antiquity have been desalinating their seawater as well.

Not only did the Coliseum generate water pressure to ensure that water would get to every quarter of the city, they also delivered 100% clean mineral drinking water for all. The most advanced features were sand filtration, with v-shaped basins suitable for a superior vortex oscillation water purification mechanism. Five hundred tons of iron wiring in the arches ensured magnetism of water's minerals. Stone pipes could be used to transport cold water and the lead pipes in stone tunnels for hot water – maybe even to generate heat. This is an easy explanation for all the pipes.

They would have clean, pure water with this 'closed pipe' system in place. Basically, you get one side of the pipe that goes deep into the earth, and then the water will heat up because the earth is warmer the deeper you go. Then it goes up into the house, once it is nice and warm, it cools down and goes back down through the pipes to reabsorb the heat again and returns into the house.

The most amazing thing about this is that it is all-year-round FREE ENERGY generated by warm water. They built lead and stone pipes for the water reservoirs. I think this is a good summarisation.

A place for uncivilised retarded morons or an architect or marvel of hydraulic engineering made by an advanced civilisation.

Which one do you think?

Resonance
Now, this is going to buzz you out. I did introduce this concept in my last book, but if you can stretch your imagination, think of churches as sound resonance machines.

The ceilings have cymatic patterns, and if sound is played inside a tower, with organ pipes, water will vibrate. When reaching a certain tone, for example, 4,3,2, the sound resonates and leaves a pattern it creates on the surface.

Now that pattern would be hard to see on the water alone but, if light arriving from a window opening reflects like mirrors and passes through crystals or lenses then, through the resonating water, you will get a projection onto a white screen. This device could project cymatic patterns on a ceiling – to be copied as a template, maybe? Or for a window? Is that what they did?

What this type of technology proves to us all is that the previous generation of humanity was using sound as light. Sound and architecture are very closely connected and the perfected architectural qualities found in churches are definitely a resonating mechanism which is used to great effect for healing.

It seems that antiquity had very advanced energy and purification mechanisms and desalination processes. All of this is evident all over the world. It's in America, South America, Mexico, Africa, India, Asia – everywhere. This is what they were practising in the past. This is how much we have been robbed.

Gladiators? No wonder they put so much money in that bloody film. Makes you think how much you've been deceived.

Evidence of advanced high cultures?
Historians will lead you to believe that Göbekli Tepe is the oldest archaeological site on earth. According to their dating techniques, the temple is 6,500 years older than Stonehenge. To me, though, it's another hoax designed to either distract us or to lead us away from the truth. Why do I think it's a hoax? Göbekli Tepe portrays dinosaurs and they depict things that are not around today.

The site has been precisely constructed in proportion with sacred geometry. Bear in mind they've only excavated a tiny proportion of this site. It was found by a farmer who was walking across the dry, dusty land and he came across the stones sticking out of the earth. He brought the experts in to excavate it and found what has been described as the oldest site on earth but, there were no signs of human habitation. No signs of tools. No religious aspects to it either. Why did they build it?

Göbekli Tepe was a place that people would travel to on a pilgrimage, but I do think it is some sort of hoax to permeate their globe myth. Göbekli Tepe is about twelve miles away from a boat that was found on the side of a mountain; Noah's Ark. They've also found stones with modern-looking drill holes in them. Weird, don't you think? Are they some kind of ancient advanced culture? Who were these people? Where did they come from?

Looking at maps of the North Artic and a model from the Vedas, the hyperborean seems a likely answer. The civilisation that I believe has just gone before us used to move blocks that weighed up to twenty tonnes. What makes me question the narrative is that we can't move them now with our own equipment, yet we believe that these polygonal blocks are from the late bronze age. The thing is, you cannot even get a razor blade in between the blocks and they're too heavy for our trucks and cranes today. When you look at those blocks of stone, you have to ask, how did they do it?

Make a comparison between the huge buildings that have been carved from a massive block of stone, and then look at the intricate lace and rope examples etched out of sculptures. One fantastic example I am fascinated by is a sculpture of a statue with eyelashes that are carved so intricately. We can't do any of this with the tools we have today.

I believe it all comes from a previous civilisation, a highly intelligent culture, that has been wiped out from beneath our feet. The technology and tools that they must have had to produce such baffling structures and art don't make any sense.

There are bridges based in Eastern and Western Europe and Russia that have survived World War One and World War Two. You'll notice on these bridges that they have a line across them. It looks as though they've been built upon something from the recent past – I wouldn't even be able to give it a timeline.

Given the destruction of all the stonemasonry and architecture damaged during the two world wars we had in the i900s, it is amazing they are still there to give us clues. I think the over-bombing of Europe was not just to kill the civilians and their stories about their history, but to destroy physical evidence of a previous civilisation.

From the mining in the Belarus area of Russia, a lot of evidence remains of a previous advanced civilisation. Big stone blocks that have been carved and then left to rot gives you a clue about what people were able to create before our generation came along. I'm puzzled as to what machinery was capable of that sort of work. The grooves in the rock roads, we're told, are due to cartwheels that have rolled over these roads over thousands of years. Yet, how do wooden wheels grove out rocks?

You'll see lots of caves carved into the rock faces in the Crimea, old palaces that have been knocked down. It's all been carved into the stone. There are entire valleys that have been carved out with what seems like giant mining machinery. Things like aqueducts, bridges and massive valleys, but we're told that nature carved out these valleys. You can make a comparison by checking out the massive slate mines in Wales and the machinery we use to do that job. The size and scale look impossible but, when you compare them to the giant valleys around the world that we are told have been carved over millions of years, the ancient ones look like they've been carved by giants.

It's clear that river and rain haven't made those grooves in the rocks of the Colorado Death Valley and Grand Canyon in America. Instead, they look as though they've been carved out by giant mining machines.

Look at the maps of the i500s, you'll see the hyperborean area, then check out images from the Vedic cultures and you'll see the clues for Mount Meru. When you get to later images, all the evidence that was available earlier has gone. The same has happened with photographs of buildings from the i800s. When we get to the i900s, they've been demolished before our eyes. Hundreds of magnificent buildings in Paris, France, have been demolished for no reason at all and we don't even need to look at the maps drawn 300 to 400 years ago because there is actual photographic evidence for it.

What happened? More to the point, the question we should be asking is, why did it happen? Compare the demolition process to what happens to buildings when they decay over time. They don't just vanish into thin air.

ARE WE GOING BACKWARDS?

Looking at the fine examples of buildings such as those found in India, Japan, Italy or even Cardiff in Wales, you would think we were going backwards in time and our ability to produce such beautiful architecture has been lost.

I've been looking into the age of buildings and carbon

dating, where they take a bit of the building and then put it through a process to find out the age of it. I've got a piece of the Coliseum in Rome. As I was walking around the Coliseum outside, I heard a clink on the floor behind me and I found a piece of the building that had fallen off. It was as though the building was trying to give me a clue. I picked it up and took it home with me.

There is an energy in that stone. Apparently, it has witnessed an era where thousands of Jews were supposed to have been killed when Nero fed them to the lions. Nasty bit of business to any ordinary person anyway. It does feel a bit spooky.

When you look at the series of photographs I've made available on the Flat Earth British Think Tank page, they make you want to scratch your head and wonder what the hell has been going on with the timeline. I have a theory about what they have done and the cataclysms and what they've done to set it up.

Entropy – nature's way
What happens to buildings in the normal world? With the evolution theory, they say that gravity gathered everything together in orbs over a period of time. What they don't take into consideration is entropy which would cancel it out. The rate of entropy would be much quicker than the period of the universe. If you go with the theory of entropy, you can see how things decay in a lifetime. Quickly.

Consider sandstorms in the hot arid deserts, blasting

and pounding buildings over thousands of years. Built-in the eras when they tell us that the deserts were arid at some stage, and through the Middle Ages, there was a mini ice age period too. If you go by their geological bullshit records, then everything falls apart.

Look at the decaying locations in Europe you'll see what happens to stone and brick that is over 100 years old. There are giant stone edifices, so big that no one can move them. Look at those and you can find out if you're being lied to or not. The records are altered; one generation follows another and slowly, their history disappears, as it only takes one generation to get everyone to forget.

I looked into the decay rates of buildings over a short period of time, the town in Chernobyl, which has been closed since 1984 and the decay in twenty years has been incredible. Or a beach hut, which had been moved out ten years previous and looks like it's over a century old. How is it that some buildings are subject to entropy and decay and, yet, those that are apparently thousands of years old are not? You might have the same questions as I have. I only have to look outside in my local community to have questions raised in my mind.

Destruction – humankind's way
I'm tying this all together to make a point here about what happens naturally, compared to what humankind does to its history. What I've found is that there seems to be a concerted effort to eradicate the past through fires, wars, and the rest.

Once you start looking at the information available, you'll notice the replicating themes of domes and pillars in the building structures. Many of them look like symbols and many of them were built in Russia in minus sixteen degrees! I don't know if you've ever worked on a building site in the winter in Britain, it's horrible. So, I'm asking, how did they manage to build the beauties in Russia - in that weather?

> *What I propose is that they are remnants of a previous civilisation and they are built on the bones of people.*

We all know that Russian history has been successfully covered up for the best part of a quarter of a century with the Cold War and the Communist political parties. During that time, they've done a good job of eradicating the past.

When you look at what they've done to the people, how they've murdered millions by putting them in gulags and starving them to death or leaving them to die in camps without clothing and in freezing conditions, then you have to ask why they did this? What was the reason for this? Was it because the people knew the history and the political elite didn't want the news to get out? Did they have to get rid of the evidence – which included people too?

You'll find buildings in Russia that are built the same way as the buildings in South America – the Aztecs. Tunnelling techniques that are unfathomable have been used as well.

Make a comparison between the beautiful buildings in Russia to the terrace blocks of the late 1800s – both build in the same era.

Why did Hitler not storm Russia? What did they do in the Siege of Leningrad? Hitler basically chose not to storm Leningrad, instead, he decided to put an order in to starve the population to death. Unfortunately for Hitler, as it was winter, the lake that connects St. Petersburg to mainland Russia froze over. It was called a 'sacred road' over which the people had a chance to escape.

There were millions of people in that city and all of those beautiful buildings survived, untouched, through an incredible bombardment of the giant Howitzers. Something like 4,000 big guns were on the German side. What do you think about this? Many of Russia's ornate architecture looks very Germanic or Roman. Elegant, beautiful and impressive and many of the symbols used are part of the Nazi's belief systems.

We pass by so much architecture without looking at it. We park up on the road or the street and we miss the beauty and history that's been hidden from us. You only begin to notice it when someone points it out like I'm doing now.

What happened to these buildings? Half of them have been buried under the mud, but how did the mud get there? When you're on an archaeology site, you'll normally find a black band along the stretch of earth. It looks like there's been a massive fire or burning at some point.

We have to ask about the size of our normal buildings, the ones in London, they're bigger than they should be and they were built when we didn't even have proper roads.

There's a lot of evidence found across the world of a culture that has been eradicated. But, some clues have been left behind. They are there if you make an effort to dig it up.

Re-writing history
All the historians do is re-write our history to the way they want it so that we don't learn anything about what our ancestors achieved or the lessons they learned. They could achieve this brainwashing in a week or, as we've learned with the CV-19 plandemic, they could do it in a year. Through fear and brainwashing, we will forget the way our own fathers lived before. Our own kids will not know about the world wars that were part of our grandparent's generation.

All those lives lost. All those people died.
For what?

You think you're having a brain-fart when one day they tell you that one side won the war, then the next day they're telling you someone else won. It's how you begin to doubt yourself. You think you're going crazy, so what do you do? You shrug your shoulders and you accept what you've been told. You don't wonder why would 'Big Brother' lie to me?

You see the problem? Makes you think, doesn't it? Our history seems like it's only 500 years old. It seems like they've just been resetting it every so often and telling us what they want us to know. They don't think that we will consider the entropy of these buildings and how we are wizening up to it all.

The stones you see all over the plane look like they've been melded, or melted, in together. You have to ask what kind of technology could do that? The technology was obviously there, in this Golden Era, that we know nothing about. Humanity today is not being given information about it. Why don't they want us to know?

Talking about stones, there was one under the Queen's throne, called the Stone of Scone from brought down to England from Scotland. They moved it back up to Scotland a few years ago. What was all that about? Talk about subjugating people and making them under the rule of another nation.

When you look at the buildings all over the world, there's a similar theme in them. Wherever you go, Russia, America, Europe, Egypt, it doesn't matter. Today, in these modern times, it is a confusing place to be. People who begin to wake up from their hypnotised/programmed sleep must be really disorientated. I do believe in the world of the metaphysical, I notice the spiritual aspects of life and then see subtle realities. This is all happening constantly. If you can sense it, you've sussed it.

You get things like this that were supposed to be from

ancient history. The historians that go on the television to talk about it seem to just continue with the lies. They go with the thunderbolt theory, which says there was a great catastrophe in the past.

There was a massive industry in the 1800s that focussed on these hoaxes. Follies are common across the UK and they even created broken down monasteries so that they could get money from tourism.

It looks to me like, when we were in our Golden Age, before the Age of the Kali Yuga Age that we are in now, when our vibration was higher when we were what we truly were, we were at one with nature and the animals and the world. Some kind of evil, maybe the Archons, came along and perverted everything and messed with our minds. What we need to do is not listen to the confusion that's going on in our minds and tell them to "get behind me, Satan!"

The Elite don't appear to want us to know that the people who created these magnificent structures were our recent ancestors. Today, this construct that has been placed around us has trapped our souls and minds. Luckily for us, we're just about to wake up. If we can get our act together in time, that is.

When we do wake up, there will be a beauty like no other. No more darkness across the land. There will be pace and love throughout. For now, though, the evidence has been wrecked and continues to be wrecked. It's intoxicating us. You can see the people who are doing this. Those with their bow ties, yellow hats and monster trucks shouting, "Chop it down!" "Build it up!"

> *"Pay Paradise and build a parking lot!"*
> Joni Mitchel

Well, eff them!

3. ART OF THE APOCALYPSE

If we look for more clues as to the great resets in the past, we only have to check out the many pieces of artwork left for us. It would only take an afternoon's walk around a local museum, art gallery, or a National Trust house will give you loads of clues.

In the paintings hanging up there on the wall, you'll see the artist has left something much more than an image for future generations to take pleasure in. Clues are in the structure of the painting, the positions of the people and buildings, the landscape and the architecture. Clues are also hidden in the shapes and diagonals used, particular hues, colours and tones. Etched permanently into the artwork are also obvious depictions of surroundings.

It's as though the artist has made time for and spent effort on leaving traces of what went on before. The capabilities of our ancestors and the technology they used are all there, left as evidence, direct from an artist's mind.

Take, for instance, the narrative in the Bible's New Testament, in particular, *The Four Horsemen of the*

Apocalypse in the Book of Revelation by John. The artwork that has been created to express that story is really weird.

The Book of Revelation is about the scrolls handed from God that tell of the Four Horsemen as the first four of the seven seals that the Lamb of God opened. The stories tell of 'beings' that ride out on different coloured horses, basically, these four horsemen are a real bummer.

In i887, the Victorian era, the horses were depicted by various artists as the following:

- Death – the first horse of the Apocalypse destroys all of antiquity – his job is to Reset it. He's on the pale horse.
- War - is the next rider of the Apocalypse, astride the red horse. We're always being frightened with some war or another.
- Famine - is the next rider, on the black horse. After wars, we always have some kind of reduction in food available to humanity. Think of after World War Two and the rations our civilisation had for about a decade or more after.
- Conquest - is the final rider. He's on the white horse.

You can look upon these four horsemen as a message for a Great Reset.

These four horsemen were depicted throughout our known history. Basically, Knights on horses go about predicting what's going to happen or even go to great efforts to make it happen. In the 21st Century, I predict they're going to come on motorbikes or hoverboards.

Death on the Pale Horse by Benjamin West, i817 is another intriguing painting. Beautiful, but you can see that it looks like the Phoenicians have turned up to kill everyone with plasma charges. There are bollock naked blokes in there. They should have got dressed!

Angier's Apocalypse is a tapestry by a nun. She probably got up one bored morning and set to work on it. As with many others along the same theme, it depicts the serpent - and there are plenty of them that show the plasma charges in them.

When you look at these images, they are quite chilling. The thing is, they all seem to hint at the power that people have and that it's just a matter of waking them up to this fact.

The Sutton Hoo Hoard – O004
This is a Saxon hoard found in a hill in Suffolk. You will be led to think that these were left by the Anglo Saxons who inhabited Britain prior to the Norman Conquest. So, after the reset of 04 AD, whatever that reset was for, they got hold of this information and

they perverted it and used it for their own selves and kept the rest of humanity down in ignorance.

The quality of the craftsmanship found at Sutton Hoo was made, apparently, with rudimentary hammer and chisels. When you look at it, it seems like it's electroplated. All of it is gold with crystals and precious stones embedded in it. Some of those crystals and precious stones were imported from other countries, like India and South East Asia.

The question here is, were these people Saxons from the Dark Ages? If so, wasn't their travel ability limited? It was supposed to be a time that was fallen from when the Romans left our shores.

Not only do you have to ask how they made it, but how did they mine so much gold? And then there is the smelting of the gold and making it into such intricate and beautiful shapes. Compare what you see today, to that which was supposed to be almost 2,000 years ago. You'll find the purity in this gold is perfect. What I don't get is, how is all of that find over a thousand years old? We weren't supposed to have the ability to create such things in those days. We are led to believe that we weren't that clever back then.

One of the most intriguing things that I saw was the Death Mask or the helmet of whoever the King was. They put it back together and found that it was jammed packed with gold. There's also a purse cover covered in jade, not stone, not metal, but jade.

I propose that the Sutton Hoo find was from a more

recent time and I suggest that people had then, was more advanced technology than we have now. This hoard found at Sutton Hoo shows part of the ability of the civilisation that built all these great monoliths, or megaliths in the rest of Britain. I reckon this is in the near past. For the record:

- The Saxons were from Germany, Saxony.
- The Angles were from Southern Europe.
- The Normans were from France.

These tribes are said to have come to Britain and conquered its people. Could all of this be a hoax? I think they are definitely lying about the dates.

Hieronymus Bosch – i500s
What puzzles me is the mindset of the i500s. It was at the time of the Enlightenment when the Globe lie was introduced to the masses. The artist who will give you clues into the minds of people during that era is Hieronymus Bosch.

Bosch was born around i450 and died August 9th i516 in the Netherlands. In his paintings, he depicted sin and human failings which focussed mainly on morals. He painted demons and half-human animals as well as machines. The machines confused viewers and encouraged a kind of fear of the evil that is in mankind.

Bosch's paintings were very bleak, even at the

Enlightenment, and when the Jesuits and the Vatican promoted the Heaven and Hell myth view. Bosch digs right into the human psyche and I think it's to brainwash people. The machines in his art are very futuristic and his symbolic figures are the stuff you get in your nightmares. Go and figure them out for yourself.

The theme of his art reveals the way his mind worked - perverse and evil. I can't possibly say whether he was a good man, but he did many paintings on Judgement Day and created cities that look like they belong in your dreams, not reality. I am interested in many of the maps he painted. They give us clues to the reality we have today. He depicted the sphere and the pillars, and everything was created with symbols in mind.

When you look at his work, you have to be able to read between the lines. Bosch paints men and women who are black and white-skinned, sitting together in boats. I must ask, was that frowned upon at the time? Bosch paints an enclosed world with the land masses on a flat plane with ice all around. It is intriguing but, we never ask what's below us yet, it's something that's depicted in Bosch's paintings.

Have you ever seen the film where Leonardo DiCaprio took a map to the Pope? The map was a kind of Mappa Mundi style. In the i500s, you see maps of the globe set within a sphere, if you look closely at Bosch's paintings from i500s, can you see Antarctica? Yet didn't Captain Scott find that place?

The heliocentric model was worshipped at that time.

It seems to me that the Elite want to bring in the apocalypse and all the horror depicted in Bosch's paintings. It is a hell on earth. It must be, when I look deeply into his work, I can't imagine what Bosch was thinking.

Bosch's paintings tell me that we are surrounded and controlled by a very troublesome force. It seems like it's all from another realm – one that's very close by. There's a lot of sexual depravity going on, too and the symbols in his artwork look like they have some important meaning. Perhaps a Freemason or a Jesuit would understand them.

Bosch depicts a nun as a pig that licks a man's face. Is this saying that men and women are swine? He depicts backgammon, a game that we have now in our era. There are also giant lutes or harps - the vibration they give off is transcendental, so you will hear harp music in heaven. When I commune with the Eternity, I hear it coming through as a harpsichord, or an old organ, from far away.

Remember, in the i500s, nothing was flying at the time, yet Bosch depicted flying ships in the guise of fish and futuristic looking crafts. Beggars and nuns were begging, and a Jesus figure was often hung on the cross.

Giovanni Battista Piranesi – i700s
Think of the Coliseum, the one they've been trying to make us think it's been there for around 2,000 years and was an entertainment slaughterhouse. If you look

up the drawings that Piranesi created of the Arch near the Coliseum, you can begin to imagine the Roman Legions marching through that Arch in extreme antiquity.

The artwork of Piranesi's that gets me asking questions the most is *The Paradoxes of Piranesi*. The sort of technology that Piranesi depicted in his art in the i700s is questionable. He lived between i720 and i778 and I ask if that technology was available during that period or was he depicting it from his imagination?

If you look at St. Peter's Basilica in Rome, Piranesi depicted it in the Middle Ages. He shows you how the Basilica was still surrounded by muddy pathways and there was no solid road around it. The style of the dome and the colonnades are replicated in buildings throughout the world. They are the same type of buildings you see in the ancient Grecian and Minoan Empires.

In his artwork, Piranesi gives a clue to what has gone before us. His work depicts bridges that look like the original London Bridge, the style of architecture could be Victorian, but it's not. This man was creating these works of art in the i700s.

So, the style of architecture that Piranesi depicts can be seen everywhere. This is all food for thought for me. I'm really intrigued by this timeline and I'm hoping it's enough to get you questioning too.

THE HOLY GRAIL OF THE GREAT RESET

Camille Flammarion - 1800s
Camille Flammarion was a Flat Earther who lived between 1842 to 1925. A French astronomer and a prolific author, he wrote a series of science-fiction works about the afterlife and spirituality. I did look for his links to Freemasonry and Illuminati but couldn't find any. Interestingly, he was a member of the Flat Earth Society.

> *He believed, in 1907, that a seven-tailed comet was on its way to the earth. With the appearance of Haley's comet in 1910, he believed the gas from the comet's tail would impregnate the earth's atmosphere and possibly snuff out all life.*

If he was a Flat Earther and knew it was a plane and not a globe, how could these be his theories? Then I came across this quote:

> *Jean Reynaud, who lived from 1806 through to 1863, described a religious system based on the transmigration of souls believed to be reconcilable with both Christianity and pluralism. He was convinced that our souls, after physical death passed from planet to planet, progressively improving at each new incarnation.*

What he means is 'plane to plane' and that's how it

works. If you look at any ancient texts, they always talk about the 'plane' and that there's always a 'plane' on top of a 'plane'. Planes. Not planets. Do you get that?

What he says about 'progressively improving at each new incarnation' is completely correct. We do live life afterlife but on these planes and different planes of existence. I believe we live here on this plane, one that overlaps a different dimension. They are 'planes in synch'. I believe that eternity is not far away and that those in the other plane can see us, but we can't see them. I also believe in the Astral Realm because I have visited it - many people do when they dream.

Flammarion was known to have visions and go into a lucid dreaming type sensation. In my videos, I go into subjects like astral projections and other highly interesting topics, anomalies to do with spirituality, consciousness - the stuff academia don't cover. Most people have encountered it, but for some reason, even though many people believe in an extra-terrestrial life, which means aliens are still on the table, scientists won't touch the subject. To me, aliens are either inter-dimensional beings, or they're up in a different plane.

Though there were no Masonic ties, Flammarion did have a bit of a thing for Mars and he was into spirituality, having attended spiritualist churches, although you'll find a lot of people did in the 1800s. People of that era are said to have witnessed things like transfiguration, where the Medium host would transfigure into somebody else. Usually, for some reason, they transfigured into a North American Indian.

> *After investigating into automatic writing, Flammarion wrote that the subconscious mind is the explanation and that there is no evidence for the spirit hypothesis. He believed in the survival of the soul after death but wrote that mediumship had not been scientifically proven.*

I found this intriguing. The book that I'm referencing is his *Mysterious Psychic Forces*, which Flammarion wrote in 1909. It's a jolly good read and his legacy is science and astronomy. He leaves some cool quotations. If you subscribe to the electric universe hypothesis theory, then you'll understand what he's saying about whatever cataclysm has come before us. Here's one he's known for:

> *The end of the world will occur without noise, without revolution, without cataclysm. Just as a tree loses its leaves in the autumn wind, so the earth will see in succession the falling and perishing all its children, and in this eternal winter which will envelope it from then on, she can no longer hope for either a new sun or a new spring. She will purge herself of the history of the worlds. The millions or*

billions of centuries that she had seen will be like a day. It will be only a detail completely insignificant in the whole of the universe. Presently the earth is only an invisible point among all the stars, because, at the distance, it is lost through its infinite smallness in the vicinity of the sun, which itself is by far only a small star. In the future, when the end of things will arrive on this earth, the event will then pass, completely unperceived in the universe. The stars will continue to shine after the extinction of our sun, as they already shone before our existence. When there will no longer be on the earth a sole concern to contemplate the constellations will reign again the noise as they reigned before the appearance of man on this tiny globule. There are stars whose light shone some millions of years before we arrived. The luminous rays that we receive actually then departed from their bosom before the time of the appearance of man on the earth. The universe is so immense that it appears immutable, and that the duration of a planet such as that of the earth is only a chapter, less than that, a phrase, less still, only a word of the universe's history" Camille Flammarion 'The End of the World'

I've witnessed the Aurora Borealis myself. I was in northern Scotland, in Banff, sitting on rocks. There I was, one inch from the sea, yet the sea was so flat calm it didn't even ripple to my boots. I remember eating garlic bread and drinking a bottle of Penguin beer and I stayed there all night in awe, watching that display. I've got to be honest; it was amazing.

I found a lot of maps with loads of Flat Earth symbology in them. In the middle of most of the maps, I found a pyramid structure, which I believe to be Mount Meru, but when you look closer at some of them, they get more intriguing.

There was a specific map that Flammarion interpreted to be the opposite way around to the way we see our earth today. There's one where the North and South Poles are on the opposite ends to where we believe them to be. Most of the lands were named after scientists of the day, Kepler Land, Herschel Land etc.

As I said earlier, Flammarion was prone to visions and a known psychic and practised spiritualism. You'll find this to be a common theme among a lot of inventors of the day. It explains how you'll find that one person lived on one side of the earth and came up with an idea for progressing science while, at the same time, someone came up with the exact same theory while living on the other side of the earth. You'll find this to be true when you look at the Patents that people have registered without actually communicating with each other in the same week.

Gallica Books
When you search these old books, they depict a lot about our history. Many of them are written in French, but the images show you the history of England, perhaps because it depicted a time soon after the Norman (French) invasion. Some of the pictures show you that the place is underwater.

The books seem to begin with beautiful landscapes and buildings, but you only have to go partway before seeing the population depicted as being abused. There are images of people hanging upside down, beating each other up, cutting their heads off. They're drowning and dying in rivers and seas. They're frying children, boiling people alive. They even show bones of the dead people and people who are being cooked and eaten. Depravity to the extreme. This shows you how they got rid of people during the Great Resets of the past.

You don't have to trust me on these things, it's all there, you just need to open your eyes, do your own research and know where to look for that research. Plenty of it has been collected in the Flat Earth Think Tank. Spend an afternoon browsing the images and the books that are linked there and I'm pretty sure you'll find the time has whizzed by.

Decoding music
When you hear the song "The hills are alive with the sound of music!" unfortunately, it means the music was set at a specific frequency, and it melted the rocks. I kid you not.

All songs need to be decoded. You may have heard of the i970s/i980s rock group Queen. I think they must have been the biggest social engineering band in history. Oh my! Every track, nearly! *Seven Seas of Rye* is a reset song. *Killer Queen* is not about a prozzie - it's about resetting our arses. *"Dynamite with a Laser Beam – guaranteed to blow your mind anytime!"*

There are musical methods that have been used by civilisations in the past that are beyond our understanding now. Why? Because it's been hidden from us. As I said earlier in this book, the resonance waves used by the organs in churches were used to put healing energy into the water. How are we not using this type of technology today?

One of the Pope's back in antiquity even changed the musical scales so that we haven't got the full spectrum of music to play with. What was that all about? Why would anyone want to deprive people of something that provided beauty and harmony?

Artistic clues
Artists from a bygone age seem to depict either a dystopian nightmarish future for humanity or a past that was so horrific our minds have blocked it out from our memories.

Art, as well as music, can give a lot of beauty and perfection. We can see how the classical music of the i700 to i800s has degenerated. Today, while you can hear a film score that can break your heart with a highly emotive melody – but then we've also branched out into mindless pop that has no meaning at all.

Do I think the buildings and technology depicted in the artwork I've highlighted here are a hoax? I think they are part of this civilisation that's gone before us, but I don't believe it was that long ago. We are a civilisation in the Dark Ages now, in this present day.

Think about Shakespeare's theatre, The Globe, which was around in i500s-i600s. It was built in a pentagram style and there's a bit of controversy concerning this aspect of it. There's also a bit of controversy over whether Shakespeare existed as well. Apparently, they were ordered to relocate the theatre. A group of men dismantled it, put all the pieces on a barge, sailed it across the Thames and built it all over again - overnight. So the story goes. Maybe there were a lot of people helping with this. Is it a reality? I don't know. Some people say that Shakespeare was a complete psyop and never existed. All those plays he was supposed to have written may have been written by his wife or someone else.

The Parthenon is a place I've visited. I was told the roof was made of concrete. When you get to the top, you'll be told that rain has been pouring through the oculus, which is a big hole in the roof, for two millennia. When you look at photographs and paintings that depict this, you can see how thin that concrete is at the opening. It was a type of concrete mixed with volcanic ash to give it some sort of solidity. And the 'boxing' technique or style was to give it strength and support. There is only one door in and one door out of the building.

Originally, the Parthenon was a Pagan temple, and you'll see little boxes inside the building where they used to place little Pagan Gods. Now there are statues in there.

When you look at the art, listen to the music and gaze at the beauty of the architecture passed down to us, you have to try to imagine the civilisation that existed then, what kinds of lives they led, what did they eat, how did they work and entertain each other. If the ancient civilisations were truly free from slavery of the banks and financial systems and everything that's going on today, would they be able to build such impressive structures? They certainly would have had the time and the leisure to do it. The people of that era knew what enabled them to achieve such architectural feats and I believe it is the remnants of their civilisation that exist today – depicted in the artwork left to us from the i700s-i800s.

The history handed to us today has to fit it in with the evidence that already exists. When you go to Rome, you have to be provided with evidence to support what you see. For example, when you visit certain buildings in Rome, you'll see that there are chess boards on the floor that are carved into the stone. There are other games too, games that we play today in board game compendiums, they were playing the same games in ancient Rome.

MARTIN LIEDTKE

*Once someone points these things out to
you, you see it everywhere.*

What's really at the heart of it all is the style of the architecture. In my mind, artists from civilisations past were trying to leave their children clues. Some of those clues were subtle hints and messages for those who are astute enough to notice them. They have hidden the answers to questions hoping that they will be revealed to those who can understand them.

We have to begin to look into these things and begin to ask questions for ourselves. We should not accept the narrative being given to us as fact. So, let's get to work together to make meaning out of all of this. The answer, I think, will be in finding humanity's higher purpose.

*Listen to people, do your research, then
make up your own mind.*

4. WHAT DO THE MAPS REVEAL?

I often look at maps of the i500s, which depict the North and South lands. From these, I can tell that nothing is as we see it today. What was the medieval mind trying to show us and what were they mapping? Could it be the maps are from an earlier time?

Of course, I realise I am aware of modern-day spoofs that try to fool people, and there are plenty of them around, which is why I put a lot of questions out there. I want to ask you to get your grey matter working to question the narrative being fed to you. I would like you to go ahead and do your own research into this subject. That way, you'll begin to wake up on your own without a rude shove from me or anyone else.

The maps I have range from around the 13th through to the 16th Centuries. What I want to know is what was going on at the time. Why were so many maps showing the landmass anomaly in the North, yet there are none today that depict it? Better map-making tools? The use of far superior photographic imaging from the fiction of space? Or, just more lies being fed to us?

I usually find in early maps that the North Coast of Canada and Greenland show the lands with mountain ranges. There's the Delta and a river running into these regions, but the strange thing is these are not on today's maps. The earlier maps show the hyperborean, but today's maps don't.

There are some anomalies with the Southern projections. In maps from the 15th Century, there are obvious outlines of Antarctica which are labelled as Terra Australis Stratus Incognita. You will also see on the maps created by Piri Reis (i465-i553) that Antarctica is always depicted free from the ice and snow. Just as with many of the old medieval maps, there is evidence of an ice wall around the land.

Buddhist Maps - i000s
AE Map was made by the Wright Brothers, and their father, in India. The ideas for this map came from the 1000-year-old Buddhist map, which is known as the Kobayashi Map, from Japan.

The AE Map was in a book by Kiz (like Kizmit), he says that the map is not an Azimuthal Equidistant because you're projecting from a northern central point. This map was discovered in Hawaii in the i920s. It shows us our landmasses fanning out in the middle with a perimeter of an ice wall on the outside, an endless large continent. I believe this is the reality of our earth and that the true continents are being hidden from us. However, there are issues with AE maps only because we don't know what's missing. If you look at the maps and lay them down on to a

Kobayashi, you could figure out what's real and what isn't.

There are some castles and commons in the Welsh Valley, about two or three miles from where I live. What I find is in i540, about 500 years ago, the maps were rudimentary, well, rubbish actually. Oliver Cromwell was stationed in this location in the i600s, so there's a little clue in that period of time. All you have to do is ask what Henry VIII was famous for? Apart from marrying six times, he demolished the Roman Catholic Church in Britain and brought in the Anglican Church. He was also known for the dissolution of the monasteries, and he smashed up all the beautiful Abbeys. What if this was part of an elaborate plan by the Elite to hide evidence of the previous civilisation gone before us?

I watched a documentary by NewEarth about the *Labyrinth of Minotaur* – which is on the Mappa Mundi. I don't know the exact location, but the entire area is laid out in a labyrinth of tunnels. Apparently, Hitler sent some people there, did some strange Black Magic, and they blew up the hillside to collapse the entrances so no one else could go in there.

Many maps present a puzzle in the date and location, especially the castles dotted around the world. The people who created these things would like to think that we're all as thick as shit and living in caves – if you're not the King, of course.

The detail on the image of the *Beast on the Battlements* at Knaresborough Castle in i561 is so intricate. It makes me ask, what if they just inherited something from before? There's a lot of symbology in the images: two trumpeters, the crown and sceptres, which are symbolic of King Edward III and his wife, Philippa. The lion was presumably a statue.

On the map of the Port of Rye on the southern British coast, you can see the channel and ships in the ports and the harbour. This seems quite populated for the time, 1500s. It shows it bristling with canons and it's heavily gunned. There's always this thing about tall walls in medieval cities. Why do they feel a need for them? What were they hiding from?

Mappa Mundi – 1200s
As with the Azimuth maps, you'll see the Mappa Mundi shows lands that are not on today's maps. The tip of Scotland, Iceland, Greenland are there and then there are some extra pieces of land that are not shown in today's maps. The further 'north' you go, you'll see the lands divided into four landmasses with a pyramid centred in the waters between them. This is called the magnetic mountain, Mount Meru, which makes our needles point north.

Many of the old maps, including the Mappa Mundi, show a creature with no head but it has a face on its body. They also show mountain ranges that warn people not to go pass into the vastness where possibly the dome is.

I did visit the original Mappa Mundi. It's painted on one huge piece of animal skin. It was created around i290 and is based on the book of Ezekiel from the Christian Bible. What you'll notice is that a lot of clues are given to our ancient past and these clues show how the Elites have probably reset our history, time and again.

The Mediterranean and China are on the opposite side of what we are told today. Britain (Albion) is depicted, where you'll see the hyperborean and mythical creatures and men with no heads. On them, Jerusalem is depicted as a meridian or a central land. Some maps depict Arabs with giant snakes and an Antarctica coastline that's free of ice.

There are some weird depictions of people with no heads on their bodies. There are images of half animal half human beings and you'll see this kind of thing in all Sumerian images from antiquity. It's as though the people who created these maps want you to think they were splicing DNA back then, creating cryptoid people. These all provide clues to the past that has been reset and hidden from us.

The Piri Reis Map – i500s

Piri Reis, who depicted maps from the i500s, has always said he copied them from earlier times, possibly a thousand years before. They were maps that were probably housed in the now burned down Library of Alexandria.

Most of the Piri Reis maps are biblically orientated but, for some reason, they also include symbols and images from Greek mythology. You'd have to be forgiven for thinking that Greek was in the Christian Bible, but it isn't.

Some Japanese maps show a giant landmass at the bottom of the earth, which is ridiculously big. Again, you'll see that they have the four land masses with the mountain ranges at the northern part of the map. They show how populated the earth was, all the busy towns and cities with loads of buildings in the – and they are not there now.

There are several versions of the Piri Reis maps, each one depicts ships everywhere, but there's no sign of any ice at the Poles. Are these from a time when there wasn't any ice in these regions? You'll find an indication of a warm and arid climate, and there are mountain ranges and crops with animals that are normally located in Africa. But the animals and plants depicted are not in Africa, they're in Antarctica. One from 1550 shows a lot going on in the area, it's busy and even a place anyone could live. So, what's going on?

The Azimuthal Maps
The Azimuthal, a map that I'm really intrigued by, looks down on the South Pole, Antarctica. You can see clearly the Cape of Good Hope and how it is linked to Antarctica. What I've seen on a hundred different maps is that Antarctica is connected to the lands of South Africa and South America.

There are maps from old Scandinavian books that show you early evidence of something happening in the North. You'll also find maps with no indication of the Bearing Straights being present. There's no Asia or America either.

The maps from around the 1500s depict Denmark and the Norwegian coastline and Friesland and the northern tip of Britain. There is no giant land mass between Britain and Greenland in current maps, yet they are there in medieval maps. Greenland is depicted with mountain ranges, but there's no snow, which is kind of odd when you compare it to today's Google Earth.

The theatre of the sky and earth
Now, this is interesting. It depicts Antarctica free from ice, with beasts, lions and mysterious creatures and your usual hyperborean at the top. They also show Purgatory at the top and another map outside of it. They propose Purgatory is above the world map, and it shows the journey of souls...

> *...delivered by the ferryman to the Inferno to be cleansed by fire, thence to the next circle Limbo, where, wrapped as it if mummified, they await Judgement Day.*

There are mummies and a hellish fire — and you really don't want to go there. It's nuts.

Could these old maps be from earlier projections? Are they maps that have been locked away and dribbled out into academia from earlier times, suggested by earlier map makers?

Arab Maps
There's an Arab projection too, but these have been suppressed in Western literature. If you can find anything from them, they are awesome. The hyperborean is depicted in them too.

Of course, the Arabs could have discovered these lands over the years and adjusted them accordingly, but to be so completely different is a bit weird for people who sailed ships and needed to know where land was. To be successful sailors, they needed to know the types of oceans they were crossing to navigate them properly.

A cataclysm?
When did this cataclysm happen? They say the Ice Age ended somewhere around 10,500 years ago. So, what if we assign a 10,000-year time frame for this current civilisation and the one that's just vanished. This would fit exactly with the India Vedas and the Bhagavad Gita and Krishna, which is around 6,500 years.

Some medieval maps use Jerusalem as a meridian, with an ice ring around the land. They knew back then that the earth was flat as they hadn't been massively brainwashed by evil devil-worshipping types.

I love upside-down maps. On some of them, you'll see Asia, the Americas, and Australia. They show the map of our world, but the other way up. On these maps, you'll see some strange things, like the hyperborean. The 'fools cap map' is also quite telling, especially the Latin and what it translates as.

You should be asking questions if you find that a civilisation had a catastrophe in the recent past, and the present civilisation was not only recovering that history from the mud but smashing up anything that didn't fit with the time frame.

There are some beautiful maps available. In most of the ancient ones I've seen, the land of Greenland takes centre place and yet, above it are ships and wales but no frozen ocean. There are puzzling depictions of pyramids at the centre of the North Pole. Does this mean it's a magnetic mountain?

These medieval maps show us something intriguing. They show Africa and the Nile and a great landmass at the bottom that comes all around us. Some of these medieval maps even show our landmass surrounded by an expanse of land. Some show America as 'undefined', yet you can tell certain parts of it – like Oregon, Seattle and California. Then there's a puzzle about a massive expanse of water near the Hudson Bay. I know that parts of Canada are peppered with lakes but, in 1762, a map depicts the Bearing Straights completely different to what we have today.

Other maps define an undefined landmass north of mainland Russia. Most of them show ice all the way around our landmass.

Why are all these maps showing something different? Was map making so difficult during those times? Why do they show undefined lands – like Australia and America? Apparently, New Zealand wasn't discovered until the i720s.

5. HOW OLD IS PHOTOGRAPHY?

Photography of the 1800s
When photography was first invented for some strange reason, the first thing they decided to take pictures of was not those beautiful structures they had just built but photographs of dead people.

I'm not quite sure if it's on par with this spirituality movement that was rife during the Victorian era, where everyone appeared to be a psychic and wanted to talk to their dead relatives. Still, there seems to be something going on with that. I think it relates to one big bad event back in that time.

There was a strange need to take these types of photographs. Not long after the process was introduced in 1839, the photographs that come from that era seem to reflect the reality of Victorian life. Before antibiotics were around, infant mortality was rife, and it was the time of the Civil War. Death, then, was a constant companion. Part of the process of keeping memories of the relatives who had passed over was to take photographs of them after they had died.

Are we doing this nowadays? No. To me, it's a weird thing to do. But back then, post-mortem photography was part of 'posthumous portrait' movement. It was like portrait paintings today. Lots of wealthy Europeans and Americans did it.

The children in the photographs give the impression of being healthy and alive, but their bodies were placed alongside a host of symbols, colours and gestures associated with death. These symbols would show the viewer that the person had passed. It could be something like the following:

- a dead bird
- a cut chord
- a drooping flower
- a three-fingered grip

Incidentally, the three-fingered grip indicated the Holy Trinity. It all sounds crazy to me, and I can't help but ask, why? Why would they photograph dead bodies and not photograph the magnificent antiquity that was around them? Was it like a mass quest to take photographs of everyone that had gone before?

The popularity of these photographs, often taken in a studio, reached its height in the i850s. It's almost as though the photographic process was invented especially for this type of thing. It's spooky.

What I find of interest is that some of them were taken so soon after photography was invented. It just screams to me there had been another Great Reset then and the people wanted to capture the ones who had perished during that era.

Three-Legged Horse sand Vanilla Skies
UAP and Lee Flat Earth British have spotted so many changes and alterations on old photographs that it makes me question what was going on.

I was told about a horse with three legs in one of my videos, I didn't believe it at the time. I thought, obviously, the leg had been blocked out by a shadow or another leg. So, I wanted to take a closer look to see if this was the case. If it wasn't, then I wanted to find out if the horse in question actually had three legs and if maybe it had been what you might call 'photoshopped' into the photograph for some reason.

When I looked closely at the images of horses pulling trams or carriages or carts, I saw that some of them didn't even look as if they are connecting with the road they were walking on and one of them did indeed have three legs. There's no doubt in my mind about that. The legs shown don't block the possibility of another leg in the background, but it's clear that the fourth leg doesn't exist.

There's also another anomaly, in that you are always shown big buildings and city scenes, which look great, but the odd thing about them is that they all have grey skies with not a cloud in sight. It doesn't matter where you are, or what timescale (usually between 1880 and 1920), or what time of the day it is, there is no expression in the sky. Of course, you can appreciate that it might be a nice blue sky, but there should have been at least one cloud somewhere in one of those photographs.

Was this the photographic process at that time? I don't think so. You can see some photographs that have got skies pencilled in. There's also another strange thing I've noticed; there aren't many people in the photographs and, when you do see a crowd of people, they're all dressed the same with the majority walking in the same direction. Maybe they were taken sometime early in the morning before most people had gotten out of bed, or were walking to work, a large factory perhaps. It's as though they're all coming out of somewhere at the same time, like they've just arrived, dazed and confused.

Don't take my word for it, go take a look at any of the old photographs you can find for yourself. They're all in the Flat Earth British Think Tank, go browse the site. To me, they have been altered. The common themes among them are that they've had colours added, they look as though they've had the background blocked or rubbed out, and the houses have been boarded up. Another theme is the lack of people and you'll also find that a lot of the streets are filled with big and ornate stone buildings, but that the steps lead down to muddy roads. In most cases, there are no pavements and the only tracks that seem to exist are for trams pulled by horses.

Buildings look of similar construction and similar

styles – worldwide. Yet, everything looks altered; everything looks a bit off.

Are you intrigued by photographs of the past? Some of them don't look so old. Many photographs depict empty streets that look like they're in the aftermath of a mud flood.

Egypt
Some famous historic sites across this earth are begging to tell you their secrets. One of them is Egypt. Questions always come up when I look at old photos of the Giza Plateau, the pyramids and the Sphinx covered in sand. None of it makes any sense.

We could never decipher the hieroglyphics until a soldier of Napoleon's army, a high-up the ranks Freemason member, found the Rosetta Stone. It was located very near the Sphinx. The Rosetta Stone has the Greek and Hebrew languages and Egyptian hieroglyphics and, more importantly, it's a translation. By reading Greek and Hebrew, they were able to decipher hieroglyphics.

None of it makes any sense, though. Just like when NASA sent a probe up to a rock flying through space and called it 'The Rosetta Mission'. Unfortunately, the probe landed in a dip and was hidden from the sun's influence. As luck would have it, they weren't able to charge the panels, and they couldn't get any messages from it. To me, this could have been made at any stage in history.

I watched a programme on the TV recently, called 'Flog It' and they were in an old Cathedral with carvings on the wall dating it to i637 or i520 and there were people's signatures there. It occurred to me that they could have put those signatures in recently. We are told:

> *The Rosetta Stone is the only guide to
> what the hieroglyphics say.*

Don't you find that odd?

If we look at the Giza plateau, we'll see the whole area is a settlement that belonged to the workers of the pyramid for Keops. We only know that because there is a plaque at the site that says so. There is nothing else at the site that says Keops was building anything in particular, so this can't be a burial place.

When you look at the Giza site, you'll see three pyramids in a row, one is off-centre, but we're told that they correlate with the starts of the Orion's Belt. Only, there's a smaller pyramid which you don't hear about much and a few smaller pyramids in front of that. What intrigues me most is what is located underground.

Under the Sphinx, there's a huge cavern and a massive, elaborate tunnel and cave system. This cave system holds a library with hidden knowledge. Really unusual, as when I look at photographs from the Victorian era, I get really confused.

The photographs of the Sphinx show there's a question to be asked here. Look at the nose. The chin, the bearded bit, is in the British Museum in London. Why? We are told it got shot off by Napoleon's men who had target practice with a canon. I don't believe this story. Napoleon was really into his Egyptology, so he would not have allowed his men to do this. It would have been an act of vandalism to him. He was even reported to have spent the night in the Centre of the Great Pyramid once. The Great Pyramid is supposed to be the burial chamber for Keops.

If you take a closer look at the photographs taken during the Victorian era, I ask why would they stick a human head on an animal anyway? What's going on in the photographs that show the Sphinx up to its neck in sand at this stage? In some of the photographs taken around the First World War, you can see the suburbs of Cairo in the background and the pyramids are actually black. Yet, they don't appear to be black today. What's more puzzling is that there's normally no Sphinx in those images of that timeframe either.

When you look at the photographs of the pyramids, you would think there were only four sides to each pyramid - but there are eight. Look closer at the old photographs and you'll see that there's an entrance to a cave system. The modern photographs show the height of the base of the Sphinx and it doesn't appear to have any feet, maybe it's just the photographic angle of it, I'll give them that. What is really interesting is that, in those old photographs, there's no plaque about

Keops either.

When you have studied those photographs for a bit, go back to the photographs of the Sphinx from the late 1800s, when Napoleon wanted to get into the pyramids. The question to be asked is, how did Napoleon get inside the pyramids? Apparently, they used explosives to blow a hole in the side when the King's Chamber was found. My question is, how could it have been buried and yet they were able to have target practice at its head? More to the point, how would they have known about the underground structures? This was when everything was supposed to have been underneath the sand.

When you've looked at those old photographs, take a bit of time to compare your findings with the modern-day ones. You'll see that the site is completely enclosed with a wall and the Sphinx has new looking feet and the face doesn't look like what it looked like a hundred years ago. Compare the weathering of the Sphinx from the old to the, apparently, new photographs, and you'll see how it looks nothing like what we see it as today. It seems they've cleared all the sand in recent times also, the feet seem to have been recently rebuilt.

Was it just billed as a tourist attraction? The same as Britain's Stonehenge? When you visit Stonehenge, you'll see a board that shows pictures of Cavemen outside. This means that the people in those days built these massive monuments with their picks and axes. This is what we are taught to think. Was it a scam?

Was it rebuilt? Is it a relic?

There are photographs of Albert Einstein in front of the Sphinx, just to show you the bullshit that they're feeding to humanity. Where is the connection between the pyramids and the Sphinx?

There is some incredible Egyptian art and paintings available, as well as beautiful statues but you also see that, within a mere hundred years, the Sphinx's face has changed and, in some photographs but not in others, there's also a tail on the Sphinx.

The scale of some of the pillars are so massive, but they've been smashed up, and we're left to wonder what happened. We're told that the masonry left in Egypt was smashed up over thousands of years, yet it looks like it's a recent anomaly to me.

There is a definite inconsistency between the photographs of the Victorian and Edwardian eras. You only have to look at the differences in the amount of sand surrounding the Sphinx and the pyramids to figure that one out.

There are also photographs of creatures and cryptoids, and men with hound or eagle heads and strange creatures. Think about that for a bit. In this day and age, we have cartoons and Disney characters. Is it not conceivable that the Egyptians had the same thing going on in their time?

Why is it in ancient maps or old maps, like the Mappa Mundi, you see Africa peppered in palaces, yet today it looks as though there's nothing there? It's all just desert, as though nothing ever existed there. Yet, the pyramids give clues to the high culture dotted around Northern Africa.

The Nile Delta has flooded several times and it has wiped out a lot of the past, yet you can see ancient Egypt under the water. There are also tall pillars with hieroglyphs all over them, and there are ancient buildings where it looks like some kind of devastation has happened

When you get out of the Giza plateau, you see giant edifices and they show great age, they are weathered, yet they are smashed to pieces. The buildings and statues near Giza are defined and mint condition (for their supposed age) yet, when you move further out, some parts of Egypt are smashed to pieces. Other sites, however, show the ancient buildings and sculptures in pristine condition, as though they were hewn yesterday with a 3D printer.

The devastation in the temples, shows there was a concerted effort to destroy the past and hide it.

A lot of the Victorian photographs show archaeological sites where people are working away with the locals. But, anything they brought back to the UK was basically stolen property.

There are too many questions from the Giza Plateau. To me, it looks like they've dug it up recently and restored or rebuilt it.

TIME LIFE MAGAZINE

Have you ever looked closely at the 20th Century photographs in *Time Life Magazine*? *Time Life Magazine* is a glossy magazine that depicts the history and current affairs of humankind. In fact, their historical images are interesting to look at as they show you a world that seems to be a bit on the fictional side of life. You can see them in the videos on my channel and look them up for yourself on the internet. They are a mind-boggler – especially the weird-looking paintings. I was scratching my head at times while looking at them.

One of the first photographs (I think is their worst) is the image they chose to represent the blue marble they call our earth. It doesn't look real. In fact, I'd say it was computer-generated. Especially when you compare it to the Google Earth images that come up on the search engine today. It looks like a painting or a computer-generated image, not a photograph.

People
When you see the photographs of Francis Ferdinand in his car before the First World War began, apparently, he was testing out the first bulletproof vest in history. Unfortunately, in his case, it didn't work. Apparently, a member of a terrorist organisation threw a hand grenade into his car - and triggered the First World War.

There are many photographs of the soldiers in the

First World War, where 25 million men from Britain were mobilised and many millions were killed. Needlessly. I don't think even one family got away untouched by that war.

There's a photograph of Rupert Brooke, the poet. After the First World War, he went into depression and was diagnosed as mentally ill with shell shock. In the *Time Life Magazine* photograph, you can see the haunted look in his eyes. He must have gone through absolute hell.

There are also photographs of Queen Victoria and the Russian Tzar and his family. Paul McKinley, Evelyn Nesbitt, beautiful lady for her day, plus, people not found in the BBC archive. There are images of people in Arabia (who are not cutting people's heads off) and there are also photographs from i902, of Helen Keller, the lady who couldn't see, hear or talk. Geronimo is in the *Time Life Magazine* too. The skull used by the 'Skull and Crossbones Society' at Yale College, USA, is supposed to be his.

There are also photographs of 'the lady with the lamp', Florence Nightingale. I did notice that there was no photograph of Mary Seacole from the Crimean War. There are some photographs of the tanks from Ethiopia from the i914-i918 war, the war to end all wars.

There are lots of images in the entertainment industry, music, film and theatre. Lots of movie stars and theatre actors. Danny Kaye, West Side Story, Pamela Blair, Cats.

In the photographs that Time Life Magazine depict, I've noticed that they didn't worry about what they showed you. For instance, the photographs of the Russian Revolution show you that they didn't seem to worry about taking pictures of people who had died. There are photographs of twenty to thirty people lying dead in the street and a father lying down, dead, you can see from his position that his last dying effort was to protect his daughter from the bullet fire.

The *Time Life Magazine* even went as far as to show the blood-splattered wall where the Russian Royal Family were murdered. Apparently, they stood there waiting for a family portrait to be taken - until the men pulled out the guns instead of cameras. I know I could be considered a bit cold when I say this, but I notice that there's not a lot of blood in the photographs. There's no evident pools of it on the floor. In fact, when you look at the photographic evidence, there doesn't seem to be any blood at all. You would think that there would be more from eleven bodies. They were shot and then bayonetted to make sure they were dead.

Buildings
When you look at historic photographs depicted in the *Time Life Magazine*, you would be thinking the same as I am in that I can't believe no one had an Eastman Company Brownie camera before 1880.

I've researched Expositions and the buildings were in every Australian and American city – yet, all of them were burned down. In 1904, Louisiana, they said there were 108 unique palaces scattered around - and they're all gone. These palaces were apparently built for just that occasion. Ok, so how long would these stone buildings, with ornate details, have taken to build? There was the Russian star and the American Eagle on each of those buildings – and there was always a dome too.

Ask yourself, when there's a fire of a building, what remains afterwards? Does stone burn? No. Buildings are normally just gutted, and the stone is left. Which is weird.

Crystal Palace, in the UK, was prepared for the Great Exposition so that Queen Victoria could show off to the nation all the achievements of the industrial age. There are pictures of the palace everywhere, a beautiful, big, ornate building. Can someone explain to me how glass and metal burn? Every city had them, so what am I suggesting?

Maybe the people of the Victorian era inherited these buildings from a previous civilisation and, then in the history books, the governments or Controllers of the time lied about their original use. How would we know? We wouldn't unless the Native American Indians came forward and said, "Look," pointing at the palaces, "White man was here. Long time before."

What I find intriguing are pictures of the Manhattan Underground being laid at the turn of the century. Horses and carts are dragging all the debris out underneath New York. Then you only have to look at the overhead railway lines before they were put underground.

It has been reported that five hundred workers killed themselves by jumping off a factory roof. Why would five hundred workers kill themselves all in one go? Doesn't anyone question the narrative?

Woolworths basically sold out because they didn't keep up with the internet generation. For some time, they had the highest building in the world, in New York.

There are even photographs of the remains of the buildings after the Dublin uprising in Ireland. After the Howitzers were ordered to bomb the place. When you look at the building structures, there's nothing inside, they're gutted. We are told there was a huge battle where Collins and his boys fought against the British army because they didn't want their sons marching off to the First World War.

Vehicles – Air, Sea and Land
The *Time Life Magazine* images of the Kitty Hawk (referred to as *The Wright Flyer*) was the first successful heavier-than-air powered aircraft, and the magazine doesn't appear to show the aeroplane in a good light. It's just a plywood design covered with cotton sheets. Yet, just one decade after the first photographs were taken of this machine in flight in i903, they were flying in WW1.

Henry Ford showed his mock-up for the Model T, which went on for sale at $820. Not bad price for that day. There's even a photograph of the Titanic. Cool. A photograph of the (Masonic) Captain who was willing to, basically, do an insurance job on his ship in 1912. The strange thing is that no one seems to link the Titanic's sister ship, the Olympic, which had a weird ending. It's down at the bottom of the Mediterranean Sea.

After the Titanic went down, the Olympic was taken into the dry dock, they gave her a double-skinned hull, made sure all the partitions were sealable so that that tragedy would never happen again. It was only a year later that the Olympic went down after being, apparently, torpedoed.

All the Elite of the day were on that ship, the Astor's included.

WHAT'S THE TRUE AGE OF PHOTOGRAPHY?

This Flat Earth is the answer to everything. Everything comes back to the Flat Earth. Who we are, what we are, and the timeline, which I'm beginning to break apart and expose. I caught a couple of videos by NewEarth (who isn't a flat earther) about Baalbek and the ruins in Armenia. When you look at them, and then the people standing next to them, the people are like ants in comparison. I'm talking massive!

I have to ask, what kinds of civilisation went before us? When you look at those buildings in those photographs, you can only conclude that it was recent. Eff the Ice Age. I've washed my hands with it all. All of it, I really have. About a decade ago, I started digging into the origins of the Ice Age because of this text I had read about them getting rid of the evidence in the 1700s. They were talking about the stones that had been left deposited across Britain after the Ice Age and that they cleared them for agricultural purposes. After that little revelation, alarm bells started ringing for me.

Some people will tell you that the Ice Age was a long, long time ago - millions of years actually but then you'll find in the alternative research from authors like Graham Hancock, who will tell you that it was around 10,000 to 12,000 years ago. Who is lying? More importantly, why are they lying?

Link to Freemasonry
I study old photography and have lots of 'first' images. One of the first images was of Cornelius, who looks like he's dressed in garb around the Napoleonic era. When did people stop dressing like that? Georgian times? Around the 1830s? The way he was standing, dressed in that garb, with his hand in his coat, gave me a clear sign that this was Freemasonry. Therefore, one of the first photographs ever taken was of a Freemason. The later photographs were of American Presidents who, incidentally, were Freemasons, too. Then I looked at all the oldest photographs and they all seemed to be tied into Freemasonry.

What if the photographic plate was invented before they say it was? What if these people lied about the true age of photography? And, what if the photographic plate came out a long time before the mid-1800s? Then we'd have to ask, well, why didn't they take photographs of the Battle of Waterloo? The Battle of Trafalgar? Maybe those events didn't really happen?

Let's put the Spanish Armada into perspective. During the reign of Queen Elizabeth I, in the i500s, apparently, we were going to be attacked by the Spanish. It was reportedly the biggest armada outside of D-Day. As you may know, Sir Francis Drake was playing bowls in Plymouth when he saw the fleet sail past. He was reported to have said that he would finish his bowls game and then go off to Chatham and sort them out later.

A picture of divine intervention was painted because the Tempest blew up when the Spanish were in the English Channel. The wind apparently blew them right around Britain and they lost most of their ships on that journey. Some were wrecked on the coasts near the Scottish Highlands, in the Hebrides, and some met their fate on the Western Coast of Ireland. They were said to have come up around Britain and smashed to pieces on our coastline. Apparently, there was no fighting at all.

Apparently, Britain was going to be invaded by the Spanish, just as with Operation Sea Lion with Adolph Hitler, but they never actually got here. It seems the only person in the history books that had seen this was Cromwell. You'd think while they were coasting the English Channel, they would have laid down a heavy artillery bombardment on the coast of Southampton and Portsmouth, but there's no record of this. Were they really there? There is no evidence for it. It only makes me believe more in the fact that what they have given us in our history books is all bullshit.

Think about it for a bit, if there was a massive wind that blew up around them, as experienced sailors, they should have been able to navigate stormy seas so they would have sailed directly into the European coast and took harbour until the bad weather passed. I just can't believe they would have sling-shotted all the way around Britain and carnaged the entire Spanish Armada. To me, the Spanish Armada of the 1600s was a psyop.

If you think about it on that basis, even though photographs weren't around in the 1600s, there seems to have been many remarkably realistic depictions from that era.

There's evidence where some photographs show you the centre of Moscow in the early 1800s when photography is supposedly in its infancy. What's strange about the photographs is that many palm trees outside of the Palace have been completely smashed up. There's photographic evidence of another identical Palace in the city of St. Petersburg, which has palm trees there as well. I looked into this a bit deeper and apparently, the zoo in Moscow had semi-tropical plants and elephants.

Weirdly, the photographs show that in the early 1800s, the weather was a lot warmer in Russia. Therefore, we must explore the climate change bullshit that has been pulled over our eyes. Many researchers have found a cooling period in Medieval times, it was so cold that they were able to hold a market on the frozen Thames. Britain was that cold. Photographs of this event exist as well as paintings.

My question is, are the photographs from further back in time? Are they showing us a time when they say our weather was cold? I think what has happened is that Britain was warm and we could have arrived at what they would postulate as 'nuclear testing', or what I would call the 'industrial revolution', during which things heated up and then the weather started to plummet.

Some people will put forward the notion that what started this cold snap was the Krakatoa volcanic explosion at the beginning of the 1800s. Krakatoa was reported to have spewed out enough debris over the whole of the planc to cause a sort of nuclear winter which cooled things down considerably.

However, I ask you, what if everything we've been told is in reverse? What if it hasn't been cool at all? What if it has been warm? Would that explain why we've gone into a recent cold patch in the last century? There's a shortage of information past that date about this kind of thing. The records that have been given to us from the late 1600s through the 1700s and 1800s - are from our controlled media.

> *Unfortunately, we cannot prove how old photography is, but it looks like the truth is being hidden – perhaps by Freemasons.*

A VERY PECULIAR DISCOVERY

While looking over an old image of San Francisco, i909, I found a very unusually flying airship and wondered what it was doing in an old photograph on my website. I wondered if it was an advertising stunt or if someone was playing silly beggars with me.

When I came across the image, I looked at the sky, a modern-looking skyline from i909, I noticed a pirate ship in the clouds. After a bit of investigation and a bit of discernment and a bit of digging, its truth became clear.

The first question I asked was, is this actually the same shot? After looking closely at it, the conclusion was that it was the same shot, and it wasn't a photoshopped image either. Then I wondered if it had been airbrushed over.

The ship was an airship with sails, which didn't exist when the photograph was taken. I had been in possession of that photograph for close to two years and I never noticed that before. Someone had taken the time to paste this image in, and it had been done to a highly professional standard. Now, either it was an advertising stunt, or someone hacked into my computer, stole the photo, airbrushed it, and put it back - just to make me go crazy.

After further investigations, the image was of a fictional ship from the pirate Air Ship Card Game. It was an Abney Park Airship. I tried to find a picture of the airship at the angle in the photograph, which was really difficult. If you want to investigate it yourself, check it out and see if they're messing with me for whatever reason.

I found an image of *HMS Ophelia over Mohammed Ali Mosque in Cairo* and another one of the airships in a photograph that was of a picture entitled *Eisenhower announcing Ophelia's arrival campaign trail in 1952*. The photoshopped airship wasn't in that one.

I'm puzzled. It doesn't appear real, as you can get the image pasted into photographs, but the strange thing is that all these photographs you see of the 1800s period have modern-looking people in them. It's unusual. It's strange. It's mind-boggling. Is someone trying to change our history right before our eyes? I don't know what to think, but I'm willing to investigate whenever I see these things. For one thing, it teaches you to discern these things, to check them out and to keep your mind open.

JUST FOR LAUGHS

Photographs can be messed with at any time. Today, we know that it's easy to mess around with photographs if you have the knack and the skill to do it, but I believe they had the technology to airbrush over photographs from an older period.

I've seen some old photographs of a creature called the 'Tasmanian Devil'. There is actually another version called the 'Tasmanian Hound' as well. It's a crazy looking animal that's extinct now – as is the DoDo, which was another weird-looking creature, a bird or reptile-type creature, but don't say anything about the DoDo around a flat earther! The Tasmanian Devil had the front end of a deer and its rear end resembled something like a tiger. Actually, there was one in a zoo in Wales at one time.

When you see the photographs of Captain Saunders or that bloke who invented the Southern Fried Chicken monopoly, you have to realise that he couldn't have been alive during the American Civil War. Why? Because there are photographs that look like him, standing together with Alice Cooper - in the i970s.

Then if you hunt down photographs of Edward Snowden and his boss, the CIA grumpty, they're in a photograph together. There are many portraits of people who are laughing in your face while they deceive you with lies about the way of the world.

Look at old photographs of The Quarry Boys, who were the original Beatles, and what becomes apparent is that the photographs of Paul McCartney don't look like Paul McCartney at all. Although I love The Beatles very, very, very, very much, they're still part of the Tavistock Institute and not really a 'real' thing. They were manufactured to sway the masses into some kind of hysteria and make them forget, or not notice, what's going on around them, which is another way to 'distract' people while managing the next Great Reset.

There's a photograph of a group of people in Bangor, Wales, and there were a lot of pop stars in that photograph: Donovan, George, John Lennon, and Mia Farrow. Mia Farrow had an interesting little life. She was the star actor in 'Rosemary's Baby' where, you know, the Devil gives her one (has intercourse with her). Ms Farrow was married to Frank Sinatra, part of the Rat Pack of the day and some even say the Mafia, but what did Ms Farrow do at the said Hindu Festival for meditative purposes? Drugs.

Then you look at the tons of photographs available online of Adolf Hitler. They're all contrary to the mainstream narrative. There are some photographs of him having a laugh with a bunch of gals and doing whatever Germans do – but not molesting their nieces or pissing on them like we're led to believe from the NSA or the CIA narrative.

You don't see many photographs of Hitler's Bunker, the ones you do see raise questions as to how he would even have stayed in something so small and menial.

I also saw a photograph of something that should really come with a warning before you open it. It's one of Satan's daughters - I mean Nancy Regan and 'Mr T', you know the massive dude from that bonkers television series. You can see in the photograph that Mr T is saying, "They don't pay me enough!" And she's thinking, "Ooh, I'm rising up in the air!" Nancy, the little thing that could snap in half if you dropped her. She basically married Ronald Regan after he walked out on the beautifulness that was Jane Wineman and Reagan's brain was left in the walnut dish - they basically hid him because he went nuts. Apparently, Regan kept trying to press the red button, and they kept slapping his hand and saying

"No, Ronnie, no. No nuclear war today!"

"But what if aliens come?" he would ask.

Then you see photographs of Marylin Monroe. It really annoys me when you hear people saying she was a dude, as that is clearly not the case. Arthur Miller, who was with her, was a bit of a crazy fella, but he wrote a good book (*Death of a Salesman* – yes, I read it. Alright. I'm a geek).

You know what I mean by all of this. Oh, and I may have made some of that up. But, as I said in this section's heading, it's just for laughs.

6. WHO ARE THE MAJOR PLAYERS?

First off, some family dynasties run this earth and, as you can imagine, the people who do are from certain bloodlines and live a longer timeframe than us ordinary mortals. So that none of their truth comes out too early, everyone is killed off - and one way to do this is to have a Great Reset. If you don't believe it's possible to do this, you only have to look at what's going on around you today.

Today, it feels like a bit of reshuffle is going on with this global plandemic. The Elite have probably got a warehouse full of clones ready to repopulate the world after this reset. This is probably where all these dazed and confused people come from when you see them in the old Victorian photographs and the mental asylums I mentioned earlier.

Whatever happens or, however you look at things, whatever obstacles you come up against, you have to stay awake to all of this. If only to protect yourself from these crazy-arsed people who want to control you.

NOSTRADAMUS A FLAT EARTHER?

It seems the prophet, Nostradamus, was a Flat Earther and I have some evidence that the quatrains he wrote refer to a flat earth. Who knew?

The first time I ever heard the name, Nostradamus, it shook me to the core. I kept asking, "Whatever is that?" People told me, "He's a man!", then I asked, "What was he?" I asked again. "He's a prophet!" This man blew my mind.

The best source on Nostradamus you can get is from the author Erika Cheetham (1939-1998). The book is written in quatrains, in Hebrew, Latin, French and English and in allegory. More to the point, they're written in code. Codex, to be exact. You can make of this what you will but, the evidence in them is quite thought-provoking and they show clearly, that Nostradamus was a Flat Earther.

Nostradamus' story ties in perfectly with what has been going on in the world today. You can look at his story in two ways, either:

- He's a guy that didn't exist at all
- Or, he existed.

You might think that it's all just a bullshit psyop that's been made up, but I get the feeling he did exist. I've seen his birthplace with my own eyes, mind you, there's nothing of note there. It's just a cobbly building on the corner of a street in the South of

France and there are not any touristy-type signs there – not even any shops. It's just a normal corner of a street which doesn't even look 500 years old.

Nostradamus was an apothecary, a doctor, and his fame, or renown, was for treating people who suffered from the Black Death by using Rose Water. He made the Rose Water simply by putting rose petals into the water, then he put the water directly onto the sores and blisters under the arms and in the groin area. Nostradamus wasn't affected by it.

When you look into Nostradamus, things start to tie in with the story of what's been going on over the years. Nostradamus did his work in quatrains to hide it from the Inquisition that the Vatican implemented so cruelly at that time. This was in the i500s, so it was smack in the middle of the Reformation period.

At the same time that Nostradamus was alive, Copernicus was around. Galileo Galilea was in this period, but he was under house arrest, so he wouldn't spread the word about his geocentric ideas. Galileo Galilea's work is tucked away in the Vatican archives even today.

It turns out that Nostradamus was a Jew by birth, but it says in Erika Cheetham's book that in i502, two years before he was born, Nostradamus' family converted to Christianity. His grandfather taught him Hebrew, which I find intriguing as we don't even know who the Hebrews were because they've disappeared entirely.

The only thing I can take from this is that either Nostradamus was completely free of Judaism, or he was what you call a Crypto-Jew, which meant he was practising secretly. In the days of the Reformation or the Inquisitions, they had to as being found out meant facing torture or certain death.

Nostradamus wrote his quatrains about prophecies which have, mostly, been validated. For instance, take the day after 9-11 in America. If you go on Google and look for 'top searches' the day after 9-11 and you'll find that it was "What did Nostradamus say about the Twin Towers?" In a later version of Cheetham's book, either Nostradamus or his son did some watercolour paintings and one of them shows two towers burning and in flames.

Nostradamus mentioned the Kennedy's, he also called Hitler 'Hissler'. He wasn't too good in his prophesies with World War Two, though, because he mentions nuclear bombs - but *the bomb* was used to devastate Japan.

When you look at Nostradamus' citing's of Napoleon, a couple of centuries after Nostradamus lived, things start to get interesting because his predictions are so spot on. It was Napoleon that completely changed things.

As you may be aware, all world leaders must submit to Rome, even today. The ceremony includes a part where they have to bend over and kiss the Pope's ring. That includes the British Queen, PMs, Presidents, etc. At some point, they all go and pay homage to the

Vatican. However, that's not what happened when Napoleon made himself Emperor.

Nostradamus predicted Napoleon's achievements. He said:

> *"A Prince of Corsica makes himself an Emperor and Rome will submit to him."*

Napoleon was from Corsica and did indeed make himself an Emperor. In the i500s, the thought of anything submitting to Rome was not really conceivable. But, Napoleon placed the laurel on himself, called himself Emperor and made the Pope kiss his ring. This was unheard of, and this is where things began to change.

Incidentally, the same laurel on the UN flag was put on Notre-Dame de Paris (also known as Notre-Dame Cathedral) by Napoleon. I'm convinced this laurel is significant, it's the same laurel that Julius Caesar wore.

The Bible Code
You can read into Nostradamus's prophesies what you will, it's a bit like the book *The Bible Code*. If you ask *The Bible Code* a question, even you will show up. Yes, you. It will say that you are asking a question. It's that direct, but it goes onto a multi-skip code, and there are trillions of permeations. However, there aren't many permeations with a quatrain.

We know what the languages of Latin, French,

Hebrew, and English are, but it's not written in a way you'd understand when you read it out to yourself. For instance, he could say something like, 'From a great hill rests a man and a man would look down on a flat plane,' so there was a bit of confusion.

It turns out Nostradamus thought there was an edge to the flat earth, but he thought it was either somewhere off Western France in the Atlantic Ocean (they had discovered America by then), or he thought it was further North, near Ireland.

The Victorians were very much into the prophecies of Nostradamus, so this has been out in the open for a long time. Some people believe that Nostradamus didn't predict anything because he was a remote viewer. I do agree with this idea and have found that he used a few techniques as follows:

- Water – basically a still body of black water where he would see a 'looking glass' reflection and be able to interpret things there
- Crystal ball – which is as valid as it ever has been
- Incantations – with candle smoke and incense, partaking in psychedelics

Remote viewing
Either one of the above methods is how Nostradamus remote-viewed. I've looked into remote viewing all my life and one of the best remote viewers of all time

was Ingo Swann, who was born in September i933 and died in January Z013. Swann was depicted in the film *Men that Stare At Goats*, and there is a lot of reality to that film. That operation did happen, and psychic spies are a reality, the Russians and the Americans have them. Ingo Swann was one of the main psychic spies.

Basically, these investigative organisations were able to find someone who was missing off the radar and, through remote viewing, could pinpoint exactly where they were. They would say that, "he's in a café, upstairs, second room on the left," and the FEDS would turn up and there would be the person in the exact spot that was told to them.

What I can make of Nostradamus is that he was a Jew that attended Catholicism. Because he hid his quatrains from the Vatican, I can only guess that they have some crucial information in them that he didn't want the church to know about.

Greenhouse Effect
The interpretation of Nostradamus' idea that the earth was flat comes from Nostradamus' ideas about the greenhouse effect. After the Biblical flood, Nostradamus reckoned that everyone started to burn the trees to clear the land to make things better again for the generations to follow. This caused too much $Co2$ to be chucked up into the air, which caused the Greenhouse effect, which then caused the climate to change, which brought on the last ice age.

Even after the flood, he spoke about the last ice age, which we are told ended 12,000 years ago. It's an intriguing insight as Nostradamus seems to have been able to see into these timeline events.

Nostradamus' quatrains are not easy to read, and they're not a pleasant read either, but some of his writings can blow your mind. When I read them, I'm constantly asking, "How could he know that?" His predictions touch upon recent history like the Vietnam War, President Kennedy being shot, as well as 9-11.

Timeline Tweaking
Although I'm excited to find out that Nostradamus was a Flat Earther, I have to be careful as it could be more bullshit, and it could all be a bunch of lies. However, having seen Nostradamus' birthplace and the trail he left behind, I believe he was a real man who lived 500 years ago. I think the 500-year timeline is accurate because you can trace the i600s, i700s and i800s. Tudor England was still there at around the i500s, with Henry VIIIs castle, Hampton Court. Hampton Court is still there, and we're told it was built in the i500s.

I think the timeline has been tweaked around the time that Nostradamus was around, by a few hundred years, and I believe the last Reset happened before the Norman (French) Conquest of England, back in the Saxon times. This gives a good argument as to why you can't go to a church in Britain and figure out what date those buildings were constructed. We are told that my local church in Cardiff was built in i110, but there's no stone reference that proves it was built on that date. That's the best part of a millennium, which I find fascinating - there are no gravestones from that era that remain.

Controlled thinking
The reason why I'm interested in Nostradamus is that no one seems to have picked up that he was a Flat Earther and that he came out of the 'dark age' period – after another Great Reset. They came out of this depressing era, around the 1500s, into a new era of art and forward-thinking. It was a time that ideas that were beginning to flourish, but it was controlled 'forward' thinking.

Oxford and Cambridge were set up about 500-600 years ago specifically so the Controllers could control that information. All the information that came out of there was what the Elite dictated would be. So, every single piece of information through our educational system is handed to us from them. Therefore, sadly, nothing of our history or way of life can be believed.

Of course, there are bits of truth in the educational system, there has to be. If you could follow the crumb trail back to somebody's burial point, Karl Marx for instance, you'll find the grave of Marx in Highgate Cemetery in London. I followed the crumb trail of Nostradamus, and I found his hometown. There is enough evidence and I think he is definitely a key to all of this.

It all seemed to be that, during that era, there was a

fight to bring information out, as it was all being closed down around them. The information was being controlled chiefly by the Inquisition upon orders from the Pope in the Vatican. This change, or fight for information, came when the English language was being introduced to the people. Even the King James Bible (1611), was being translated into English at that time. So, the Controllers must have been trying to hide something of importance from the people.

It all seems to tie into the story of the Jesuits and right into the story of the Vatican control system. It also ties into the prophesies, probably because they're apocalyptic by nature. With this and other works of a similar nature, you put ideas into the mainstream, basically for predictive programming purposes. You have to ask if there is any reality to any of this?

KING HENRY VIII

Henry Tudor was a Welshman and the father of Elizabeth I with Anne Boleyn. He reigned during the Reformation and the Great Enlightenment - the heliocentric model was being introduced during this period.

The Mary Rose was the flagship of King Henry VIII. After being brought up from her grave at the bottom of the Solent in the 1980s, she was restored and put on display in Portsmouth, UK.

As you know, Henry VIII is known for his many wives and, the story goes that because he wanted a divorce, he chose to opt-out of the Church of Rome to introduce the Anglican Church - the Church of England and the Protestants. He also gave orders for all the monasteries to be demolished and for their gold to be stolen. We all know this part of his story, but what you may not be aware of is the Mary Rose. If you look at this from a context of a Great Reset, you have to ask what did the Mary Rose prove?

The Mary Rose was brought up from the Solent, located between the Isle of Wight and mainland England, the narrow seaway called the Solent. There's an annual regatta held on the Isle of Wight, in Cowes and it was there that Henry VIII was up on a stand, probably in the Portsmouth area, to witness the Mary Rose sink. Nobody really knows what happened as it was out of the blue. She was quite an unbelievable ship.

I'd like to know why so much money was spent on bringing her up. As well as canons on board, they recovered Long Bows, which was intriguing. This was the only evidence that the Long Bows existed, which solidified the story of Henry V at the Battle of Agincourt, which apparently took place in i415. Did it? I wonder if all this expense to re-float her was to infuse a fake history.

History states that the English won the Battle of Agincourt using the Long Bow where 'the sky was blacked by arrows'. We all know Henry V from Shakespeare which is where the story of the Long Bow started. There's also a tale about the fingered V-sign, which indicates to someone you point at means: "Eff off!" This was something the English were encouraged to do to the French, who would cut off their fingers when they caught a British soldier, so they wouldn't be able to use the bows again.

On the Mary Rose games were found, board games like chess, 9-man-morris and draughts. People were playing the same games we pretty much play today. When you think about it, 500 years is not a vast distance of time, so how is it that our information from 500 years ago is so sketchy? When you check out Hampton Court, the Palace that Henry VIII lived in, it looks like it could have been built by London Borough Council in the 1950s. I'm not joking. It's a very advanced looking fortification for the Tudor period.

I think a psyop entered the equation as the Mary Rose went under. Today, she's protected by being hermetically sealed. The engineering and the techniques of building that ship were so highly advanced, we couldn't even build it today if we copied their technology.

The Mary Rose was televised as it was being brought up in the mid-1980s. It was worked on over a long period. The documentary showed how a gantry was built underneath it, how they placed airbags under her and how they brought her to the surface. It cost millions. Why did they invest all that money into raising a ship?

There seems to have been some information in there somewhere - something they badly wanted. I don't think the Tudors, or the people of the 1500s were anywhere near as backward as we are led to believe. It's just a different style, but everything worked just the same. Look the Mary Rose up online and check out the size of her canons, they are massive.

This is of major interest for British history and I think the ship was brought up to show you the scale of it, which is impressive, and the technology they had on board. Remember, they had all of that 500 years ago. So why is the information around this period so sketchy? Possibly because of the Great Reset of that time.

On that ship, they had everything but not the electricity we have today. Does it give clues to our past?

Agincourt and the Somme
We're told that the Archers of Agincourt blackened the skies with their arrows from the Long Bows. They are said to have had the technique of mass bowmen shooting arrows all at once, which helped them win against overriding odds. Apparently, the British were outnumbered 24 to 1 against the French.

Interestingly, Agincourt is on the same site where, almost five centuries later, the Somme in the First World War was fought. Am I the only one who has made this link? Is it a thin one? Is there some meaning in it? Again, as at Agincourt, on the Somme, the British were outnumbered.

In this place, trenches and battle lines were drawn up around the city in 1915. I've spent a lot of time visiting the trenches of Ypres, the D-Day landing sites, the artificial harbours, the giant docks called the Mulberry's. When I was there, the sky went an inky black, and I had this terrible feeling all over me. It was a horrible fear. The atmosphere in that place is unbelievable. The trench systems are still there, and you can freely walk up and down the same tracks that soldiers walked over 100 years ago. When you walk in those trench systems, I have to say, it's a nervy experience.

The historians and volunteers have kept the trenches in good order over the years, so they look like they did in WW1. When I walked through the trenches at Ypres, I could see the Cathedral from them. Ypres was one of the most contested battles over a relatively small stretch of ground – only eight miles were ever recovered.

Some of the photographs you see from WW1 are fantastic - and horrific. You see soldiers sitting in the trenches, some preparing to go over the top, some getting themselves forty winks, and some being shot. There are men who are dying and men who are dead, there are men lighting up a cigarette and a brew, and there are men writing letters to home and to loved ones. Almost a million British men died in WW1 and, considering the population at the time, that's a huge percentage. I do understand why the French didn't want to go through it again in World War Two, a little over twenty years later after the First World War.

SABBATAI THE 17ᵀᴴ CENTURY ANTI-CHRIST

The deeper I look into this character of the self-proclaimed Messiah, the more troubled I become. Today, his followers are underground, continually pulling the strings of our re-written history. Of course, I'm exploring the tip of the iceberg and the first thought that jumped into my mind was why did Sabbatai's followers permeate the race hate by jumping to the Jews and the Jesuits? Because that's their tool of choice and this kind of thing ties into every bit of the unfolding story.

Let's get one thing straight: Sabbatians are crypto-Jews, not the Jewish people. The Sabbatians, who use Kabbalah, went missing when millions of his followers went underground. While they did, they infiltrated all other religions.

Sabbatai Zevi, also spelt Shabbetai Ẓevi (1626-1676). He lived in Turkey and was a Jewish Rabbi active in Kabbalah throughout the Ottoman Empire. He specialised in rewriting old history and bringing it into the present day and he studied how to set a paradigm. People claimed Zevi to be the Messiah and anyone who stood close to him was said to have had visions. His followers were big into reversal and had mystical powers.

I have a big collection of history books, yet none of them say anything about this man. So, I'll start with the story of The Satanic Law of Reversal, written by Zevi and Jacob Frank. Here, you'll find something sinister as to why Frankish Jews promote anti-Semitism and wars. I cannot believe that these people have not been highlighted throughout history. It seems that they are the culprits of all that has been going on in the world throughout history and is still going on today.

Jacob Franks, who set up the Illuminati, funded Adam Weishaupt, a Jesuit who managed the Satanic political expansion globally and established the Illuminati in Bavaria in the latter half of this century. Zevi's religion infiltrated Islam and Catholicism because, according to him, 'there's only one doctrine' and they all follow one man.

In February 1666, six months before the Great Fire of London, upon arriving in Constantinople, Zevi was imprisoned by the Grand Khalif. After being moved from prison, he was accused of fermenting sedition and was given the choice of either facing death by an ordeal of some sort, or converting to Islam. Zevi chose to convert and got a 'generous pension' for his compliance.

Bear in mind these people don't care which religion they follow, so he may have converted, but he still told his followers that they could follow any religion as long as they followed his cause. Let me repeat: the cause they followed was Satanism. This was orgiastic, ritualistic and sacrificial, basically, the whole works of evil.

The movement went underground and, from there, they infiltrated the whole of society to bring about the evil works you see about you today.

Shabbatean Movement

The Shabbatean messianic movement was the religion associated with Zevi, in fact, he was thought to be the Anti-Christ. He came along on the Winter Solstice, on December 21st i665 and, when he was old enough to know better, he declared himself Messiah. Apparently, millions of people followed him and the notorious 'has sasins' (where Hashish was named after) assassins worked for him. One of the most well-known men was Jacob Franks, who set up the Illuminati in Bavaria in the i600s.

What I've been trying to find out is how much truth there is in all of this. Was it just a Jesuit psyop? Did this man really have millions of followers? Was he really like this anti-Christ figure who had a Satanic religion of reversal?

This role reversal thing, the perversion of the human form, everything anti-God, orgy-istic behaviour, is the same as Aleister Crowley's theology, which millions of people have followed. Crowley was born in October i875 and was said to have died in December i947. He was an occultist, magician, poet, painter, novelist, oh, and a mountaineer of all things. The religion he founded was called Thelema and he saw himself as a prophet who needed to guide people to the Æon of Horus. Apparently, the ideology got so out of hand, the 'powers that be' tried to get Crowley, but he apparently disappeared, and nobody knows where he went. So, how come they know he died in i947?

I've asked people who have authoritative knowledge of the Jesuits whether or not there is any reality in Zevi's people going underground after he went missing and dictating our reality today. It is known that Jacob Franks, who was Adjutant to Zevi, funded several famous people and organisations who had influence in the world's direction of thought and actions. Franks was supposed to have influenced the Illuminati, Freemasonry and their temples, Jehovah's Witness movement and the splinter groups. From that, he was able to organise big events like the fire of London and rebuilding the architecture of the big cities around the world.

Christopher Wren
Zevi was brought out the same year as the fire of London, 1666. One of his operatives, namely Sir Christopher Wren, began the fire, after which Wren got the privilege of the contract to rebuild the city on the structure that you see today.

When these people began to build Masonic temples in the early part of the 1700s, Sir Christopher Wren was said to have secured his contract to rebuild London in 1667, after the fire of London of 1666. However, plans had already been put down for a stone structure of the new London skyline, based on the geometry to fit the Satanic nature of these people. The trouble was the old style of buildings had to be gotten rid of before this work began, which meant they also had to demolish the old Anglican church that was St. Paul's Cathedral. It had to be wiped out.

The fire in 1666 stopped short of the Tower of London, Westminster and the Bank of England. The fire never touched those buildings as it stopped at the very end of Fleet Street. What were the chances of that? One in a million? This was so obviously a set-up to wipe out lands and basically give Wren permission to build 72 churches and rebuild all the Masonic Halls in London as well as Queen's College in Cambridge. Funding came from the Illuminati. This is an important link to the globe lie and the Great Reset.

Wren also got funding to build the Royal Observatory at Greenwich, where they appointed the first Astronomer Royal, Isaac Newton. The heliocentric model lie was permeated using Isaac Newton's idea of gravity (a theory which came from an apple falling on his head).

The Carnegies' & The Astors'

Zevi is linked with the Zionists. I couldn't say who is really in charge, but this organisation have agents all over the world, check them out for yourself. In America, they sent Andrew Carnegie, from the Carnegie dynasty, to influence the world through his building empire.

The Astor family was also involved. The Astor's were a massive dynasty in America, but something must have happened because when Astor was on his way to America, he travelled on a ship called the Titanic. As a result of his death from that sinking, his wealth and fortune passed to Lady Mary Astor, who carried it on to the present day. The Astor's were known to be

Jesuit agents.

So why were these rich and famous families sent to America? The goal was to overturn the American Barons and we all know how successful that bit of business was. Before this, it was these organisations that started the French Revolution.

Rothschilds
Waterloo, as you will probably know, was a complete psyop. You might know of the story where the Rothschild's benefited from a lie that changed the history of the world. We are told that a 'false' courier was sent back to England with information that proved a winning formula for the Rothschild family.

As a result of the lie, that the British had lost Waterloo, the Rothschild's bought out the Bank of England through stocks and shares based on that lie. When everyone thought that the Battle of Waterloo had been lost, the banks sold all their stocks at rock bottom prices – that's when the Rothschild's bought them all up. Then, the real courier rocked up with the true news, that the British had won the Battle of Waterloo. By then, it was too late. The Rothschild's ruled the world.

Mad King George III
The French Revolution nearly spilt over into England, and we very nearly had a British Revolution. It looked as though our monarchy was going to be toppled but, luckily for King George III, he was a Jesuit agent.

As you probably know, the 'Mad King George' was said to have gone doolally and lost the colonies – this was portrayed in the film *The Madness of King George* but, if you dig into the information available, he never lost them. The surrender at the American Revolution was left as an open armistice - in fact, there's never been an official surrender. I'm not saying there's an official state of war now but, it's basically still open.

New World Order?
Shabbatean-ism, their doctrine, which emulates those of the Councils of Trent and of Zion, gives us the information we know about the New World Order. It all whittles down to the man Zevi, but it's easier to research Jacob Frank than this Zevi dude.

Aliens?
When the biggest fleet outside of D-Day turned up outside of Washington, what did they do? They turned tail and left. There are a whole load of stories about what actually happened that have not been made public. Especially at Bunker Hill. Apparently, Washington had visitations from UFOs, and I've heard that the aliens inside those UFOs told the government at Washington what to do in order to change history.

Throughout history, there have been a lot of people who have had visitations from UFOs. Constantine The Great apparently started Catholicism in Roman society because of a vision he had. The story goes that he was on a campaign when his army stopped by a lake and he witnessed a large fiery cross in the sky - a UFO by all standards. Constantine took this UFO sign in the sky as a Divine message and turned it into Catholicism.

All these ideas seem to have been put into our psyche, and the course of history has been externally interfered with. Is this true? To get to the truth, you have to find the source of the information, which is, unfortunately, more often than not all too elusive.

THE TALE OF THREE COUSINS

You might already know of the three cousins and their part in the Royal Families of Europe. This is part of the structured paradigm we experience today. Three jolly chaps were grandsons of Queen Victoria. If you don't know of it, it's an interesting story to get to know because their lives give you an idea of the structure of today's society and how it came about. The three kings I'm talking about were:

- The Englishman: George V, Prince of Wales, soon to be king.
- The Russian: Tsar Nicholas II
- The German: Kaiser, Wilhelm II.

A petty indifference and jealousy set them apart from each other and set the world alight in World War 1. This, as we were led to believe, was 'the war to end all wars'. My story starts with the Englishman, George, and a quick look at the family of Queen Victoria.

Two of the brothers, George and Nicholas, looked very similar to each other. So much so, they could have been twins. The other one, Wilhelm, was different. George and Nicholas couldn't stand Wilhelm, which must have made him feel very left out. When George and Nicholas were boys on holiday and playing together, the story goes that Wilhelm would want to play and the two brothers wouldn't let him. The reason given was because Wilhelm was full of it, he was bigoted, and he even laughed at his own jokes.

Now, even though I know they are an elitist bloodline who want to subjugate the whole of the human race, I have some sort of affection for the old Royals. But, firstly, I'm going to check out George V.

Prince of Wales, King George V
Now, George V, George Frederick Ernest Albert III, was born in June 1865. He became King of the United Kingdom, the British Dominions and also the Emperor of India on June 10th – until he died in 1936.

George V was the second son of King Edward VII and the grandson of the reigning British monarch, Queen Victoria. I don't want to go too deeply into his life story here, as I aim to give you just a brief outline. He had an interesting life, and you can check it out for yourself as it is well-documented.

George V saw the rise of socialism, communism and fascism, but I don't want to go into his political aspirations. Let's just say that the man was ridiculously over-educated, and he was so completely different to Wilhelm. Wilhelm had to be forced to learn because he wasn't a very good student. However, George V absolutely lapped-up the learning. He had a powerful fire in his eyes.

George's father, Edward, however, bullied his son because of his speech impediment and, as the whole world knows by now, Edward abdicated his throne and went off with his divorced lover, Mrs. Simpson. Unfortunately, Edward was a 'high end' Nazi and good friends with Ribbentrop. They regularly went off together with Adolph and his wife.

There are lots of photographs of George and, yes, there is a spooky resemblance between the fiery-eyed George and his cousin, Tsar Nicholas. Those two were really close.

I can't really fathom how this family must have been affected by the wars because all of Europe was at war because of them. My question is:

> *What gives this family the right to dictate the lives and deaths of millions, so they can stay stinking rich?*

However, it was an exceptional era and, to me, there is a kind of romance to the photographs of the time, especially when you know about the characters.

George was super intelligent, super quick-witted, a hell of a bloke, and his wife was Princess Margaret. Fiery old George was a true Brit. In the war with little Willy (Wilhelm), he would plead, "Do we really need to carry on with this fiasco? We're going to have to draw a line in the sand somewhere. Millions are dying, you know." But out of vanity or whatever reason, they carried on for four years. For what? To redraw the maps for the family.

They were an exceptional family. The funny thing about these people was that they had their pomp and ceremony and all their official staff, but they lived in gilded castles or cages of their own making. They lived a fairy-tale life that had nothing to do with reality, and they were totally disconnected from the population they ruled over. The Russians were the most guilty of that sin, but the British were too.

Following the Industrial Revolution, Britain was ravaged by the slums that never got cleared until the Second World War. Not that they cleared at all, we still have some in Cardiff, in Wales, today.

It was this little chapter of history that gave us the structured life we all experience today. No matter where you are on the plane, if you're in Australia, Thailand, or America, all of this family dictated our existence and still do today.

Kaiser Wilhelm
Kaiser Wilhelm felt very proud of himself, and you have to ask why. Wilhelm II was George's cousin, but he wasn't as intriguing. In fact, he was a bit of a loser, as far as my research tells me. Wilhelm was the type of man that everywhere he visited in Britain, he took his pomp brass band with him. The Oompah Ooompah had to be played everywhere he went. Apparently, it

deafened everybody about him, and nobody could actually speak to him because of these bands that pissed everyone off.

When he arrived for the Regatta's in Cowes, on the Isle of Wight, they couldn't wait for Wilhelm to go. He used to block the Solent with his two German battleships, which annoyed everyone. Wilhelm was the type of man that would walk through the ranks to inspect his troops, and all he would hear were sniggers behind his back. It's a shame because he desperately wanted to be liked, he was the kind of man who persuaded people to like him, basically by sucking up to them. For a Royal, he was a bit sad, if I'm honest.

Wilhelm looked up to the British and our pomp and ceremony. He was totally impressed with the visits he had to the UK, where the British had 9,000 people lining the route of his railway line, all waving to him as he left. This left a lasting impression, and he wanted that kind of ceremony for himself as he travelled through Germany. He hated and loved Britain at the same time.

Wilhelm was a bit of a problem child, sickly, it was surprising he survived at all. His birth was breach, and his doctor snapped his arm while he pulled him out. If he hadn't, he would have died. But this left him with a bit of a gammy arm. For him to be made Emperor of such a powerful nation that had such an incredible future coming to them, what with the unification of the German peoples and the soon-to-be Austro-Hungarian Empire and the Ottoman Empire, it was a bit strange. They were to become an unbelievable power, formidable enough to take on the might of the British Empire.

Wilhelm was born in England on 27th January 1859 and died on June 4th 1941. Believe it or not, he's buried beside a little house in Holland. He was the last Emperor of Germany and King of Prussia and ruled Germany and Prussia from 15th June 1888 through to 9th November 1918. The Armistice at the end of the First World War brought about the end of the German monarchy.

Wilhelm was the eldest grandson of the British Queen Victoria and related to many monarchs and Princesses across Europe. Crowned in 1888, he dismissed the Chancellor Otto von Bismarck in 1890. He then launched Germany into a new course of foreign affairs that resulted in his support for the Austro-Hungarian crisis of 1840. This is the key to what ties these three cousins together.

Traditionally, Britain and Germany were allies – that was until this period in 1888. For some reason, during the Boar War, Wilhelm trolled Queen Victoria to the German press. Wilhelm had no support, but after the First World War, in 1918, he had to go into exile in Holland because the Royal Family were not allowed in Germany or Russia. The only place for the original monarchy to exist at that time was in Britain.

Wilhelm believed there was a conspiracy - from Britain, Russia and the Jews - and he wanted no part of it. Basically, it was the same rhetoric as Hitler was spouting off. Wilhelm wanted Tsar Nicholas to like him, but Nicholas was having none of it, believing Wilhelm to be an imbecile.

Wilhelm was a member of the Freemasonry, and photographs show him dressed in his regalia with symbols all over his uniform - including the Knights of Malta. He was also a holder of the class of Iron for doing nothing, as Wilhelm was the kind of man who would have run from his own shadow.

As a child, Wilhelm was very pampered but disfigured because of his sickness and his gammy arm, which makes me feel sorry for him in a way. When you see Wilhelm in photographs, you can see how unpopular he was just by the look on his face.

Wilhelm wouldn't take any advice from his High Command or any of his goons as the only one he would listen to was Queen Victoria, his grandmother. He loved his grandmother, and she loved him too. She would tell him firmly and persuasively what to do. She sent him letters. Because of this, I have to ask why he would upset her by saying things to the German press. The Queen did ask him to sort it out, but he didn't (or couldn't) do anything about it. As we know, she died in 1901, before the First World War. I sometimes wonder if she had lived, would there have ever been a Great War?

Wilhelm thought of himself as a Napoleon-type figurehead, the way he dressed and, in particular, his helmet with the eagle on top, harked back to the Roman Emperor past. In contrast, the British press,

Europe and his own German people portrayed him in cartoons as a silly man who rode a donkey with a potty on his head. The Germans were quite nasty to him and gave him terrible nicknames. Sadly, he didn't have a very good life.

Tsar Nicholas II of Russia
There are a lot of photographs of Wilhelm and Nicholas together. Tsar Nicholas was (and still is) well thought of by the people of Russia, people are so much in awe of him, he's taken on a religious-life status.

Tsar Nicholas is the most intriguing, the most charismatic, the nicest, but his family is the most haunting. His story is tragic actually, as everyone is aware, he was murdered with his whole family. If that happened, of course. We have no way of knowing as we have no photographs and we weren't there.

Tsar Nicholas was Emperor of Russia, and the Russian Empire was one of the greatest in the world. He was given the nickname 'Nicholas the Bloody' and was seen as weak and incompetent. His military defeats led to the death of millions of his subjects. He had no connection with his people as he lived in his fairy-tale castles, the Hermitage and the Winter Palace, or visited his family's palaces in Britain. They lived in unbelievable wealth and opulence.

There was an uprising through the Bolshevik Revolution, funded and set up by Freemasonry and Jewish and Protestant Bankers. The Rothschild's had a part in this too, but their name was kept out of it.

The Russians suffered a defeat in the Russian-Japanese War. Then they had the Second World War with Germany, and in the First World War, around 3.3 million Russians were killed. Tsar Nicholas was a bit of a buffoon when it came to war.

Behind every great man is a great woman, so they say, and Tsar Nichola's wife was no different. Wilhelm was rumoured to have met the future Tsarina, and he told his brother, Tsar Nicholas, to "Go get the girl!" The story goes that Nicholas went off to this bandstand at the park and told the future Tsarina that he loved her. Apparently, he cried his eyes out, she did too, and well, the rest is history. Secretly, I believe Wilhelm loved the Tsarina. She had an illness called haemophilia; it was an illness that Queen Victoria also had. The records show, she lost a son because of it.

The Tsarina was a Lutheran and, to start with, she shunned Nicholas. To be married to the Tsar meant that she would have had to become a full Russian Orthodox. But when she did become a Russian Orthodox, she joined it full-on and went extreme-o with it. She didn't do things by half though, and she was every bit Nicholas' intellectual equal. Apparently, she dictated everything to Nicholas. When Nicholas was made Tsar, she was said to have said, "You stick your head up high and you let them know who you are!" She was the power behind the throne of Russia.

What makes history interesting is a 'horny mystic' and there was one tied to the Tsar's: Rasputin, who stunk like a dog. Rasputin's knob (penis) is on display in a museum in a very large jam jar. This is true, as you can go and visit it. Apparently, he was hard to kill. You could shoot him, you could poison him, and you can put him under a frozen lake, yet he would still be looking at you.

Rasputin was rumoured to have cured the Tsar's son, and there were many more rumours about him relating to his sex life. Many of the women in the Russian dynasty, or the Court at least, had had sexual relations with him. Apparently, the rumour was that the Tsarina was one of them.

When you look closely at photographs of Nicholas and the Tsarina, he seems smitten with her - but her? She's got a cool, hard intent in her eyes. Remember, it was Wilhelm that brought his cousin and the Tsarina together.

All the aristocracy overlooked the Tsarina and yet, she's the central figure to the whole of this story. To me, her mind structured our humanity or our paradigm. She dictated how the war was to be carried out.

The family were shot by the Bolsheviks with German machine guns. There are some stories that the Princess Anastasia survived. In fact, a lady in Swansea, Wales, came forward years ago and said that she was the Princess. I wonder what really happened to that family. There's no absolute proof of their being killed, and I can't see Bolsheviks machine-gunning a royal family - kids as well.

Anastasia apparently had diamonds sewn into the material of her dress. It was the diamonds that saved her as the bullets ricocheted off of her.

The people don't care about people. They are all in the same 'boys club' and they're all in it together. Don't believe anything they tell you. They lie. They don't give a shit about their subjects. They have only been chosen because there's something different about their frequency and bloodline from ancient times.

There's one little thing that links these three cousins together.

> *The Last Emperor of Germany, Kaiser Wilhelm II had this to say about the Jewish Bolsheviks: "The Jews are responsible for Bolshevism in Russia and Germany too. I was far too indulgent with them during my reign, and I bitterly regret the favours I showed to prominent Jewish bankers." July 22nd 1922 – Chicago Tribune*

That's a very intriguing bit of information, and it provides a key here to what happened in the bloodlines, the banks, and everybody else. In fact, the whole shamoley and it should be starting to make sense.

If you're wondering what this has got to do with the Great Reset – well, everything! I'm trying to show you the links it all together with the shadow government, with the blue-bloods that we know for sure.

The thing about the three cousins is that they were all Knights of Malta. They were cousins, they were pen pals and were linked together, sipping brandy and laughing. They lived in a make-believe land while their countries starved, while our men, women and children died in their millions.

MY LOCAL AREA

On a personal note, I can see how these organisations and individuals reset our history and change our timelines because they are not so secretive today. They dress up and make the most of it with public ceremonies and big parties. They even parade around the streets of Cardiff. They might be seen to be doing good things for charity, but my trust in them is a bit limited.

There's quite a bit of Masonic presence in Cardiff. There's an island called Flat Holm, which is about six miles off the coast of my city. Half of it belongs to Wales, the other half belongs to England. This is where the listening posts are located. Queen Victoria put massive gun placements there, she was apparently protecting the coal ports. It was built by the Irish navvies. When the guns went off, they recoiled, deep into the underground. You can still see them today.

At one time, there was somewhere in the region of about 60,000 ships a month entering into the Cardiff Docks. Cardiff was the biggest and busiest coal port.

On the island was a cholera hospital and anyone infected would isolate in that hospital.

The story goes that one person had the bubonic plague and, naturally, he died. They burned his body in the crematorium, which was unfortunately burned down too.

There are parts of what was a radar station and what you'll find is that there are many underground buildings. There's a lighthouse with foghorns in place, and there are lots of gun emplacements.

I think that all of this was just a psyop. It was t create something to deter people from asking questions. It's really interesting when you dig into what they created and what they were actually for.

HOW DO THEY RESET HISTORY?
You don't need religion to be Godly. All these wars, all these people suffering, starving and homeless, what's that for? Because of wars over religion? Religion is just to control people. We just need to be aware that there is a Higher Power, a Creator, if you like. I couldn't be more spiritual if I tried. I walk with the Creator constantly, and I'm not basing it on any religion.

Imagine for a remote second that around the 1666s, the Jesuits or the Shabbateans found a way to collect all the literature around Europe, burn those books and take master copies for themselves. There is evidence for bonfires outside of every town around this time.

The Jesuits have been known to hide under any denomination, any race, any peoples. They're an organisation of people who don't care which religion or organisation or sect they belong to, as long as they can do the work for the devil based on the Shabbatean movement.

There's a crazy-arsed role reversal going on around us, and Grenville gives a good, if horrific, example of this. It was the fire that spread dangerously quickly in the block of flats in London on 14 June Z017. The story was all over the news for a couple of weeks. My argument was, where were the bodies? We are told that 72 people died in that fire, 70 were injured, and over 200 escaped. We didn't see any funerals. The thousands of relatives from all over the world that would attend those funerals were notably absent. If as many people died as we were told there were, then there would be loads of people attending funerals.

Imagine for one moment that there was a way to reset this whole plane and our history. Our current reality regarding the Covid-19 pandemic puts this into perspective. If we continue the way we are, what's to stop them from hiding the master copies? All they'd need to do is start with the internet by turning Kindle off and then rewrite the established history while deleting the essential bits from the big books. Essential bits like important pieces from the history of the Roman Empire. Incidentally, by focusing on the history of the Roman Empire, this conveniently hides the Carthaginian Empire, which was a civilisation as established, as advanced and as populated as the

Roman Empire. This history has been air-brushed out, along with the Byzantium Empire, too.

There would be bits of truth and lies woven together into a new narrative, and it would be written to suit themselves. This would then cause religious wars and strife - brother against brother. As we have been doing for the past few hundred years.

When the slaves were shipped to America, in the time of the thirteen colonies, this was found to have had links to Zevi, and the reason for doing it? Preparing for the future - as a way to cause race wars.

The idea was that they wanted to keep the slaves in such bad conditions so that, in the end, these slaves would bite the hand that fed them and kill all white people in America. This was their way of getting the American Civil War going. People read the books, fiction and non-fiction books like *Uncle John's Cabin*, which makes people think, "Oh how terrible!" The Amendment says 'All Free Men' and they thought, "Well, they're men, why aren't they free?"

This was the argument put forward to begin the American Civil War - but this wasn't the reality of what was going on. Lincoln was just propping up the military complex with massive contracts to build weaponry. Those contracts were worth millions at the time and, of course, he wasn't going to let that go. It goes deeper than this as we now know that Lincoln was also a Jesuit agent. I can find traces of Jesuits infiltrating every aspect of society everywhere I look. They seem to dictate the course of our reality.

Not that I'm saying this is real but, imagine 1666 (because it's the Devil's number – 666) as the reset date. Just imagine that the great fire of London was a contrived event to wipe out the civilisation of London, then rebuild it with all their Masonic symbology in the buildings they constructed in their style.

This Zevi man had followers in the millions, and they were probably in one of the main centres for Europe at the time, Constantinople. Wars have been held to keep Constantinople within the hands of the Elite. In the First World War, we lost a hundred thousand or more men in the Gallipoli campaign. It was an absolute disaster. It was a campaign by another Jesuit agent, a Jewish man (or his mother was Jewish), Winston Churchill.

Having learned all I have about Winston Churchill, I now see him in a different light. He seems to be one of these satanic orgy-istic types. You usually find that when a person or organisation has so much money or expensive trinkets around them, they become rotten to the core, so much that they want different things to what the common man wants. They have different aspirations in life than the rest of us who just want to get on with each other, looking after our families and working to put rooves over our heads and food in our bellies. These Elite group of people don't.

They seem to want to destroy everything in their path, all to grab power.

To me, they're like a cancer and they're doing evil

things to a good society to bring about what they want. You can see it happening now - and it's not slow-mo anymore, it's happening quickly and it's all right before your own eyes.

What needs to be done is to find out more about this Zevi character, to find out if he was a real person and what his mission was. That would be a cool thing to achieve.

7. WHAT PART DOES SATAN PLAY?

BETWIX THE DEVIL AND THE DEEP BLUE SEA

The Flat Earth British Think Tank has a great host of people doing all sorts of wonderful things to help the channel succeed. A member of our translation team, Matt Ferguson, has given us some brain mashing and incredible information, which I'm going to take you through in this chapter.

Matt has looked at a i611 French *King James Bible* that is not exactly in line with the same one released to the British Isles, Little Britain. If you look at the original versions, and compare them to what you see today, you'll see that there have been some obvious changes.

You may know that the Lord's Prayer has been changed in the King James Bible. Some people put it down to spooky mandala, but I put it down to something definitely going on with the Phoenicians. This chapter shows some more correlating evidence that solidifies the Phoenician evil plot.

We're going to go a bit further back in time to Sir Geoffrey Monmouth, who spoke of the Phoenicians doing said matters early on. I think the Phoenicians came early, set up the buildings, the pumping stations, the star forts - and then flooded it all.

So, let's get to that Bible, the one you may be aware of, the original *King James Bible* of i611. The translation into English began in i604 and was completed in i611. Forty-seven scholars were involved in the work, with the Old and New Testaments and the Apocalypse, which I understand to be Revelation. All the scholars were members of the Church of England.

On the cover of the Bible, there is the double-crossed fasces and there are images of the reset, the chemcloud, the birds with the wings open, the two pillars, in fact, many of the images that were revealed to be of importance in my previous book, *The Holy Grail of the Flat Earth,* are in there. It shows the people bringing their laws such as 'Thou must doeth..." etc., basically telling the population to do it their way.

Before the book starts, there are a set of depictions and this is what they say in Genesis:

> *Light was created.*

Naturally, my question is, why is the guy who is delivering the message standing on mud?

The following image says:

> *The firmament was created.*

The third image says:

> *The waters were assembled.*

And the final one states that:

> *The luminaries were created.*

There's an odd-looking picture at the bottom of the page with some strange creatures on it, not whales or fish, but it says:

> *The water produced reptiles.*

Which is kind of weird. Then the final image states:

> *Man was made*

The reptiles in the water show a huge connection with another book which we had translated, *The Phoenicians in Haiti*. It tells how the Phoenicians took over America and Haiti early in humanity's history, then how they took over South America, Central America, the Meso-Americans, the Aztecs, Incas, Mayans, Olmecs. These countries were under Phoenician control, they put in their own language and their own new ways – so out went the old Golden Era we once had.

The Flat Earth British Think Tank has all the images you will need to see and more. It's a great book and you'll see some great depictions. The thing is, it shows more trouble from the Angels from above. Strangely, there always seems to be a bit of a bad thing going on with them.

Late on in the book, there's an image of a house floating on the water, which obviously depicts Noah and the great flood. Both *King James Bible* and *The Phoenicians in Haiti* have a 'serpent' theme going on.

> *In speaking of serpents and their followers we are reminded of the existence of symbolic monuments representing the etching of the serpent on the ground in North Africa. The one in Avebury, England UK, in Ohio, America close to Bush Creek River, Adam's Country, which are highly significant. There is an immense serpent feature, partly coiled and partly uncoiled, it is wave-like. Its mouth is swallowing an oval enclosure in which centre you can see a small oblong burial mound depending on what we can see. The inundations of the folds of the snake represent the movement of the ocean waves that will swallow the enclosure.*

This could be an emblem of Atlantis being swallowed by the sea. Basically, I believe the serpent is a waveform that travels through this place.

Back to the Bible. For some reason, the Lord's Prayer has been altered and, in the modern Bible, 'the firmament' has changed to 'the expanse', whatever that is supposed to mean. I do wonder why they changed it and, knowing this, might lead us to some clues to how this place works.

There are a dozen more books about the Phoenicians available on the Flat Earth British Think Tank, we have found one from the first millennia, the dark ages, from Geoffrey of Monmouth. He's an early writer who is one of the best sources on the subject of King Arthur around that time.

Geoffrey of Monmouth says in this book that King Arthur was directly related to the Tudor dynasty, Henry VIII, then Elizabeth I, both of whom were Welsh. He puts a direct connection to them from Arthur in their genealogy which is interesting. Geoffrey says that Merlin was an Atlantean survivor, which is why he had these magical powers.

Now, you won't have to tell me about another Welsh historian, Alan Wilson, I'm completely aware of his work and have been for years. Wilson deals in chronologies that I don't, but I will talk about the events of this period and bring it all forward.

So, the Phoenicians were indeed here at this time in this first millennium AD. In *Babylon to Britain*, they talk about Brutus, the Roman, who was supposed to be killing Cesar, having Phoenicians along with him. It's an excellent read, and it documents all that went down in this first millennium. More evidence that the Phoenicians were here in Britain at that time.

I find it quite interesting learning about the King Arthur's (there were two of them) being related to King Henry, which brings it all into the Middle Ages – around the i590s. It does say that King Arthur was supposed to have been defeated by the Saxon conquerors and the Welsh were big players in this period of history. The Welsh, Scottish, Irish and English were a recent political union with the Phoenicians. Britishness is still often seen as less primitive. I believe the British had it going on before the Phoenicians arrived – we just didn't need them.

The British King Arthur was an appropriate royal ancestor from i486 to King Henry II. So, there's a direct link to the Plantagenets from King Arthur, which I find extraordinary. The Phoenicians took over the UK and most of Europe, Africa, Mediterranean, America – soon after, it all became Tartaria. They seemed to want the tin mines and there are plenty of tin mines in Cornwall.

Another book I came across was *The Fabric of Britain*. Basically, it explains mysticism and myth in architecture. It is an extraordinary book which tells you the mechanism of this place. It depicts this place as a tented canopy, domed, and it gives you the same example in every single ancient culture. The only ones who disagree with it are the Sciences and Western Philosophy, which, in the very beginning, tells you that they are lying through their teeth. Here's a brief reading from the first chapter of *Tales of Ages Long Forgotten, Now the legends of creation, Once familiar to children* – *KALEVALA*:

> *If we erase from the mind absolutely all that science has laboriously spied out of the actual facts of the material universe, and ask ourselves what would have been the thoughts by which man attempted at first to explain the image from the natural order, we may put ourselves in sympathy with the notions that at first seem absurd. We may see that the progress of science is merely the framing and destruction, one by one, of a series of hypotheses, and that the early cosmogonies are one in kind with the widest generalisations of science – from certain appearances to frame a theory of explanation, from phenomena to generalise law.*

This tells you what this place really is, in ancient cultures. It's easy to believe the television and the computer screen, but what about reality?

> *So, like the wonder of the sky and the might of the sea or rather, the two phases*

> *of the same question by which we may realise the early systems. For in those things at least, concepts were immediately linked with words, words which were descriptive comparisons.*

So, is the sea the sky? It goes into the mechanism. The Phoenicians are also in the book, and the Chaldeans have a version of the sky-tree:

> *The Chaldeans describe such a tree as growing at the centre of the world: its branches of crystal formed the sky and dropped to the sea. The Phoenicians thought the world like a revolving tree, over which was spread a vast tapestry of blue embroidered with stars.*

The Norse, the Maori and the Egyptian cultures also subscribed to a flat earth theory.

> *The earth is a flat plain surrounded by the sea, and the sky forms a roof on which the sun and moon and stars travel.*

Like so many other people, the Polynesians thought the sky descended at the horizon and enclosed the earth, still call foreigners 'heaven bursters', as having broken in from another world outside.

They describe a 'sky roof' where the rain comes

through and that if someone climbs high enough, you can visit the dwellers above. It says that these people look and talk very much the same as the people on the earth. The Paraguayans of South America say:

> *As above the flat earth, so below it, there are regions inhabited by men, or manlike creatures, who sometimes come up to the surface and sometimes are visited by the inhabitants of the upper earth. We live, as it were, upon the ground floor of the great house, with upper storeys rising one over another above us and cellars down below.*

The book goes onto observe that this theory went on for so long that there must have been some connection between the world structure described and the buildings made by man.

The description of the earth was as though it was in a chamber, or a box, with the lid being the sky. It describes a 'vast mountain' in the middle over which the 'crystal or metal heaven of the fixed stars revolves about it'. The metal observations may explain all these strange anomalous sounds we hear today. Even the Bible's *Book of Enoch* describes the earth in such a way. This all comes from the Norse Mythology, which is growing in popularity now.

All these books from ancient cultures give endless proof of what this earth is. As I said, believe in

Western Science and Philosophy at your peril.

The Phoenician theme usually depicts two pillars with a giant lady in the centre and a dome above. It could be that the pillars hold the dome up and they oscillate, go up and down, and cause a somatic pattern that makes the mud go in with the water table. So, this might cause liquefaction and mud flooding.

There's always the unicorn and the Phoenician lion. Some beautiful tapestries have been created throughout our colourful history. In the tapestries, they always depict bees and the Phoenicians considered them very important. Coincidentally, bees are going to be part of the Notre Dame Cathedral. Someone burned the roof off of it, and now they're building an Avery with a glass dome and, apparently, there are going to be bees in there too. The Phoenicians are just bonkers about bees. I think it has something to do with electromagnetics and there's more going on with bees.

While all of this gives us a foundation of what part religion plays in all of this, it needs some more investigation.

SATANIST DATES AND BRITISH DISASTERS

I wanted to look a bit closer into the subject of the Satanist Dates and how they are closely linked to the disasters we have experienced in Britain in recent times.

Looking at it closer, the biggest disasters in recent

years checked against the dates of the Satanic Holiday list. One of the events was close to my heart as it was in Wales, at Aberfan. There, 177 Welsh school children were killed in a slag heap land slip. I also recall the Hillsborough Disaster that happened in a football stadium in Liverpool.

When you couple these disasters to the Satanic calendar, you come up with a horrific list aligned with them. Though there are an awful lot of disasters happening on this plane, I'm keeping this basically to Britain as it seems to be important for their Agenda.

Aberfan Disaster
On 21st October 1966, around the Halloween period, a slag heap slipped onto a school where 177 children were. Look at the Satanic calendar, Halloween is covered between 13th to the 30th. Halloween seems to be linked to specific events where abductions of humans, especially children, for sacrifice are done.

I've visited this place and it's a pitiful thing to behold. It's filled with little white crosses. It rained the day of the disaster and the slag heap slipped down and covered the school. The community are a proud people, but it's a heart-breaking place to be. Good people all over the world raised millions to help this community rebuild their lives again.

The Hillsborough Crush
There was a football match at Hillsborough Stadium in Sheffield, South Yorkshire, England, on 15th April 1989. A police constable opened the gates that allowed

thousands of fans to flood into an area far too small for them all. Many fans from Liverpool were crushed to death. They threw the book at the man who caused this. Look at the demonic calendar: 26th April.

Lockerbie Disaster
In Lockerbie, Scotland, the Pan Am flight 103 went down on 21st December 1988. Two hundred and seventy people died on that flight and eleven died on the ground. The 21st December is the date for the 'real' Christmas and it's also the Winter Solstice.

Dunblane School Massacre
Sixteen school kids and a teacher were massacred in Dunblane, Stirling, Scotland, on 13th March 1996. This event was covered up completely by the State as there were too many questions about it. Thomas Hamilton was named as the shooter, but we'll never get all the details as he shot himself as well. Interestingly, after the event, the Firearms Act was brought in and people were encouraged to sign petitions to stop gun ownership.

Interestingly, Andy Murray, the tennis champion, was the only one who survived. In 2019, Murray reported in an Amazon Prime documentary, *Andy Murray: Resurfacing,* that he knew the shooter as he shared car rides with him to the Kids Club. When you see footage of him, Murray looks messed with, there's something up with him as he's not a relaxed child.

From 1st March through to 17th (typically, the 15th) there's a famous event, with an equally famous strapline assigned to it, called the 'Beware the Ides of March'. It is the 74th day of the Roman Calendar, notable for Romans to settle their debts by this date and it also refers to the date when Caesar was stabbed in the back in 44 BC.

When any of these dates, you never have to look too far to see that there's always money involved somewhere along the line and that these events always seem to have a link to the Satanic calendar where events mean something to the devil, and where sacrificial events take place.

THE VATICAN ARCHIVES

I have always been fascinated with the Vatican Archives, but I'm puzzled why they don't open them up to the public. What do they have to hide? It's an underground archive that's kept suppressed. The books that are in there mention maps and inventions and even have the works of Galileo and Michelangelo. Why are these not available for everyone to look at?

What I've found is that there's a war on God, our Creator. We need to find out where, when and what we are. Where are the answers to all the questions we ask? If the answers are anywhere, there's a good chance they will be located in the Vatican. There are about 53 miles of corridors beneath the city of Rome. That's bigger than the perimeter of the city of Rome. What I wonder is how that many miles of corridors were built in there. Who built it and when?

Interestingly, it is the most heavily guarded library in

the world, the most secure fortress outside Fort Knox. The Vatican Library is a fortress. You have to ask why.

I've been reading quite a bit into the Vatican Archives. In the vlogs, I present to you on the YouTube Flat Earth British site, you'll find all the links to documents and books. There's a lot of information on the Vatican Archive. There's no way you can get access to the Vatican Archives, but Napoleon got close in the early 1800s. He and his army sacked the city of Rome and took loads of books out of the Vatican to Paris. Did he give them all back, or did he have 'dibs' on some of the best books? If so, who has them now?

We're always told that 'All roads lead to Rome' - really? I think that's allegorical because the Ho Chi Minh doesn't lead to Rome, does it? I've been to Rome twice, so I know the place quite well. I've chucked money into the Trevi Fountain and have been told that, when you do that, you will always go back to Rome. That's no lie because I did.

I'm not going to go on too much about Dan Brown's book *Angels and Demons* because it's obvious to me that it's Satanic by nature. However, I will say that Brown's book gives you keys to what is hidden in those archives. Brown actually goes into the works of Galileo Galilea and Copernicus, as well as touching upon the heliocentric and geocentric models.

In Brown's book, when his character, acted by Tom Hanks, goes into the archives, this is a clue that they are going into the fringes of telling you about Flat

Earth. How would Brown know? Is it just guesswork, a great imagination, or does he know something that we don't?

Brown goes into the Vatican archive and looks into Galileo's works concerning the geocentric model, then he looks at Copernicus's work and mentions the earth's orbit after Copernicus. It's classed as fiction but, it's a good exposé into the operations of the Vatican.

There's a lot of Illuminati symbology in the Vatican, as we see in the Phoenix too. For some reason, it seems like the Vatican is a fort as it even has its own army, the Swiss Guard.

There is a lot in Brown's book about CERN and the Big Bang. The Big Bang, to me, is an absurdity in itself as all you get from the Big Bang is Georges Lemaître (1894-1966), who was a Jesuit, and Edwin Hubble (1889-1953), who was a Freemason.

What about the Parthenon? It is otherwise known as the House of Devils and has an Oculus in the room. It's an unusual place, and you will be told that that roof is made from 2,000year-old concrete. It's not very thick, yet it's been up there for that long. Sorry, but I have to question that. It was actually a Pagan church, with only one door in and one door out. There are inlays where the statues of Pagan Gods have been replaced by Christian ones.

I think all the answers to the questions we ask about the Flat Earth and who we are, are in the Vatican

Archive. There is a conspiracy concerning the Latin name of the Vatican. Why is that a secret? The Vatican Archive has around 35,000 catalogues. We are always told that any documentation before the thirteenth century is scant, however, according to the Archives, the oldest surviving document dates back to the end of the eighth century. Political upheavals nearly caused a total loss of the archival material from before Pope Innocent III, who was in post between i198 and i216.

From i198 onwards, complete archives do exist. They include documentation on:

- Henry VIII's request for an annulment
- The heresy accusations against Galileo
- Michelangelo's letters of complaint about lack of payment for his artwork on the Sistine Chapel

Nearly all the archivists for the Vatican are Italian Cardinals.

What's hidden in the archives?
Of course, the usual conspiracies are going around, such as some people think that the Vatican Archives have evidence of ancient aliens. I'd like to know more about the maps of the earth that are said to be housed there.

The thing is, the evidence the Vatican Archives holds might even destroy the church by discrediting it. Yes, it probably holds evidence that the earth is flat and that it is supporting the heliocentric model by evil means. The Vatican Archives have books that hold information of historical events that the rest of the world is ignorant of. It also holds documents that date back to before the Norman invasion of Britain, right back to the year 800.

It is reported to also have documents that began the Protestant Reformations, the information about Pope Leo, i521, when he excommunicated Martin Luther. A petition is said to exist, signed by eighty-five English clergymen and Lords who asked Pope Clement to annul King Henry VIII's marriage to Catherine of Aragon in i530. The many names signed on the document were fixed by a red ribbon, which is where the expression 'red tape' originates. Clement refused, of course, which led to the formation of the Anglican church and the Protestants.

There's also a document in the Archives that shows how Michelangelo di Lodovico Buonarroti Simoni, known simply as Michelangelo (i475-i564), warned that the Vatican guards hadn't received pay in three months and that they had threatened to walk away from their posts.

Another interesting document was produced a year after Columbus was supposed to have landed in North America. Pope Alexander issued a Papul Bull, i493, which split the new world between Spain and Portugal. There are letters from Abraham Lincoln and Jefferson Davis, who wrote to convince that Pope Pious was an innocent victim of Northern Aggression. What I find puzzling is that neither of these men was Catholic, so what were they doing writing to the Pope?

There's also a parchment from i854 that gives information about the Immaculate Conception - that Mary gave birth to a child without original sin. Also housed in the Archives are handwritten transcripts of the Vatican trials. This includes those of the Knights Templars of the fourteenth century and the trial of Galileo Galilea.

Hitler and the Vatican
There are lots of books available in the Vatican Archives giving information on where Hitler got his money. There are details about Hitler's training and the support he received when he was in jail. The judge was basically 'buttered up' for Hitler's trial and, when he was released, Hitler received enough money to become a multi-millionaire. This is probably how he was able to pursue his dream of a Fascist Regime. Many documents provide evidence of Hitler's business with Pope Pious and the Catholic Church.

Did the Vatican and the Jesuits create Hitler and the Nazis? The funny thing is that Hitler made a speech in i940 where he talked about anti-capitalism and indicated that the newspapers were really edited by the 'powers that be'. Even then, there was no freedom of the press. If nothing else shows you what this world is about, then this should give you an idea that for the past half-century, at least, we have not been thinking for ourselves. We are not in a democracy where we think we are free with liberty. There really no freedom at all.

There are lots of photographs of Pope Pious with the Nazis. If you research into the Jesuits, you'll find that they have an oath, which pretty much gives their intentions away. These people create wars by bringing in chaos and then provide the solution to that - with their vision of order. They've been at it for years, which is why they can do it so well.

Hitler's Pope was published in 1999 by John Cornwell, a British journalist. In it, he examines the actions of Pope Pious before he became Pope. Apparently, he assisted in the legalising and legitimisation of the Nazi party – the fact that they would do the Sieg Heil salute is enough information, but the Catholic church also smuggled out thousands of Hitler's SS Elite after the war. There were also allegations of anti-Semitism within the Catholic church.

There is evidence of Papal coins with rams heads, on one side and on the other, there is the UN or Roman sign, which is a laurel together with a devily-type thing. On Papal seals and keys to the Archives, there are dragon-type images. The keys are always held by Egyptian deities. In the Vatican, you will see lots of images depicting the dragon.

I think most of these symbols are to do with the Pineal gland. There are some images of the lion and the tower - Nostradamus painted the tower on fire. The tower means something to these people.

8. WHY ARE WE ALWAYS AT WAR?

DID THE JESUITS PLAY BOTH SIDES?

It's weird the way I keep getting answers to questions that I put out there. God seems to be delivering the messages to me thick and fast. The answers I'm getting take the finger-pointing away from the Jews and towards the Jesuits.

It's becoming clear to me that, like the followers of Zevi, the Jesuits don't seem to care which nationality or religion they sign-up to. They seem to pick an organisation or group and then infiltrate and infest it with their own ideology.

In this chapter, I'm taking a quick look at wars and their causes. Bearing in mind my thoughts on the Jesuit conspiracy, did the Jesuit Papacy play both sides of the American Civil War? Was General Stonewall Jackson murdered by the Jesuits? I have a mind to believe this was indeed the case.

Stonewall Jackson was a real hero, a Confederate General, born in 1825 and died in 1863. He would tell his regiments to stand fast during battles, and the men who loved and respected him would do this, even though all the others ran away. It's well-known that all Confederate and Union Generals studied at West Point Academy. Robert E. Lee was the Confederate leader and Ulysses S. Grant was the Union army leader and, during the Mexican wars, they were friends.

Jackson's military career spanned the Valley Campaign of 1862 and services to the Northern Army of Virginia. Stonewall Jackson was a victim of 'friendly fire' when he took two shots in the arm and one in the hand by his own men. Today, this would be called 'friendly fire'. It was Robert E Lee that reportedly shot Jackson. It was by mistake, on the battlefield of Chancel Ville. Somehow, this doesn't ring true. Jackson was adored by his own men and it wasn't those wounds that killed him.

Jackson's elbow had been shattered, but he didn't die straight away. It was recorded that his elbow healed and two days after the event, they said he was feeling better. We know now that whisky is one of the worst liquids to give a person in pain as it doesn't work that well as an anaesthetic. Unfortunately, Jackson was given whiskey for an operation. Basically, whisky thins the blood and it makes the situation far worse than it could have been - and it can kill you.

Even though Jackson had his arm amputated, the operation went well. They used chloroform for him, and this can go either way. If the person giving it to you knows what they're doing, you can stay under during the whole operation or, you can wake up halfway through to see a man standing over you, sawing your limb off with a hacksaw. Not all that pleasant. After the operation, Jackson woke up. He felt ok - as well as you can after having your arm sawn off. But soon after, he went down with pneumonia and eight days later, he slipped into the end. I think it was the Jesuits who committed this crime and I'll tell you why I think this.

Were you aware that the Jesuit Papacy Bill played both sides during the American Civil War? The Jesuits controlled both the North and the South during the American Civil War or, rather, between the States or, better yet, The War of Northern Aggression.

The Jesuits controlled Davis, Benjamin, and Lee, as well as Lincoln and the Red/Black Republican Party. After Gettysburg, though Lincoln was known to have undergone a true conversion to Christianity and was a devout follower of Jesus Christ. After this, he was reported as opposing the Jesuits and their operations. Charlie Cinque and General Thomas Harris, both former priests, didn't notice a Jesuit link to the North.

For an answer, we have to look at the policies of Rome at the beginning. They have an open but false policy for the world to subscribe to and was also a secret, but true, policy only known by the higher echelons of the Jesuit hierarchy and the Pope himself. For example, the Papacy openly opposed homosexuality and paedophilia, yet lawsuits have been opened that show that they have never practised what they preached. These crimes are institutionalised amongst the Roman Catholic organisation.

Another example of the Jesuit policy is the war in Afghanistan and Iraq. The Pope openly states he is against it yet, evidence that spans years is available of his plotting for this to be brought about. Evidence includes the 9/11 catastrophe via George J. Tennent, a Knight of Malta or CFR member and DCI.

Returning to the American Civil War, or as it was commonly called, the War of Northern Aggression, what needs to be examined are the details from a century before this. We need to return to the time just before the American Revolution of i775-i783. At that time, a battle was going on between the Anglo-Saxon and Celtic people – of Protestant and Baptist religions. In i760, George III became King and would reign for sixty years until his death in i820. From the first day King George III put on the British crown, he was a known Jesuit.

If you doubt the Jesuits are the cause of what is going on in the world today, then I think you need to look closer at this organisation. All my avenues of enquiry point to the Jesuit organisation as the instigators of the world's problems in our known history. All the wars and the paradigms we experience, the ancient past that has been hidden from us, the history that has been rubbed out, all of what we know has all been given to us by this organisation.

Human history is repeated to fit with the current mindset of the time, for this reason, we cannot trust anything we read in mainstream books, magazines, newspapers or programmes. It's hard work, but we have to dig deeper if the truth is important to us.

After the French/Indian War, George III declared Roman Catholicism to be the religion of Quebec. There were no French people in the region, so naturally, every British Protestant was angry. At that time, George III also increased the London-based African slave trade. The major players during this period were white, Roman Catholic and pro-Catholic Anglican Lords. It was then that the Royal African Company held the monopoly over this wicked trade which was owned for many years by the House of Stewart.

In the Act of Settlement of i702, the Stewarts legally became British sovereigns. The Stewarts were ruled by the Jesuits and intermarried with the German Hanoverian dynasty to gain control of the monarchy right through to the i900s. You have to ask why. Why did the Jesuits use the British crown to import slaves from Africa into the British colonies?

At the beginning of the American Revolution, there were 2.5 million white Protestants and Baptists and half a million African slaves. The underlying reason for bringing African slaves to America seems to have been to bring a different culture into a liberal civilisation to start a huge race war. This war was intended to annihilate the white Protestants and Baptists - with aid from the Native American Indians. Thomas Jefferson always said that the black Africans would rise up and kill the white men of America.

These deeds were put in place by the Jesuits. Please

understand that they are up to the same tricks today. The black and white race war is still in the making, and hate is being encouraged against mankind, and it is done by causing divisions and race wars.

SEVEN YEARS WAR

When you look closely at the sequence of events in the common history books, the war in Europe and America could have been created to bring about another Great Reset. In fact, at that time, everywhere on this earth, there appears to have been wars.

The Seven Years War, as it turns out, could have been the real First World War. Fought between i754 and i763, the main conflict occurred in those seven years and it involved every great power at the time - except the Ottoman Empire. It spanned five continents and affected Europe, the Americas, West Africa, India and the Philippines.

This was the conflict that split Europe into two coalitions. One side was led by Great Britain and the other side was led by France. For the first time, France aimed to curtail Britain's ever-growing might, so it was during this time that the French formed a grand coalition of its own. This ended as Britain rose to the world's prominence, which altered the European balance of power.

The conflict between Great Britain and France broke out in i754 when the British disputed French positions in North America and seized hundreds of French merchant ships. Meanwhile, the rising power in

Prussia was struggling with Austria for dominance within the Holy Roman Empire in Central Europe. This all culminated in the French Revolution.

These countries are included in the war known as the First World of Conquest, but there are different names for it. A lot was going on in 1755 – only about 270 years ago. It seemed as though the whole world was in flux and reeling from a catastrophic sequence of events, including comets and apocalyptic events, giant earthquake and tsunamis.

I ask, is God responsible for resetting our arses for the Phoenician paradigm? Are we being judged? Or is advanced technology, like the fasces, being used to reset our way of living? Or, could it be the black magic arts?

Lisbon
There are many depictions in books that show Lisbon and huge areas of the Mediterranean completely wiped out. At one of the richest Phoenician ports, there are what looks like FEMA camps of the time.

The city of Lisbon was completely smashed, yet the police were doing public hangings and battering the shit out of everyone. Everything was smashed and there was a load of looting - but there was nothing to steal. Apparently, as the narrative goes, there was a giant tsunami, after which everything burned to the ground. Books on the subject of this catastrophe mention a comet that brought major floods. It was far from anything the Creator would have put in place –

mainly because it smacks of being man-made - partly witchcraft, partly technology.

Lisbon was a massive city, not on grid patterns like America, but they had giant architecture and massive ships. From the images the Flat Earth Think Tank managed to dig up, Lisbon was a beautiful city, but the strange thing is that all the people depicted were living in tents. The city of Lisbon had a huge amount of masonry and, in the images depicted of it during this period, all of that masonry was just floating away.

Lisbon had an expansive Star Fort system and the whole area, up to Gibraltar, Saville, was mud-flooded from previous events. All of Europe, even Dunkirk, Gent, Dusseldorf, Cologne, Hanover, Frankfurt, Hamburg, were all involved in this kind of thing.

Some of the Star Forts like locks - as though you could just put a key in them to turn them on, then the cogs would move into place. Everything seems to have a connection to water, it gives the impression of giving birth into the canal, birth in a bay – perhaps that's where the word *obey* comes from. From what I can tell, there seems to have been a pattern of events that followed like this:

- a giant earthquake
- a tsunami
- a plague
- a scorching/burning event
- a reset – a calendar shift, a rebirth

What is left after these events is pure mud-flood. My question is, how did they manage to build the cities back so quickly?

In i755, even though this period wasn't attributed to war, the whole world was at war. It wasn't only in Lisbon where there are so many devastating images coming from that period, it was all across the Mediterranean. The whole place was in flux during this time.

Plagues
Theoretical Philosophy (i755-i770) gives a lot of information on dreams and dreams of spirits and focuses on a cult philosophy, anti-Kabala. It also gives details of the comets and links them to plagues.

There's a lot of discussion about the plague, smallpox, cholera, and many other germ theories, but they are very suspect. The death tolls are in their millions across the world - around 17 million died from the Spanish Flu. If there were that many people who died of these things, you'd think that someone you knew would know someone who had died of these things. Someone would have written a book, fact or fiction, about it at some point during or after that period. It would have affected them so deeply that they would have wanted to document it in some way. I've been here over 50 years and I've never heard of anyone dying of these. I'm pretty sure there was an 'ethnic cleansing' in America, and a giant tsunami, or mud flood, wiped them all away.

The term 'Black Death' was coined in i755. The normal narrative is that the rat is blamed for infecting a tiny town, and it spread from there. There's no evidence at all for this.

The year i755 was only a couple of hundred years ago, it's not like it was aeons ago, so what was going on? The official narrative was that 40,000 good people died, but it has to be a lot more than that. I have to ask, what was the population?

The calendar shift is documented too. The year started on a Wednesday of the Gregorian calendar and the common year started on the Sunday of the Juliana calendar. 755 year of the Common Era (CE), at the start of the i750s. The Gregorian calendar was 11 days ahead of the Julian calendar. That hasn't been the only one, but this event of i755 seems to have been terrible.

Strange phenomena
Five hundred years ago seems to me like another reset date. In that time, everything is in flames, trees are gone, and they're trampling everyone to death. The Phoenicians seem to turn up on elephants with their fine silks – after which everyone ends up dead.

There was something significant about the shields they used while in battle. They seem to be blank plaques or mirrors and the images in the books the Flat Earth Think Tank find, give the impression that the tools they used were very futuristic. The authors like to attribute the period to the i700s, but the images of the things they used look modern. Many of the buildings are mud-flooded and yet, so many of those buildings are elaborate and ornate, far advanced to what we could create today.

Another odd phenomenon I've noticed is that some of the images coming out of the Middle Age period depict something like a 'projection glass' where there's a skull on one side and the face on the other. The hourglass is often depicted and strange 'hobbit-like people.

I've also come across some ancient texts that list a type of chronology. In it, it says that dog heads are the Kings or the rulers. Why were people with dog heads ruling about 500 years ago? This is so weird and trippy.

All the history that has been handed to us today is given by the Controllers – so it is a lie anyway. And this is why we can't verify anything coming from the first millennium.

The Ice Age
I have a lot of respect for David Weiss, who goes deep inside the rabbit hole. Weiss' podcasts propose an ice wall around our earth's layout, and outside of that barrier, there are other continents and other lands.

There are two versions of the last Ice Age, but there is some doubt about whether it happened at all. For my money, it did. Why do I think this? Because it seems obvious that the hills and dales of Britain have been carved out by glaciers and, as they carve the landscape out, the rocks get deposited all over the landscape. Unfortunately, the rocks that would have given some evidence of the last Ice Age are missing as, apparently, they were smashed up by people in the i600s/i700s for use in agriculture. History tells us that fires were lit underneath those rocks and then water was put on top of them, which caused them to crack open. This made it easier to smash them with sledgehammers.

While the Ice Age history is scientifically documented, the whole thing is making me question it. Let's just go with the idea that it did happen and see where we get with that line of questioning.

Our history books tell us that 12,000 years ago, which isn't that long ago, the ice wall came down from the north and, according to the maps, ended right here where I am in Britain. The boundaries are in Cornwall, Dorset and South Wales, but beyond those locations, it thawed out. What is proposed is that people moved South to other lands. They didn't return into the middle bit where we are because of the ice age.

The work of Graham Hancock and the Piri Reiss map shows Antarctica free from ice so, from this, the map is pre-ice age. My question is, how could there be maps that are 12,000 years old? Graham Hancock says that Piri Reiss got these maps from a previous civilisation and the source of those maps were from the Library of Alexandria, the one that burned down.

Supposing those Peri Reiss maps really are that ancient and show the lands around us that were free from ice.

THE HOLY GRAIL OF THE GREAT RESET

This would coincide with David's ideas.

I've always been a purveyor of the electric universe theory. Before, when I was a 'globe believer' (foolish me), I used to follow the works of Immanuel Velikovsky (1895-1979) was a Russian-born writer who wrote The Worlds in Collision (1950). Now, this is not strictly out of the bounds of possibility. As you see, the stars are God only knows what. When you get up there, they disappear, and they seem only visible from the earth's surface. This gives me the idea that they are 'locked' up there somewhere.

When you consider the planets, they wander, so they exist, and they've been charted throughout history and even in our recent news when they were bragging about the Cassini Probe and humanity being able to travel between the giant gaps of Saturn's rings. I question whether it is possible a probe can travel that distance (we're told 1.36 million miles), and send signals via Earth's Wi-Fi.

Velikovsky proposed that the worlds, or the bodies that we know nothing about, came really close to the earth's surface. You can read about this in the Iliad. He says that Venus came so close to the earth that it actually rained petrol. How did the people of this time know this? How did that story get passed down? How did they know what petrol was? What was it used for?

Other people, like Plato, wrote about the mythical Atlantis, or Shambala. If you've been looking into the hollow earth theory, you will have been told that there have been civilisations before us. Where have they gone?

If a second body came from a neighbouring pond, this would have caused a giant electrical arching. The sort that would rip this place to shreds and could create great landscapes like the Grand Canyon. That's the idea that Velikovsky has put forward but what response did he get from academia? Let's just say that he got a pretty shitty career out of it.

I've always thought about deserts. They are a bit of a mystery to me. Why they are encroaching? Why they are getting bigger? The science says it's because they're on the 'sunbelt' but that can't be true. I only have to remind you of the equators to show you the sunbelt is not a sensible thing to link this idea to. Something else creates those deserts.

A species in amnesia
What I propose is that we are a species in amnesia. We are in an amnesic state because we don't want to remember the cataclysms that came before as they were too horrendous. There was probably a flood and a pre-diluvian ice age. Even if it turns out not to be true, it's an intriguing idea to consider. I like to tie ideas and theories together, ones that resonate with me. Some of this might be sitting true. Every day a new sun. Every day is a new day.

Indus Valley
There is some evidence of radiation in the bones of the people from the Indus Valley, Pakistan. Does this

indicate an ancient battle took place and wiped out everyone?

I've been interested in this civilisation for quite some time. As you know, I like to dig into timelines and make correlations between them. The battles between Krishna and Arjuna are well documented in the Bhagavad Gita and the Mahabharata written in ancient Sanskrit. I keep asking these questions about this:

1. Is it all just rubbish?

2. Is there an element of truth in it?

When India was not part of the Raj, it was outside of Western indoctrination or manipulation. The existence of Sanskrit text is listed in the ancient cosmology of the Vedas and these texts will tell you of the battles that took place and the weapons they used. If you take the time to read them, you will find that civilisation was far in advance of today's technology. They tell of flying carpets and spaceships, but though you can't get detailed the schematics for the spaceships in this cosmic, hyper technology, there are depictions of these machines. Those machines had extraordinary power and even projected holographic armies, which had the ability to show an army on a hillside that wasn't actually there. From the descriptions of their weaponry, today the only equivalent piece of equipment we have is the nuclear weapon.

The ancient centre for the Indus Valley civilization was in Southern Pakistan, one of the earliest civilizations in the world. They flourished in North-West India and

Pakistan. The cities were well-planned, bricks were used for building and they had proper drainage facilities.

Geographically, the Indus Valley civilisation extended all the way to Egypt. According to radiocarbon dating (which I don't buy), it existed between i3,000 – 3,500 BCE. The people used to live on the banks of the Indus river yet, our history books tell us that only during the Bronze age, did people start living as civilized societies.

Does this go some way to explaining the advancement of humanity? Is it more plausible than we find ancient Rome to be? I'm putting this out there for you to consider. The Raj ruled for over 200 years and this civilisation was wiped out. That was about a million people just up and disappeared.

A Vimāna looks like advanced technology, it is about 5,000 to 6,000 years old and could shoot like a nuclear weapon. In the last few years, I caught some rumours that said the military dug out something like a Vimāna in a cave in Afghanistan. This could possibly give a reason for the war created there, first by the Russians, then by the Americans.

When you look closely at the ornate buildings in India, they look just like a Vimāna. There are some intriguing clues to ancient technology from not that long ago. For instance, does the floating city ring like a bell? There are stories of them in China, and also the Battle of Hastings in Britain is rumoured to have had something like it.

I've always found the Vimāna's true because the ancient, untampered texts mention them. Why would these stories live so long if there was no truth in them? I don't believe the teachings of Krishna were false. I believe they were from a civilisation that has been wiped out.

I've said it before and I'll say it again, something has happened in the past and we have forgotten about it. The 1% are using more than the ancient technologies, they are harnessing some subjects from the library of Alexandria and are aware of what is available to humanity. Yet, the true nature of reality seems to be hidden from us, the masses. Why?

Signs of vitrification are freely available online. The bodies of the dead lie where they fell on mass, and those bodies have signs of radioactivity in them. Even stray dogs and animals wouldn't eat the corpses. I think firestorms would give a decent amount of radiation and be enough to do this type of thing.

The bricks used in those ancient buildings look modern to me, even Henry VIII's Palace in England, Hampton Court, has modern-looking bricks. The sewerage systems, the building shapes and the blocks they used, the cuneiform writing etched into stone - all of this screams the same technology was used by a civilisation that lived not long ago. And I believe they were living in pockets all over the earth.

Subconsciously, I do think we know what's going on. We have an idea of what has happened in the past but, it may have been such a terrible event that our psyche has suppressed it. Today, scientists seem to be trying to replicate and reverse engineer what they have found so that they can use it today.

What was going on during that time to that civilisation? Why are we not being told of their achievements? Why are we being deliberately deceived and lied to about all of this? The evidence is there, but there seems to be a consistent attack on the truth. I would like to know why it is so important to hide this all from us.

LEST WE FORGET

I wanted to get to the nitty-gritty of who funded Adolph Hitler. It seemed like Hitler got arrested for taking part in a revolution, the Judge gave him a token couple of months in prison, which was in a really high-class castle. Don't think for one minute he was being given 'slops' in a dingy dungeon. There are photographs available showing him and Hess strutting around. And, after his time spent in that castle prison, he came out a millionaire.

According to the book *The History of the Jesuits*, Hitler was trained by them and began to take over Europe. He started the advent of what would have been a type of New World Order. I guess it would have been based on 'nice' disinfected streets and everybody being 'perfecto'. I mean, what happened if you had a kid that was born with something slightly wrong with it, but you love it to death? In the regime they were creating, they would have gotten rid of it.

Now, we don't have regimes like that on this plane. We don't promote any eugenics or ethnic cleansing. Not yet, anyway.

The origins of Hitler's power can be traced to the Jesuits, the Vatican and his American backers. It was not a war against the Jews, as we are all convinced it was. Hitler was funded by Pope Pious of the Vatican. It is well-documented that the Vatican supported the Germans. Hitler was probably a Jew too, as his father was a Jewish descendant, and his father was probably a lot of other things that Hitler hated. Pretty warped human, to be sure.

The Allies and Axis forces of World War Two show they were all in it together. After the war, the Freemasons, bankers and politicians were free of responsibility for their actions. The surrender of Japan meant that Emperor Shōwa (known as Hirohito) (1901-1989) was left completely unhindered at the war's climax. Hirohito was never brought to justice for countless crimes against humanity, e.g. for the raping and nuking, and the atrocities of the Burma Railway and brutally torturing soldiers. This, together with the fact that the Queen, and other world leaders, attended Hirohito's funeral in 1989, proved they are all players together in the big game. They all sit at the same table and we, my friends, are just numbers to them. Just mice in their maze.

The Peterloo Massacre
Surfdom came to an end after the Bubonic Plague in the early 1800s. You would think then that the poor

would have had it good. The Plague had killed off a good percentage of the aristocracy after a third of Europe succumbed to it. The blessing was that it had left a vacuum for the poor to attempt to change the system. As there were no more Barons who owned the land, many people were not subservient to the aristocracy anymore, so people believed they now had a chance to make a decent living from their own skills, experience and knowledge.

In i819, the world started to get back onto its feet. The Napoleonic wars had just finished in i815 and, afterwards, the people were starving from the famine and chronic unemployment.

The main reason for this catastrophic sequence of events that followed was that the Rothschild's had bought out the Bank of England - through fraud. They had scammed the country with a courier that lied about the result of the battle of Waterloo. Rothschild was able to force people to sell their stocks, then when they got to such a low price, Rothschild bought them up. This effectively made Rothschild the 'owner' of the banks – and the world. The whole sorry lie crippled the country and, as a result, ordinary people suffered.

It was as the government introduced the first Corn Laws that people got angry. At that time, the country was in such a poor economic condition that political radicalisation resulted. A group of people worked towards Parliamentary Reform - the Parliamentarians and the Whigs. Henry Hunt organised demonstrations to take place across the country to bring this about. In one demonstration in Manchester on 16th August 1819, there was what was to become an infamous massacre.

It was soon after Henry Hunt began the meeting, with almost half a million people present, the local magistrates called in the police to arrest the organisers. The Cavalry charged into the crowd with sabres drawn.

Fifteen people were killed and 400 to 700 were wounded. It was called The Peterloo Massacre because it was similar to the Waterloo Massacre four years earlier.

The death toll is vastly underestimated. Obviously, with sabres and horses, how could only 15 people be killed and 700 be injured? Based on what we've seen from our own battles in the past and in our own time, do you think this is a realistic ratio?

The charge was ordered by the government against its own people. The government is still doing this to its people today via the police forces who charge into and kettle demonstrators against a system that is being put in place today.

Sadly, we seem to be going through it now -again. History always repeats itself, especially if you don't learn from it. Because of this experience, I need you to be aware that you are not safe in a Satanic Police State – even today.

More recently, in Manchester again, there was a

supposed explosion that killed lots of people. I have noticed that these events seem to be deeply coded. The dates and times were coincidentally in line with numbers that have hidden meanings. Am I wrong to believe that they all culminate in their demonic cosmological numbering system? If you think that this doesn't happen, that governments do not terrorise their own people, that they don't keep their people in perpetual fear, think again.

Victoria Station is connected to the Manchester Arena and I saw some images of the supposed suicide bomber, who went to the shop in the train station to buy some nice 'smellies', obviously to make his house smell nice before he blew himself up.

I keep pulling premonitions out of the air, the day before it happened, I said that Oasis would make a comeback now, after the Manchester attack. It's as though it's all scripted. They had a mini-marathon in Manchester, and the lead singer of New Order was there, he is so heavily into the Matrix. I saw about twenty minutes of New Order and left. No thank you.

Some people say that I'm fear-mongering – no. The complete opposite. You look outside your window and you hear the birds tweeting and all the nice things about you. Yet, you go back inside, look at your tel-lie-vision, and you get hypnotised into bombs going off and shit going on everywhere. It's all designed to scare the shit out of you, to turn neighbour against neighbour, friend into enemy. It's a 'divide and conquer' tactic.

Many more cases can be found of governments attacking their own people, not just with police charges, but with experiments as well. Many innocent people have been killed because of the Controllers greed, their grabs for power, their selfishness. They don't seem to really give an eff about the populations that vote for them.

You need to follow this trail of breadcrumbs because I can honestly tell you this is not the end of it. Something is going on now and it's a big one. The bombing in Manchester was announced as the worst in Manchester's history, but it was definitely not the worst, even though it was horrible. You only have to look back to the Peterloo Massacre to debunk that.

The Dresden War Crime
I've been thinking about the atrocities carried out by Bomber Harris and the RAF and the Allied bombers. The attacks were at the end of February 1944. The city of Dresden had no military significance, but it was the victim of significant destruction. To me, this is all part of the deception and I wanted to explore it.

The Dresden atrocities have disturbed me deeply. It contributes to my thoughts about how our history is hidden and resets happen without our knowing. I'm a bit of a history buff, especially military history and I'm in a country where the narrative given to us is all a lie. I'm also in a country where my fellow citizens and I are portrayed as 'the bad guys' – in fact, I agree that our behaviour in the Second World War was not befitting of gentlemen. It's sad. Especially as we are taught to believe we were the heroes.

I know everyone likes to think about the Germans as being bastards, there's even a sketch on a British comedy show called *Mitchel and Webb*, where they portray two members of the Death Head squadron in the trenches. They had a skull logo on their caps, and they looked at one another while the bombs were going off around them. I can't remember it word-for-word, but they said to each other something like the following:

"We have skulls on our caps!"

"Yes, I know."

"Does that mean we're the bad guys?"

Then the sketch ends and you are left with that narrative that the Germans were actually the bad guys. I'm in Britain so, apparently, I can't even discuss this.

The thing that I can talk about is the Dresden bombing. It happened right at the end of World War Two, and it's only briefly touched upon in the history books. If you are unlucky enough to see any of the footage or photographs of this event, then you will not get it easily out of your consciousness because it is that bad. For some reason, Churchill and the Allied powers took it upon themselves to eradicate the German population by bombing Dresden into oblivion.

As a city, Dresden was a beautiful place, filled with

museums and works of art. It was often regarded as the Florence of Germany. There were no military bases whatsoever located there during the war. It was considered a safe haven for Germans who were escaping the raping-Russian hoards it was jam-packed with women and children. No soldiers, or armed men, they didn't even have any air defences.

It was as late as February and March of 1945, right at the end of the war when the Allies had already more or less won and they were at Hitler's door. Churchill and Bomber Harris, who I'm pretty sure is damned to hell, made a decision to do a bombing raid on Dresden.

The bombing raids happened quite a bit all over Germany, but not to the extent that happened in Dresden. The only way you could compare the catastrophe is if you check out Nagasaki and Hiroshima, which, we are told, were annihilated with nuclear weapons. Note that it appears there was no evidence of nuclear use in this area, but there is a hell of a lot of footage of radiation burns and people who suffered for years after as a result.

What was really going on? Did they put radioactive material into the bombs they dropped? Is anyone else asking these kinds of questions? Will we ever get to the truth of it?

Dresden was a true holocaust and a devastating injustice to humanity. The level of destruction defies the imagination. The estimated death toll was about 300,000, but that's only an estimation because no one knew how many people were in the city.

The first bombing wave entered over the city in late February 1945 and was ordered by Bomber Harris of the Royal Air Force. Incidentally, my grandfather was part of the Air Force, he was an Air Marshal who guided the planes in with paddles that looked like table-tennis bats. In the raid, they lost six Lancaster's. this tells you that Dresden had eff all anti-aircraft defence positions around the city. Thousands of tonnes of high-end explosives were dropped, followed by thousands of tonnes of bombs that caused firestorms.

The situation with a firestorm is quite horrendous. I don't want to nasty your mind out by being too graphic – so don't read the following if you're a bit squeamish or sensitive as it is effing horrendous. These firestorm bombs suck the oxygen out of the city.

What you find is that everybody is crowded in the streets, shoulder-to-shoulder, because the buildings are on fire and then the air disappears from the streets. Basically, people's heads do this Hiroshima thing, where they swell up like balloons and what's left are two little slits for the eyes and mouth. There's plenty of evidence for this. One pretty brutal image I saw was of a father and a son, laying down together. It was very sad to see.

So, after the bombs are dropped, what follows is a firestorm. Tornadoes, or fire-twisters, go up and down thoroughfares and they suck people up as they went. It is akin to a fiery dragon that would just pick people up and throw them down burned to ash.

You'd think that one wave of this kind of battering would be enough, wouldn't you? But no. They sent in another wave later the same night, then the Americans paid them another visit the next day.

They put two SS divisions to work in dealing with the bodies. Everyone was dead. The whole population was piled up in the streets. A lot of people were boiled alive as they had hidden in the cellars. The temperatures had reached a thousand degrees or more and the water systems just burst and poured in on them. You don't normally get these sorts of temperatures in burning cities.

The state of Dresden was disgusting. There was nothing left of the beautiful city that it was. This sort of act was replicated in other cities like Hamburg and Berlin. Some people did escape, but not many.

There are a few nasty stories about Britain being bombed, but not like that. Dresden was bombed on a Biblical scale. If you don't know about it, it's not surprising. Why? Because our government doesn't want us to know that we are responsible for such crimes against humanity.

They say that the Germans wanted to conquer the earth. Hitler was a megalomaniac, apparently, he wanted to take over the world. Don't get me wrong, I don't empathise with what Hitler did to the people he put in the concentration camps during World War Two, but his ruling the world wasn't the way things panned out. Remember, I've mentioned how Hitler was funded and trained in another section, so check that out for yourself.

It's not a subject I ought to say much about, as I'm from Britain and, as I said, my grandfather served his time in the RAF in the war. Though I have a little bit of pride in that, I am ashamed about what happened in Dresden. Dresden was an effing crime against humanity. I know the London blitz went on for months, but we're talking different levels. We're talking about five hundred bombers, all loaded with thousands of tonnes of high-end explosives. The buildings, the marble and alabaster, were just being smashed up. It wasn't really razed to the ground, it was incinerated – including its occupants.

I know many of the different battles and bombings that happened – plenty on Hiroshima and Nagasaki but, Dresden? That was something else. Dresden should be a by-word for the level of the lie. The lies told to humanity about what really goes on in this world and why.

I'm bringing it to your attention because I don't want it to escape your consciousness. This kind of event gives you an idea of the level of the lies that are fed to us. I hate to think that the Controllers that run this world could be so evil. So sadistic. But they are. The important thing to remember is that people all over the world have the ability to be barbaric – especially when they say they were 'just following orders' – which is no excuse. In the end, it's up to the individual to wake up and make up their own mind as to how far their conscience can deal with when they consider harming another human.

FLAGS & NATIONALISM – IS IT ALL TO DIVIDE US?

A couple of years ago, a very interesting man spoke with me, he was a Vietnam Vet who had spent twenty-six years in the US Marine Corps, to me, he was a hero. We discussed how flags and borders create nationalism and how it's nothing to do with Patriotism at all. What he understood was that it's all to do with:

Divide and rule of the masses.

I attended an online chat session to commemorate Memorial Day in America and I couldn't help but well up. The worst thing this man had experienced was when he returned and the 'non' hero's welcome he got. You've probably seen the films where the Vietnam Vet returns from war and is rejected by society because of the film footage and media coverage they had got before those men returned.

We have to keep reminding ourselves that, even though we have all this bullshit going down around us, we are brothers and sisters together and we should work together.

BOMBING ALL OVER THE WORLD

There was a long comment from one of my follower on my YouTube channel, which I thought was valid.

He explains what is going down in our present reality and how this is bringing about a Great Reset for our modern era. When you put it all together and join the dots, so to speak, it all makes sense. It's from Charles and I totally agree with it:

> *I can only speak for myself. I live in the US and we have had many false flag attacks. The biggest so far was 9-11 but also the Boston bombing, the Sandy Hook event and even an airport.*
>
> *Sandy Hook was used to take rights from people while saying children were killed - but no bodies were ever seen or blood found. Not even a body bag. Sounds bad, I know. Who wants to see kids in little bags? But it never happened. There were so many holes in the story it was crazy.*
>
> *If you look at the Boston bombing, how were they doing a training exercise a few blocks away?*
>
> *From what I have seen here on what happened there, why do the people in all the interviews smile and seem happy? If you really go through something traumatic you sure as hell wouldn't be smiling! And the set of parents shown*

> *there, if that was my son, and I have one 11-year-old son, I could not even be on a damned camera.*
>
> *So did people die? Well, I know the picture used was of a girl who died four years ago. Her mother called them out on it. Did young people die? I don't think so. But most only talk of the sound and running. No real facts. Mainstream news here or there can't be trusted. More rights will go away and people will thank them for it.*
>
> *It's the way to feel safe from the bad people. One day we will get up and feel the rope around our necks. But it will be too late. I know and I get it, you can't make this shit up. It's a bad movie that will not stop.*

Charles goes onto mention the FEMA coffins and the guillotines. Why is no one mentioning this? The news media is not taking any notice of it, it's like it doesn't exist. Yet, ordinary Americans can see it going on in their beautiful country. And, if those who spew out the false news think they'll be immune from these things, they've got another thing coming to them.

Charles hopes, as I do, that people will wake the hell up – and quick. I agree with every word he says. If we don't, we'll soon be embroiled in yet another war. So,

God Bless you Charles.

There's a lot of suicide bombing going on. At least there was before the Covid thing hit the world like a sledgehammer. Strange the way that's all stopped, don't you think? The white van man attacks in London were becoming quite regular. However, since the plandemic hit, not one. Odd.

LOCAL 'COLD WAR' HOAX BUNKERS

Why are the nuke bomb bunkers so cheap and nasty? The mode of thinking with the Cold War, like a Flat Earther, I do have questions about these bunkers. I've never seen a nuclear bomb go off, from the i950s to today, where nobody has let one-off. No pun intended.

I think it's safe to assume now that, since the emptying of the bunkers, that it was all bullshit. I thought to myself, well, what about all these listening stations dotted around the place? There has been a massive investment, all over the world in silo's all over the US and bunkers all over the UK.

I got thinking on this subject because Leckwith Woods, just north of where I live, looks like a giant hunk of concrete sticking up out of the ground. A couple of years ago, a documentary was made of it, by the BBC. The journalists got right down into the heart of the building. The public can't go into it, but there are a couple of bricks at the back, and you have to climb over a really high and dangerous steel fence to get in. It's not easy.

THE HOLY GRAIL OF THE GREAT RESET

This is a question for the critical thinker: If you were to invest in a nuclear bunker, a building that's going to keep you alive (it will be to keep you safe so you can rebuild humanity after the bomb has been dropped), wouldn't you expect more money to be invested in building it? What I mean is, don't you think they would have created a massive, elaborate underground 'hive' type system? Well, they have got them, but this isn't what they're showing in the photographs they've released.

The one near me was closed as recent as 1990. It's a listening post and it is one of many that are dotted around my city, Cardiff. While I was looking at the photographs of the inside of these bunkers, it occurred to me that they are all built to a substandard. Basically, they are shit. We are told that they're built so the Government can survive what is basically Armageddon, and yet, where they stay, they have a diesel generator. Think about that for a second.

Why would they need a diesel generator? Think of those fumes. Would they want to breathe all that in? Would you? Surely they have some sort of set-up where they could get fresh air.

Some of the photographs show people in an underground tunnel which looks like a disused tube station and they're working at a switchboard. It's just a thought. You should check them out. Search 'underground Britain' and they'll pop up.

LSD in Wales

When you look at what was (or is still) going on in Afghanistan with those poppy fields and what happened when Britain took over Hong Kong with the Opium Wars - that brain of yours has to start ticking over. Is there a link somewhere to all this?

Back in the 1970s, half of the world's LSD was produced in a mansion house in Wales. A big Operation, called Julie, took down all the kingpins of the drug trade in Wales. They found that the man who owned this massive mansion house where Acid was being produced buried tens of millions of pounds worth of sealed LSD in his grounds somewhere. That stuff would be as good now as when it was made.

This was the largest drug bust in history. Think about it. HALF the earth's amount of LSD was produced there. Who was accused of creating it? A bunch of bloody Freemasons.

Why would these powerful drugs be important enough to begin or continue wars? To eff with our minds? To derail us even more from what we really are?

9. ARE WE HUMAN GUINEA PIGS?

It may be a bit strange, what I'm going to present here, but bear with me as there are some important topics to talk about. One is focused on the 'hearts of gold'. You've heard them say 'he talks from his heart' or 'he has a heart of gold'. We know that people die of a broken heart and feel physical pain through emotion that comes from the heart. What is the heart, exactly? A pump? Is it a torus field? A real muscle? We'll find out more about it here.

Another topic is the 18th Century Wig out that was in what seems like a post-apocalyptic era. Even the official narrative shows that the elites were in deep shit during that time. Here, I'm going to look into why in the i700s they were all wearing facial powder and wigs. Was there something going on?

I also look into ritual magic and how this has been used to control the masses. 5G technology and harmonics are also topics that I open up for discussion here. The more we discuss these things, the more we will understand them and become aware of what they are capable of doing to us.

The most important thing I talk about in this chapter is our children's freedoms. If we continue down the road that we seem to be going along, we are letting them down. Our grandfather's fought horrible wars and lost their lives so that we could have our freedom. We must do the same if we are to bless our kids with the freedoms we have enjoyed.

Before I talk you down the rabbit hole of how I think we are being used as guinea pigs for the Controllers experiments, I'd like to give you some hope. For that hope to come alive, all you need to do is look at the world's ancient cultures. For instance, look to the Chinese and Indian ways of living, of being and of doing.

IN-HUMAN ABILITIES?
There are Buddhists in Tibet practising some sort of advanced technology simply by controlling their own body heat. I've seen an experiment where a Buddhist monk is covered with soaking wet towels, and he's sat in the snow, freezing cold. He sat there and literally advanced his body temperature so that the heat evaporated the water in the towels. They took the towels off, and they were completely bone dry within ten minutes.

There's another guy I've seen called the Ice Man. He could take his shoes off and run across the tundra in a pair of speedos. Nothing happened to him. He didn't get frost bite. He didn't lose his circulation. His feet didn't go blue. Snow, ice or extreme temperatures didn't have any effect on him. Is he just a freak? Or has he managed to tap into something we don't understand?

Some people can dive deep down to the ocean floor and have the ability to hold their breath for so much more time than anyone thinks is humanly possible.

If you doubt any of this, remember before Roger Bannister broke the record for running, no one believed it was possible to do what he did. Soon after, though, everyone was achieving the same standard.

Every single one of us has the same abilities inside of us. That's what I'm thinking is important with this Flat Earth Awakening. I think that human consciousness has something to do with it and if we are to avoid the next Great Reset, we need to tap into this hidden technology or become aware of our abilities.

WAS THE BUBONIC PLAGUE A HOAX?

There are some inconsistencies with this disease and some evidence exists that doesn't fit the official narrative. We are constantly scared by rumours of disease and death, and we're reminded of it through the horrors of our fake history. The question, was the Black Death a Hoax, is intended to get you to look at an alternative historical timeline based on what we can prove. As it turns out, the narrative is set in mystery.

The origin of the bubonic plague is still under contention today, they say it came from a flea that lived on a black rat, but note, not the black rat itself.

The Black Death was from i346 through to i353, and it covered all of Eurasia - Europe to Asia. It was said to have been one of the most devastating pandemics in human history, resulting in the deaths of about 200 million people. Just think, that's almost two-thirds of America-land. Gone. Later on, there was a plague, the one that Nostradamus was famed for curing people with rose water - that's pure, clean water with rose petals in it.

There are several theories of the cause of the Black Death, but the questions I ask are: How were they able to analyse DNA? Are we to believe DNA? Does DNA exist?

I have a chromosome 13, I'm told it's because I came from Estonia, in Scandinavia. A village in Scotland never had the Black Death simply because the people who lived there had this chromosome 13. It was this chromosome 13 that seems to have stopped us from getting the Black Death. So, does this make me immune to some diseases?

I think that diseases are some kind of infection and not germs. While any natural nutritionist or Eastern philosopher will tell you that disease comes from within the body, Western medicine points to the horrors that we are to avoid coming from outside the body into our own. Why is this?

When you watch the adverts on the telly about bleach, it makes you question the validity of germs. Bleach kills 99.9% of germs and it even used to say on the back of a Dettol bottle (it doesn't now, perhaps because it doesn't fit with the narrative we're being fed) that that stuff can kill coronavirus. Why do we need the vaccine then?

I've seen church parish records listing people who died of the plague, but I've also seen statements of people who lived through it. As I've said, there are competing theories, there has been analysis (Z010-Z011) from several different people from Northern and Southern Europe that indicate the pathogen responsible for the Black Death was a bacterium that resulted in several forms of plague. They believe that it was formed in Asia, travelled along the Silk Road from China through to Europe and reached Crimea in i343.

Bubonic plague still shows its face today, in India and North America in recent years, and they have it in vials in a laboratory underground in Cardiff where, apparently, they keep all pathogens. Oddly, this appeared in *World War Z* with Brad Pitt, and the guy who wrote the book comes from Cardiff.

The fleas that lived on the Black Rat have been blamed for a plague that decimated the population and caused many religious, social and economic upheavals. That tiny bug caused a change in European history. The history books will say that this wiped out serfdom, where Squires and Lords of the Manor (think Sheriff of Nottingham and Robin Hood days) died alongside the common man.

There are statements from historical records that say, outside of most towns, people would see someone, or something, in the fields akin to the Grim Reaper. If that was a reality, then think of it as some sort of chemical warfare. It is a known fact that men were dressed up in masks and capes and spread smoke everywhere. People called them Doctor Death. I've been looking into this for years and it may not have been like this. The reason why is that I see the stories of Nostradamus who cured people with Rose Water.

We know that the ancient civilisations did practice biological warfare, and many of these pandemics were started by man. Even the Native American Indians were wiped out by Smallpox that was given to them through the blankets. However, some inconsistency exists with the origins of the plague - no one knows whether it came from the flea on the back of rats.

The plague was depicted in the film *Monty Python and the Holy Grail*. If you've seen it, you might recall a scene when they shout, "Bring out your dead!" then some guy comes along with someone over his shoulder and askes the collector with the cart to bung a person on the pile, of bodies and he says "But he's not dead!" Then he replies, "Alright then, how much do you want?" Then he gives him a few quid, bumps him over the head with a giant ladle, kills him and Bob's your Uncle. Another one bites the dust. They give you the impression that if you're not the king, you're knee-deep in shit.

A group of workmen, who built the foundations for the London Railway all the way to Canary Wharf, but had to stop work when they came across a cemetery. There, they found bodies were laid down sporadically.

What they're saying is that there wasn't a Plague Pit for London. What?

I remember when I worked on an archaeology dig and I rebuilt a medieval village - where I mixed cow shit and clay to build walls. The people in that village apparently died of the Black Death. I retrieved items from there, but no one was worried about whether the pathogen was still alive and if they would infect us today.

There's something really wrong with the narrative of the Black Death, and I'm sure anyone who looks deeply into it, would come to the same conclusion. The Black Death was supposed to be around in i348 and arrived through a shipping port. It eventually killed 30-50% of the population. This whole narrative makes me ask too many questions.

There's absolutely nothing to fear. It's still in debate today and its origins aren't even known.

The virus that shut the world down in Z020/Z021 has made us all into guinea pigs. We are being experimented on by a bunch of sicko behavioural scientists. NLP programming tactics are put out via the media and television programmes, after which they observe how the population react, collate their data and then put recommendations into action. That's how we're being played today. We're the lab rats.

ALCHEMY
The Philosophical Epitaph and Hieroglyphical Figures of

Somebody's Tombstone is incredible. It talks of giants and the reset. It shows some mind-blowing alchemical symbols flaming heart, the bell, and the Masonic compass which points straight to the heart. Nobody's shit would have been stolen if it wasn't for the flood. Remember when Moses came down from Ararat and every one of the Israelites was worshipping a golden calf? There's a brief of the golden calf, the world's idol.

Printed in Little Britain, in J693, the graph of the air, earth, water depicts Mount Meru, the domage and the chaos down below what they call Tartarus. Then right down at the bottom, they've shown a picture of Hell and who they call Satan.

The incredible narrative goes on about Lucifer's relationship with God and how they hit it off; oh yes, in this, he's a good guy. But there's a weird story in that the Phoenicians, or Jesuits, bring in this period the double VV (making a W). They have the hieroglyphic scratchings, their philosophical mottos and explanations with philosophical mercury, the nature of seeds and life, and the growth of metals. Then there's the discovery of immortal liqueur: the elixir of life, the salt of Tartar, volatilised and other elixirs with their differences. It's crazy stuff. Everyone was worshipping the Calf on earth:

> *Discovering the rarest miracle of nature*
> *how by the smallest proportion of the*
> *philosopher's stone, a great piece of*
> *common lead was totally transmuted into*

> *the purest transparent gold at the Haig in 1666.*

Now, the Midas Touch, everything Midas touches turns to gold or a new chemical light demon.

> *Rating to blind world that good gold may be found as well as in cold and hot regions and can be extracted out of ground stone, gravel and flint and, to be wrought by all thoughts of people.*

> *Jesua, the next one is the day of dawning of the light of wisdom containing the three principles of the origin of all things.*

Then it goes into the Creation, and it basically explains what this place is - but in a Jesuit sense.

> *Whereby are discovered the great and many mysteries in God, nature and the elements hitherto hid and now revealed.*

It's still mind-blowing and there are quite a few secrets in this. From what I discovered, there is an obsession with gold in this period which is connected with death.

If this is a reversal, and we're not alive or dead, is someone prolonging death with this stuff? It says here:

No man is happy before his death.
Mercury bringest the best after death…
All in mercury that wise men seek.

And this is interesting…

If thou dissolvest the fix it maketh it fly.
And maketh the flyeth fix.

In this field, we are aware of the levitational application of mercury. Basically, it looks like a recipe book for alchemy. In it, they tell you about green gold, which the Flat Earth British Think Tank know to be electrum.

The applications for the gold for these people in the post-apocalyptic society could be wealth. If they are transmuting lead into large amounts, as they state in this book, one gram of this load stone material would transmute - and you could get sixty tonnes of gold from it.

Lee Flat Earth British has posted some 'handbags' that you see the Sumerians carry. They look like 'man bags', with the watches, these could be the load stones which could be a way of transmuting or making currency on arrival.

The philosopher's stone could be a real thing.

THE HOLY GRAIL OF THE GREAT RESET

The Worlds Idol, The Rarest Miracle in Nature, says that a great piece of common lead was totally transmuted into the purest resplendent gold with the rarest of transmutation experiments. That was carried out in 1666 and they go into great detail about how it was done. But they refer to monotonic gold as systematic gold. On page 60, there's an interesting piece that needs to be read:

> *Before I describe the hieroglyphical pigmy*
> *conquering giants in the theatre of secrets*
> *suffer me to transcribe some of the*
> *elements words out of the book of the tree*
> *of life I am content, says he, to believe*
> *there is a stone to make gold and silver.*

I was juggling in my mind the question: was the greatest mining operation in Tartaria for quicksilver? I thought it was about mirrors, but there are other incredible applications for gold and silver. The people who wrote this book don't understand gold fully, as it's a mind-blow to science.

I was also thinking about Neil Young's song "Everybody's looking for a heart of gold", and I wondered why we say that until I remembered Apocalypto (2006), the film Directed by Mel Gibson. He stood on the top of the pyramid, ripped a heart out of someone's chest, held it up to the sky and said, "This heart has the gold!" From this, I can only think there is a specific gold in the human body. Not just any old gold, though.

MARTIN LIEDTKE

Gold is a miracle metal.

Gold is the most malleable element; one single ounce of gold can be beaten out of a sheet that is 300 square feet and the sheet of gold can be made thin enough to be transparent. But the unique properties are what we want to look at. Gold can:

- conduct electricity
- be resistant to corrosion
- have catalytic properties
- be exceptionally malleable and docile
- be a biocompatible
- be a nano-gold

Gold is mind-blowing. Some strange things happen when it is melted, there are all sorts of strange non-explained events with gold. This might be a long shot, but do you think this why Australia (AU) has been called by that name because the whole thing was a mining operation and that's why it's all like a desert. I think so. I think that anywhere with AU in its name is related to gold mining spoils.

Hearts of Gold

From what I've discovered, from the 'powers that should not be' the alchemists and black magicians have learned something about the nature of human existence. It's not a great stretch to link this to the metal in the human body. We are all aware metals are in us and the highest concentration of gold in the body is around the heart.

A radioisotope of gold has been developed, the AU195 isotope, which will give you an image of blood containing structures within the heart, a process called 'heart imaging'.

> *Ok, now we have gold in our heart.*

It is said that the gods, or Zeus in particular, bled gold and that it was called plasma. Incredibly interesting, don't you think?

This is one of my hypotheses, hopefully it's not true:

Gold occurs in places in our bodies and we contain about 0.2milligrams of the stuff, most of it is in our blood. You need 45,000 people to make 8 grams of sovereign. Is this dead or alive? Either way, that's a fair bit of gold.

If you're fortunate to be alive after a Great Reset, then there will be millions upon millions of dead people – and they'll all have that gold in them, around their hearts. That's tempting. Yes, I think you might know where I'm going with this.

> *After a Great Reset, the Controllers might be harvesting our dead bodies for gold.*

Not just any old gold, mind. Specific gold. Gold like monatomic gold. This is in our bodies, along with all the other elements and metals. We could be like a little mining operation in ourselves.

Remember when we're dead, in Christendom, they rip us apart, they cut all our organs out and weigh them. Why do they do that? It makes no sense to an ordinary person who knows nothing about this kind of stuff. The Egyptians also had all their organs removed and put into Coptic jars.

It must be about metals in the body.

My other idea, after I stumbled across something to do with a par-syntax, an algorithm called gold, I thought gold is in our hearts and it affects our emotions. Gold is also used in microchips and processing panels in computers. All our emotions seem to be housed in our hearts, where the highest concentration is gold.

Therefore, I ask the question: have the Controllers processed a programme in our bodies? Or, more to the point, are they programming us now?

It seems as though gold is being collected from us. If you're wondering why it's such a special element, look what white powder gold does:

> *Monatomic gold allows subconsciously held beliefs and worries to surface and become understood.*

There is a big psychological impact with this. Think of

this after a Great Reset, after the collection of a massive amount of gold. It's not for the Anunnaki as Zecharia Sitchin says, they're not mining gold for some aliens out in space because it's not out there. It's in the water, it's in us. Consider this:

> *Monatomic gold acts on the pituitary gland inducing an increase in hormonal production and is thus is a rejuvenating agent.*

It rejuvenates, and this stuff could keep you going for a long time.

> *Monatomic gold strengthens the heart and improves the production of red blood cells. It's in the bone marrow and it increases the production of semen. It can be manufactured alchemically out of 24 carat gold.*

I've just said the highest concentration of gold is in the heart and the blood, the plasma. The research also says that monatomic gold mustn't be confused with colloidal gold as this retains its metallic nature. Now, look into the colloidal gold, as the health aspects with gold and silver are mind-blowing.

I always wear silver and a little bit of gold, but that's just to pay the Ferryman. The applications are its amazing conductivity. It hasn't really got any electromagnetic properties, but what is brilliant for conducting electricity is electrum.

Electrum is worth a lot of money and it's a naturally occurring alloy of gold and silver. This is what was put on the top of obelisks and pyramids in antiquity. It is this that forms a part of this great Tartarian mechanism of free energy. It also applies to health, long life and a higher state of consciousness, which everybody had not long ago. Positively charged silver ions create a conductive field that creates electromagnetic radiation away from the body.

What I'm doing is making a couple of suggestions about the amount of gold in our body. It's a horrible thought, but are humans being harvested for the gold? Are we being programmed with metallic elements and gold?

Gold can act in a specific way, as some sort of electrical conduit or circuitry. Plasma is a big thing, but I always ask, who owns all that blood once collected via the Red Cross vans. All those blood banks, all over Britain, where does the blood go? Certainly not the NHS or the medical companies that own the blood. It goes to the monarch.

This information is coming undone now and the trust has gone. To get a bit of sympathy, they'll probably resort to killing one of them because no one cares about them anymore. People are not condoning these people leeching off us while they seem to be some kind of paedophilic, psychopathic murderers. This whole system is insane. People who put up with that, well, it's just beyond me.

If they are increasing gold into their bodies (not too much as it might get dangerous with all those heavy metals), they could make themselves live longer and it would protect them from electromagnetics.

The Elite are deeply in this shit because they're always trying to prolong life and improve their health.

> *Colloidal silver steers electromagnetic radiation away from the body. It stimulates the body's natural conductivity and improves the blood circulation, body temperature balances and encourages general well-being. It can also fight against harmful infection and disease.*

Some of this information might be making sense now.

> *For those who are sceptical, the University of Southampton has proven that wearing a specific type of silver ring can help alleviate some symptoms of arthritis in the hands, and the benefits include reduction of pain, it prevents hyper-extension of the finger joints, which is common in those suffering from rheumatoid arthritis.*

I wish I had known about this years ago when my

mother was suffering, but the doctors filled her up with drugs.

Southampton University, in England, found that there were many healing benefits to the colloidal silver. It balances moods, it's a powerful anti-bacterial agent that helps fight infections and helps prevent colds, flu and viruses. It also helps with wound healing and heat regulation and circulation. Cardiff University Hospital in Wales has researched for a cure for colds and flu.

I find it amazing that scientists can fly us out to space, but they can't find a cure for the common cold. Why won't they do this? Because Big Pharma makes billions on it.

There are many health benefits to wearing gold as well. It's an all-natural mineral and there are no side effects to wearing it, plus it has also been shown to have a relaxing effect. It regulates oxygen flow, which helps keep you fit and wearing gold can improve and alleviate arthritis.

Through the alchemical books, there's an obsession with alchemical and monatomic gold. There seems to be a need for it in post-apocalyptic times.

Wigs
You'll see many, many old Masters paintings by William Hogarth and in the i700s, everyone appears to be 'whiting out' and either wearing a hat or a wig. I believe this to be another post-apocalyptic time frame.

The reason for wearing wigs was that people had bald patches, which explains radiation poisoning. In John Bunyan's book *The Pilgrim's Progress*, a man's wig falls off and he is completely bald – all the characters in the image are shocked.

In that period, there was a lot of shame in having a bald head, and a lot of people were known to kill themselves for just such a thing. Anyway, what were the wigs about? Usually, you find that by the late 18th Century that the trend for wigs was dying out. The British stopped wearing them after William Pitt put a tax on hair, so short natural hair became popular.

One thing I find odd is the powder people were putting on their heads. The powder was made from finely ground starch and scented with orange and lavender. It was worn all over the Colonial world. Why were they doing that? What was it for? Probably because they stank.

The people who wore these wigs were the Elite and the wigs were made from goat and horsehair and, because they weren't properly washed, they smelt horrible. In the official narrative, everyone stank and was diseased. The trouble was that the wigs tended to attract lice and, to combat the odour of the parasites, they bought powder to put on their skin and wore little love hats.

All over the depictions you see from the i700s, there are fountains, water features and aquatic everywhere. It seems odd, therefore, that they couldn't wash their wigs properly. They appear not to be able to access the water. They also seem not to be able to access the water because their fountains were full of mud. This is where it gets weird.

For nearly two hundred years, powdered wigs were all the rage, but the chic hairpieces would never have become popular if it hadn't been for venereal disease. The story goes that syphilis became the worst disease since the Black Death. I think it was a bit like the AIDS virus in the 1980s.

The hospitals were filled with people who had open sores, blindness, dementia, patchy hair – everyone seems to be rancid with sexually transmitted diseases. If it wasn't an STD, then there was something else going on which I think links to an electromagnetically transmitted dis-ease.

Samuel Pepys wrote that his brother wouldn't show his head as hair was such a big deal. People got very depressed when they were bald and they got blood sores too, so they hid them under the wigs. Many rich people had these problems and wigs became a way of flaunting wealth, as each one cost around 25 shillings.

One clue about where all this originated is in the 'Happy Hats', which seemed to be made of metal, they were probably Faraday Cages. This is the sort of narrative that follows the 'tin foil hat' brigade around who have created these to protect themselves from electromagnetic fields and mind-control.

You see, in depictions of that period, the Russian nobility and rich people wore large round hats that look like decorative metal plates. Then you see in the 1920s, they wore tall decorative feathered hats. These types of hats have an extremely decorative, chain-mail latticework design. Conveniently, they cover the pineal gland. In fact, in most images, the whole brain is covered.

I believe these were a type of electromagnetic shielding weaved with golden or copper thread. They look like lace, but we don't know what they're made of, and you'll see the Phoenicians with these hats on too. In the film *The Cell* with J-Lo, she wears one of these lace hats as though she's dressed like a Phoenician Queen.

Everyone in the 18th Century seemed to be losing their hair. They had the biggest dose of syphilis which killed more than the Black Death, there was the insanity and also the dementia that they suffered.

I ask, is it electromagnetically connected? Is this why, in this chemical era, they were collecting sympathetic/monatomic gold, which has all those incredible properties in it? Was this a post-apocalyptic society after a Great Reset?

The official narrative of people wearing wigs during this time frame stinks. Still, I'm thinking of it in a different context, that the diseases showing mental illness etc., are because of the increased electromagnetic activity in the ether, following a reset. There seems to be a couple of resets every 500 years.

RITUAL MAGIC AND CHANGES IN CONSCIOUSNESS

Is ritual magic practised by the Elites to change our consciousness? There is enough evidence of it about and if we keep turning a blind eye to it and do not learn about what this is about, we will be forever preyed upon.

I've had my mind blown on this subject and it's another piece of the jigsaw puzzle that falls into place. Because of some things I've seen, I've had my suspicions of how reality is being manipulated for some time now. As I've explained in my videos and my previous book, I was in the Merchant Navy, studied archaeology, and saw things that don't exist in this physical reality. I can assure you, these things are real and other people have experienced them too. They've been written about from time immemorial, but I believe it hasn't been a very long time.

Ritual magic is something that was used by the Nazi's. We're all familiar with Adolph Hitler, a seemingly insignificant little bloke who was a loner in the First World War. He was a failed artist, yet, he managed to have thousands of people in the palm of his hand. Not only that, they worshipped him as a God and gave Life Oaths to him.

Whether or not people thought, in the beginning, that this man was insane, I don't know, but later on, they just gave up their lives to him. Otto von Bismarck, head of the German states at the time, was known to have said, "Over my dead body would that crazy man come into power!" So, how did this happen? Was ritual magic used?

When you dig into Himmler, the third in command after Goebbels, he had a strange cult of manifestation going on. They had something called HeartMath, which is the technology practised by the ancient religions, brought to us from Thoth, possibly the Atlanteans, or people from other ponds in recent times.

There are stories that Hitler got hold of a mandrake root which he dug up from the village where he was born and he placed it under his bed. This is a kind of ritual magic and when you look at ritual magic closely, you can see how it is managing to change our reality. You can't deny that things have altered and it's not the Mandela Effect. I mean, you can see how this technology can be used to get one man (Hitler) to get an entire race of people in the palm of his hand. That's true ritual magic and where power comes from.

Himmler's Castle
When you look into Himmler's castle, the Castle of Wewelsburg, in Buren, Germany, you'll find clues about the ritual magic they have used. There is an underground temple of sorts, when you look into it, there is what is regarded by many Flat Earthers as the Black Sun.

The people who built this knew something. In Himmler's Castle, some temples would have had openings next to the pillars, where soldiers would stand and there, they would do some sort of ritual magic.

Incidentally, we are told that Himmler was a chicken farmer and a Jesuit. Possibly a Jew too, but a Jesuit for sure. In his Castle, you'll find a link to the pineal gland, which is calcified by using fluoride and if we had the true clear pineal gland, we would have the power to create reality the same way these people do.

There's a link between Himmler's Castle and sacred geometry and who we truly are. The Black Sun occult symbol, which tourists can plainly see there on the floor in one of the towers, is evidence that they used ritual magic.

I am starting to believe that the SS Elite knew a way through to an Atlantean location, a place where Thoth came from across the ice. I believe Hitler's SS found a way through, which is why they sent a rather large fleet of submarines there. But there's no proof of this. The place is vast, with difficult to pass mountain ranges.

Blood Flag
Adolph Hitler used the Blood Flag, which was magic of a sort. The blood was from the dead people of the rebellion he took part in when he was trained by the Jesuits in the prison after said event.

Techniques used by magicians of old, it seems, are used today by the powerful. The art of creating changes in consciousness in accordance with will is practised today in every great city in the Western

World.

Have you ever seen the film *Dark City*, where, at night they get a group of people together, link minds and chant to change the reality of the situation we are in? When people wake the next morning, they know nothing about the altered situation.

Ritual magic was a practice for mid-Victorian materialists which was regarded as a sad relic of a past focused on absurd notions. It was doomed to be wiped away from history, however, it has survived and even thrived.

If you've ever wondered how we could have believed the narrative that we've been given to us, it's because the brainwashing was so powerful. Because of the mind programming blocks that are being battled with, people are getting angry. Naturally, they don't want their paradigm shifted.

It's impossible to know how many people are involved in ritualistic magic, but there does seem to be a lot of it about. You only have to look at the thriving businesses that supply their needs. In England, a large company catalogues a large selection of magical paraphernalia, such as candles and incense or anything that is needed for a ritual. While this satanic ritual magic is being used against us, we should not forget that nothing is cleverer than the human being. Humans have the ability to use techniques that will make all creation our own or do our bidding. But, do we learn this? If not, why not? Why has this kind of thing been kept from us? Are we all so crazy mad that we can't be trusted with it?

In my mind, it's not loads of people that use ritual magic, it's just a few. The governments of Russia, Americans, Britain and Europe, all know the Controllers are using it against us. We're going to have to get jiggy with this - I'm telling you. We need to get serious with whatever is happening about us, or we will be doomed as eff.

We need to understand what has been going on. This is a Big Time Spiritual Battle. It's a spiritual warfare that we are encountering on a daily basis. Ritual magic is being used to alter our consciousness. But, we need to know how is it done before we can do anything about it ourselves.

Essenes
This group of people are an ancient sect who originate from ancient Judea on the banks of the Dead Sea where the Dead Sea Scrolls were found. Parts of these scrolls have been deciphered and they tell of the secrets of ritual magic. They describe it as follows:

> *You envision reality using the pineal gland, as though the event, or day, has already happened. You go on from one event to the next, throughout the day, without any doubt.*

The Essenes knew this knowledge and practised it. The ancient civilisations knew this too.

5G - FASCES RESETS TO BEDLAM

I mention fasces in my last book because this bunch of rods with an axe put in it was basically electromagnetic weaponry. There are many allegories to this weapon, while the official narrative is that they are a bunch of sticks bound together, indicating unity. They are put on their monuments, on their pillars, and on their buildings of antiquity. The Masonic pillars are ribbed and they look exactly like fasces. It all seems to be related to the reset periods. As I mentioned in *The Holy Grail of the Flat Earth*, something is going on with the Eagle - with the wings open, which indicates a charge will be created.

> *They had this technology in the past, and they have it now, and it's being used against us.*

Have you got an understanding of this 5G technology? Most people in the 'Truther Community' will know what this is and what it means but, with the reverse engineering of antiquity, we have found that fasces, or microwave technologies, have been used all along to determine ages and resets - and to get rid of the people. It is a technology that basically prunes the population – commonly known as a depopulation agenda. Bill Gates even talked about depopulation (vaccines being one of his favoured options) in one of those TED Talks, so I'm not talking shit.

That's all well and good, Martin, but what can 5G technology do to us? What I've found is that it is a bunch of different frequencies – from mind control to heart failure. All sorts of things can be done with frequencies. My own city, Cardiff, has (unfortunately) been chosen for 5G as well as a few other cities like Gateshead and Newcastle.

Recently, a few giant cranes were set up in my local area, and they were putting what looked like giant speakers on the top of the highest housing block. This is so that they can directionalise frequencies into the local community.

What is this? What can it do to people? As far as I know, it can be broken down into a sound frequency.

Many people are aware of the 5G as a weapon and I don't like what I see when I search the internet because it sends you directly to a link that says it will kill you. This is suspect and I don't know what's going on there. Even when you see alternative views to the ones the media feeds you with, I urge you to be careful with the information you take in.

5G seems to be designed to use the spectrum in the existing frequency range, between 600Mhtz to 6Ghtz and also in millimetre wave bands (24-86Ghtz). Of course, the Health and Safety requirements have to be satisfied, and yes, I bet that evidence is safe and sound. But, some articles show how 5G can be used to 'weaponize a crowd'.

We're told that 4G networks use below 6Ghts and that 5G uses above this. There are reports that 5G uses shorter wavelengths, so the antennas can provide 'precise and directional' control.

The companies that are promoting this technology will make it very tempting for you to get very good quality Netflix and cinema-quality films. Peer pressure will also make you feel like shit because 'everybody else' will have it and you won't. Their own words state:

> *"5G network uses nearly the same frequency as weaponized crowd control systems" (RF Sae)*

If I was you, I would stay the eff away from this stuff.

The cellular and WiFi networks that we have today rely on microwaves which seems to be a type of electromagnetic radiation. It's a type of technology that is almost over as the 5G network uses sub-millimetre waves.

The 5G technology is used today by the US military, who, incidentally, commissioned a research report to find out why people ran away when the beam touched them. They found that if you're unlucky enough to be standing near it when it hits you, you feel like your body is on fire. The US Department of Defence said that the sensation goes away when the 'target' moves away. That's gently put and ok if you're not being targeted. It's like it causes a reflex action – so it hits your nervous system and apparently, the beam penetrates a 164th of an inch layer of the top of the skin which burns.

This is pretty sick shit and is the technology being put on all the tower blocks where people live. No worries.

In my previous book, you might recall what I said about some aspects of Technasmia, as in vibrational qualities coming from church windows, using the church organs. So, bear that in mind for a minute or two when you ask the question:

How many Hertz can kill you?

You only go as far as sound vibration, which can burst your eardrums. Have you ever felt that base punching you in the chest and your stomach? Even a high pitch makes it painful for your ears. If this was ten-fold, you'd be thrown to the ground and killed. It only needs 150 decibels to burst the eardrums, but the threshold of death is around 185 decibels. A jackhammer and a lawnmower are about 100 decibels, whereas a chainsaw is about 120 decibels.

People can normally detect decibels around the 20 to 20,000Hrtz range. Over or under, these decibels can hurt human ears even if we can't hear them. Infrasound can also kill you, with lethal doses in the 7Hrtz range.

There also seems to be a link between these sound frequencies and 5G technologies and, strangely, mental illness. But before I go into that, I'd like to bring to reveal to you what has happened to musical harmonies over the years.

Renaissance of Resonance
Jim Doney, MandalaTrece, wrote about *The Pythagorean*

Harp, or Kanon. He called it the *Renaissance of Resonance*. The idea was that ancient frequencies were in the region of 4-3-2 and there have been a lot of discoveries about ancient sound patterns that may, in the future, replace the 12-note structure used in today's musical harmonies.

So far, for the past 200 years, we have been using the chromatic scale. Before this (we're probably talking about thousands of years), the scale was referred to as the Pythagorean Harp, which was used in secret and sacred music. They probably had to use it secretly in early Christian times as they were getting a lot of shit. They apparently learned these harmonies through the tunnels of Solomon's Temple, which was passed down from the Pythagoreans to the Essenes.

The Essenes are supposed to be the strange sect that lived just by the Dead Sea, where the scrolls of the same name were found. During those days, a lot of persecutions were going on, particularly in relation to the music. So, as with most things of any value, people had to keep them a secret. Apparently, Plato discovered some of this history, unfortunately, it got confused amongst the theoretical teachings of the time.

The Essenes and the Pythagoreans in Italy influenced early Christians by passing on Pythagorean Rainbow Modes as they were used in sacred music in early Rome. Sadly, in the tenth century, Pope Gregory forced the new style of music upon the people, which is why the original way of depicting music went underground.

The type of musical scale that was used was the perfect spiral of Pythagorean Rainbow Mode. They used the number 5 as well as 3 as a source harmonic. When you look at creation itself, this isn't done in a linear fashion, the Triad is simply 1, 2 and 3. Because Pope Gregory of the Vatican knew this, the sacred Pythagorean harmonics were almost lost at some point. Pope Gregory broke the solemn Trinity codes held within the harmonies of music. It is this act that takes away the natural harmonics of sound in current music. The type of music that we have now cannot provoke ascension or promote healing or, interestingly, DNA re-activation. Is this why all the music we hear today is so bad? When sound is bad, we feel bad.

This is what MandalaTrece says the frequencies can do.

- 147Hrts – foundation frequency
- 285Hrts – quantum cognition
- 396Hrtz – removes fear and guilt
- 417Hrts – breaks crystallised motion patterns, erases karma and undoes incorrect situations
- 528Hrts – love frequency, DNA integration and repair, divine miracles
- 638Hrts – whole-brain interconnectedness, heals relationships
- 741Hrts – intuitive states and non-linear knowing, awakens intuition

- 852Hrts – pure, unconditional love and returns to the spiritual order
- 963Hrts – Angelic communication

Of course, anyone who knows me knows of my interest in the sonic sounds within the pyramids. In my videos on *The Greatest Secret Never Told*, I mentioned that the King's Chamber is probably a resonance chamber for reverse electrolysis. You'll find all the ancient temples across the world are aligned to this frequency, as well as to 111Hrts.

This is all very intriguing, and you have to ask why Pope Gregory stopped it. What was his reason for doing so? Was it to doom humanity to the dust again? To trap us into another prison? What's the reason for this? Why would anyone want to take away anybody's ability to connect with the Divine or even to heal themselves?

Mental Illness Linked to Technology?
I discussed mental illness in Chapter 2, but it seems to have taken hold of humans over and over again. Lately, I've noticed how everyone seems to be acting very strange - where I live in Cardiff, people have been kicking off big time and everyone seems to be shouting and screaming. But this is not new in history, nothing ever is. It has happened so many times in our past that I'm thinking that there's something bigger going on and that it might be linked to the technology used.

There's a link to a book in the Flat Earth Think Tank, *Illustrations of Atmospheric Origin of Epidemic Disorders of Health and its Relation to Pre-despondent Constitutional Causes.* It's an old text from the late 1800s early 1900s and it gives details about the mass animal extinctions and insanity caused by something in the atmosphere. Here's an excerpt from the book (1910):

> *Plants appeared to be affected by particles in the atmosphere which do not constitute a degree of temperature or pressure. In the Summer of 1810 [coming up to the events in New Madrid] all the plane trees distinguished with rough bark became diseased to the neighbourhood of London, and for miles around, very few of which in comparison with the whole number decayed, recovered so far as to throw forth buds the coming spring: while the [...] pine trees [...] remained healthy.*

So, basically, there was an unusual state of atmospheric anomalies just before the Comet turned up in 1811. There appeared to be mass die-offs of the trees. Around this time, mental illness started to kick in, and people began to wander around and get very confused.

Atmospheric disorders, pestilence caused by an electrical phenomenon that affected vegetables, trees, animals, and people. It shows that we had some incredible high EM at that stage because of some sort of reset. There were periods of irritability and headaches every month. The chemical coding tells us that who holds the EM charge is in control.

It says that contagious diseases are influenced by atmospheric causes - something in the air was killing people on mass. There is a list of diseases from atmospheric disturbances in 1817 and 1819. This is crazy stuff.

I believe there is a link between 5G technology, harmonics and mental illness.

Imagine if there was a reset in the early 1800s, where millions of people have gone, disappeared, died, after which the 'powers that be' delivered a new crowd (the orphan trains etc. take a look at the chapter on *How Old is Photography?*) to populate the cities. It seems that whatever happens, there is always mud and there is always a massive amount of mentally ill people. When you look into the oldest mental institution in existence, which is apparently 'Bedlam' in South London, you can see that it's a massive mud flood building that could house over 600 mentally ill patients.

Now, I know this is a bit of an anomaly again, and I'm not sure what you'll make of it, but around the 1800s, there were many 'lunatic asylums, for older people, for women and for children. There seems to be a lot of big buildings that are filled with people who had gone mad. Why?

It seems that there was no shortage of the feeble-minded in the Victorian era. In the Flat Earth Think

Tank, you'll find some photographs of people inside the Workhouses in Wales. The age of the photographs that I see would depict them as 'reset children'. During that hundred-year period, which sent people nuts, something happened.

If you look at insanity in the Victorian era, you will find many asylums were tourist attractions. The posh people of London would visit these people - not to care for them as charitable volunteers as we do nowadays - but those poor people were sources of entertainment. Think of *The Elephant Man* and you'll know what I'm talking about. But they did much, much worse than that to these poor souls.

What exactly happened to all these people?
It seems like a repeating episode.

There's a lot of this mental illness about at the moment - and it seems to be increasing. Is it socially engineered into our minds? Or, are these people sane when they get there then turn insane when they spend some time there? Think of the lobotomies that were done on people – right up to the 1960s? Crazy cruelty from scientists who thought they were better than anybody else! Who knows? The photographs don't lie and they show that this type of thing was on an epidemic scale.

In the case of psychiatric hospitals, the oldest one in use was the Bedlam Hospital, previously known as Bethlem. It was being used for treatment for the insane for about 600 years. However, Bedlam was not always a mental institution. I don't think the Victorian prisons were either as they look like they were used for something else. It was called Bethlehem hospital, at one stage and it evolved to Bedlam. Weird that. It's located in South London.

From i330, they were routinely referred to as a hospital. But hospitals used to be called lodgings for travellers, similar to a hostel. In depictions of these buildings from the i600s, they all seem to be surrounded by and covered in mud.

The Bethlehem hospital is a massive Phoenician-themed, flood-looking, Tartarian-type building, a hospital for travellers. Just like all the mental institutions all over the world.

The images that show what it was like
inside show a picture of dismay,
despondency, depression and deprivation –
certainly not places of healing.

As I said earlier, they used to charge tourists to enter, view these mentally ill people behind bars and taunt them. Lots of horror films were made about this place and others. Occupational therapy? That's a laugh.

DAMAGING OUR ESSENCE
I believe all the additives put in our food and water and the damage that drink and drugs and chem-trails do are all about altering our pineal glands and our DNA.

The pineal gland is our third eye which absorbs light through the skull. The ancient's realised that the pineal gland was to do with our power. Changing our DNA can be done in a man-made way where bits can be switched on and off so that, later in your life, you end up with some dis-ease so Big Pharma can be kept going by selling their drugs.

It's the same with the booze (alcohol) and the fags (cigarettes) and burgers (addictive food). You've been encouraged to eat all this rubbish that has no nutrients, is designed to make you bloat, have a heart attack or die in agony with cancer. Well, big business is basically saying:

> *"It's win, win! We've sold them shit for the last 60 or so years and now they're ill we can cash in again!"*

We, as human beings, are worse than guinea pigs. The latest covid-19 vaccine has proved this to be true. None of these vaccines has even been tested on animals. It's not that I want that, but, this time, people are the guinea pigs and this 'cure all' has been rushed out in record time – with no come-back on the companies who produce them.

Think about that for a minute. If I bought a pack of sausages and they made me sick, I'd be able to take them back to the store and even sue them for damages. But a vaccine that is supposedly altering our DNA and hasn't even been tested is protected by governments all over the world. Why?

We not only have these to face, but there's geoengineering and harmonics, 5G cell towers, HAARP and the esoteric, hermetic and black magic arts – and all this can be used against humanity.

Certain days, like the equinoxes, days on their witches calendars, are used for signs and a series of Sabbath-type 'dos' are conducted where vibrational techniques are used from another realm, realms that are not too good for humanity.

The problem is that the whole plane is Satanic by nature even, unfortunately, the religions some of us follow. If we let the world go on as it is, and we let these Satanic evil minds do as they want, eventually, our children and our grandchildren will have to kneel at the feet of Satan.

Is that what you want? What is it that you want?

According to the marketing and media companies, we want spindly, spangly happy things that shine, and we want it now! None of these is any good for us.

The same people who created the schooling system brought in the heliocentric model. When you look at NASA, the agency who brought it in, they follow orders. They're not going to worry because they're getting paid lots of money, and those people live great lives because of that money.

What about the mark of the Beast? Do you think we've already got it? Yes, the Bar Code is already coded with the numbers 666. Go ahead, take a look for yourself. Not all, but the majority of them have three 6s located somewhere on the bar codes on products. The people who deal in this kind of thing have no morals. I even saw on the BBC News that there's a plan to teach American children how to deal with transsexual or gay parents.

Some people call me homophobic - I'm not. I'm all for LIVE AND LET LIVE for everyone who doesn't harm anyone else. I know lots of people attracted to the same sex, but everyone needs to realise their Creator. People need to realise the deep implications on their Soul for the actions taken – whatever that may be. Our bodies are temples and eternity is not far away from us. God watches all and doesn't miss a trick.

There is interference from the heavenly realm, but they don't like to do that too much. They certainly wouldn't alter your DNA or damage your pineal gland. However, they will interfere to save your life. Like when I nearly walked to my death once, a voice came out of the ether to save me. It came from nowhere because my life was meant to be kept for something more important.

I don't buy the DNA thing because I saw Brian Cox doing an experiment with a rat in a glass and some orange juice, and then you'll be shown a hundred million videos of DNA that's coded. They say that it might give credence to the Creator.

I don't think that a lot of this happened the way they say it did. I think it's all Jesuit driven. I think DNA is bullshit, look up Francis Crick and read about him and his work. To my mind, there were a load of Freemasons who got paid a shedload of money to break this apparent genome code down over a decade, and the moment they finished, they unveiled a big monument to their achievements. There's a big skyscraper in London called *The Francis Crick Centre*. Whoopie do! That sort of thing makes me ask questions. To me, DNA is as reliable as NASA is, the thing is, we're not able to test it for ourselves either.

If you have doubts and think this is all bullshit, it isn't.

Have we been used as guinea pigs and tampered with, to keep us down? Have we been tested on like rats in a cage to keep us dumb, to keep us from knowing who and what we truly are? I believe that whatever has happened, our DNA has been effed with. It has been edited and bits of it have been switched off.

The scientists and biologists have said we have all this 'junk' DNA hanging around, but that's just the bits that have been switched off. Ten per cent of brain activity is what we have, with 90% of it lying dormant. Well, if nothing else, that's a bit of a waste of a brain, isn't it?

Have you seen the film *They Live?* When the main actor gets the glasses (spectacles) and he can see everything as it truly is, he sees the word, OBEY, everywhere.

MARTIN LIEDTKE

The Controllers want us to Obey, but remember we have been given free will by our Creator.

Do you remember when television broadcasters played the National Anthem at the end of the night? I do. It was back in the 1970s. The tradition in our house was to run to the telly and switch it off before the National Anthem began. If we didn't manage it in time, we said it was bad luck. This is free will in action.

The American's had this National Anthem bullshit at the end of their night's *programming* too, the words at the bottom of the screen read:

"Your country is God. You must obey."

As I mentioned previously, all this national anthem and flag-waving is all bullshit based on Nationalism, which is ultimately meant to make us hate each other, fight each other and divide us.

It is deep, high-level brainwashing. And the brainwashing that's going on now is done by Psychological Behaviourists that use NLP (Neuro-Linguistic Programming). It is used to indoctrinate people into thinking certain ways, and they put it to good use in programmes on the television, in films, and in the news bulletins, even on the radio. It's everywhere.

These evil minds do it constantly with everything and

they have no morals. They don't care about what age you are, either. Children are growing up into their teens and their minds are mentally scrambled. They don't know what's going on - we have to protect them and act as guardians to wake them up. This book is one of my efforts to do that.

At times, I can't believe everybody is missing this. This isn't even a conspiracy. This is a reality. All of it is. The Flat Earth is the biggest reality ever, yet, most people have a problem with it. Those who don't want to let go of their materialism don't want to let go of their burger. They don't want to let go of their wages, their homes, the things they've got around them.

They don't want to let go because they're frightened.

They're scared that if they change over, or if they become Flat Earthers, they're going to have to change their life. Well, they'll have to give up their life, but not their lifestyles. We can work a way out of all the bullshit.

I recommend that you don't play into them. You don't want to be licking Satan's feet forever, do you? This eternal battle of good and evil goes on constantly in the background but it's coming to a head now and it's spilling over into this Realm.

All of this is interlaced with Free Masonry, the Jesuits, and everything else. Even the M of MacDonald's and other icons, logos and signs are in your face as symbols. They are there to suppress your psyche by giving subliminal messages that you don't notice unless you are told about them.

This is consumerism at its height and it's a consumer society. All people think about is 'what's in it for me?' Well, what's in for them? A better life. A better version of reality. A more accurate vision. It's not based on Satanic bullshit made up by Freemasons or Jesuits. What's in it for people is a society that's not based on fear and pain.

This shit that's been going on all over the world, of terrorism, suicide bombs, school shootings - I've basically been going around spreading as much love as I can. I don't expect everyone to change overnight as I get it that the mentality will linger on, it will stick there, even though a few of us have been awake for quite some time, it still lingers there, it can't really help it. You know why? I'm a big believer in the memory of water.

Memory in Water
There is a lot of experimental data to prove that water has a memory. Do this simple experiment:

Get two bottles.

Bottle 1: write on the label, "you are peace/love/gratitude"

Bottle 2: write on the label: "you are disgusting/you make me feel sick"

When you look at the water the day after, you get two very different outcomes. Bottle 1, that has words of gratitude, it will look good, it will taste good and will be beautiful. But, Bottle 2, the one with the words of hate, it will look and taste like shit.

So, what caused that effect? The words.

The words don't actually have to be spoken words; they can be written. We write words in chat, don't we? We write words on people's comments. So, when you are writing stuff similar to what I get on my comment feed on my YouTube channel, extreme personal shit, it has a real fundamental effect on the person. Why? Because water holds a memory.

Water holds a memory to the extent that you could have a bucket of the stuff, drop a rose petal in it, then put every drop of water under the electron microscope. You will see a perfect photographic copy of that petal in every single drop of water. It's replicated using the Fibonacci sequence. Repeated over and over again, a million times or more. Every single drop will be encoded with that memory.

Now, that's mostly water, the rest is carbon. Carbon is crystalline by structure. There's this crystalline structure to us anyway, it's in the stones, the trees, in all matter and we have a connection to it all - more than we are aware of.

The nasty things that people say to one another are real.

Never mind the psychological intent, coupled with the words. If people say it verbally, it will be worse again.

If people understood the memory in water and who we truly are, they would not treat one another the way they do. If this Flat Earth community was filled with such bad people, how is it we can always be civil and loving towards everyone and everyone always comes in as vicious animals? How is that? Of course, people are entitled to their opinions.

YOUR CHILDREN'S FUTURE
They're really pushing the flu vaccine narrative now and all schools in the UK are planned to have mandatory vaccinations. What I suggest is that you keep your kids home from school the week they're injecting them, say they've got the flu.

In my country, Wales, they once reported in the news that there was an epidemic of measles. Apparently, many parents didn't give their kids the MMR vaccination (Measles, Mumps and Rubella). So, they were calling all the children in to be vaccinated. Now, is that good?

Of course, you want to save your kids, don't you? But, have you got the equipment at home so you can actually analyse whatever it is that's being put into your child? Do you know how safe it is? If you haven't realised yet, what we're being encouraged to do is trust a perfect stranger to stick you with an experimental prick. I don't trust them. I think we are being poisoned through:

- geo-engineering - the weather gets you down, so it lowers your body vibration
- scaremongering tactics through nuclear wars and germs, we're going to be killed any moment from a terrorist attack, a meteor hit, gamma rays, plague, alien invasion – take your pick

We're all conditioned to be constantly worried. At the back of our psyche, we get ill, lower our vibrational existence, and then die. You have got to realise what is being done to you.

It's a war on your senses.

A bombardment on your emotions. They use all types of chemicals to get this done as well. We've only just realised that fluoride calcifies the pineal gland, but it has been used for hundreds of years. It used to be put in the water in concentration camps to dumb down the people in there, so they were less sexually active. The same technology that was used in those concentration camps is being used on us today.

10. THE GREAT RESETS

The key to the Great Resets of this earth is to be vigilant for the truth. You need to be brave enough to persist with your questions and be strong in your sense of duty to help humanity escape what is, basically, hell on earth.

However much people try to make you out to be stupid when you ask questions, let me tell you one thing - you are not. Asking questions gets to the answers. If you just accept what you are told by people, they could pull the wool over your eyes and tell you lies.

To find out the truth, you might want to take a leaf out of the Essene tribe's book. You may have heard about the *Dead Sea Scrolls*, the ancient books written by a secret sect that lived near the Dead Sea. But did you know what was deciphered from those scrolls? What if we took a page out of those books? What if we paid attention to and put into practice what they did?

Usually, when we want something good to happen in our lives, we basically beg for it. We have been taught to say prayers that plead. We end up saying night after night, "Please God, gimme, gimme, gimme!" Then, we are told to wait and when it doesn't arrive, we yearn for it throughout all of our shit days.

The Essenes didn't beg. They didn't ask either.

What the Essene tribe did was to imagine whatever they wanted, as *already there*.

The Essenes got outside of their heads and inside their own minds. They planned the day out ahead of themselves by visualising whatever they wanted as already in their life. It's a bit like the power of attraction, except they used it in a different way. They used a process of thinking and feeling whatever they wanted was already in their lives. They didn't yearn for things. They didn't cry for the shit life they were living. They didn't fear the future.

The bad thing about all of this is that the powers that 'should not be' have been using these same insights against us. By hiding the information, humanity could have benefited with the Controllers. Instead, they have held all the keys and have kept the knowledge for themselves. For instance, they own and run the education systems which programme our kids' minds from a young age – in fact, the earlier the better. This education system has been structured only to indoctrinate humanity to think in a certain way.

When our children leave school, they have to deal with all the other systems that we think are normal for our daily business. Things like working, eating, entertaining, sleeping, and dealing with systems like the media and marketing. They have to deal with those who control their thoughts, guide their intentions and encourage their actions. This is done on a worldwide scale. Why?

Media entertainment companies exist only to distract us from what is really going on. The food that the massive conglomerates sell to us has no nutritional value in it at all. So our bodies become ill then, because of this, we visit the doctors who ply us with pills the pharmaceutical companies sell to them so they can subdue us. Ultimately, the whole system makes our bodies go out of balance.

We are indoctrinated with the news programmes. We are hypnotised into ignorance and submission. But this can only be done while we are asleep. It's up to those who are awake and not glued to the TV or newspaper to wake everybody else up. Remember this as we take a stroll through the collection of thoughts in this chapter.

HISTORY, BUT NOT AS WE KNOW IT
Think of this, in sixty years, our inventions have gone from the flimsy Kittyhawk aeroplane to the ultra-supersonic rocket. And it's a rocket that's supposed to go to the moon and back. Are we all that naive to think that we got that clever that quick? After thousands of years of living off the land in farming societies, how did we suddenly have the ability to reach for the moon?

THE HOLY GRAIL OF THE GREAT RESET

What makes me ask many questions about how humanity is incited to fight each other in wars comes from a book called *The Great War*. This book shows how the First World War was heavily edited and demonstrates first-hand how our history is changed and keeps changing, right before our eyes.

The Great War book I have was released the same year as the First World War ended. Because of this, it seems to have escaped censorship and there are a lot of depictions and tantalising pieces of evidence in it.

I began to look deeper into the Battle of Jutland sea chart that is presented there. When you begin to do this for yourself, you'll understand how problems show themselves. For instance, when you follow the coordinates of each of the ships, which ship sighted which, you're given the nautical mile distances they were from each other when they sighted each other. The book makes statements like "sighted the Von Bismarck at 48 nautical miles south/south-west", and there's a chart giving the actual distances that they visually spotted these ships at.

When you connect this kind of thing to the globe lie, these statements are all very telling. It's things like this that should make you start questioning. Incidentally, whenever I consider the globe model, I always ask where the seas and the waters came from. Did meteors deliver it? If so, why did the meteors stop coming? Oh, was it because it was in that narrow period where the meteors came down and bombarded the plane? The globe model has inconvenient issues and the excuses are getting a bit old.

There are plenty of ships in *The Great War* book that reveal the lies we are told today. One of them is reportedly from the time of Alexander the Great. In that era, ships had fantastic weapons and technology. There's a well-known 'clock-like device that was found on a 4,000-year-old Galley ship and brought up from the ocean. The odd thing about this device is that it is better than any Swiss watch available today. What I find fascinating is that the device showed the planetary bodies going around on a geocentric rather than a heliocentric model.

UNESCO

This is the organisation that owns everything in the world. That means all the natural parks, heritage sites, and places of historical interest all over the world. UNESCO has set up meetings and groups like the Committee for International Cooperation so that we have to follow their rules and basically do what we're told. They have their tentacles everywhere and it all just turns to shit.

UNESCO own anywhere of any importance. They run the educational systems, film and production companies, museums of history and science, media news, newspapers and magazines. Oh, but it's all 'for your own good'. CarlaRedPill on YouTube shows how this organisation runs everything you see on this earth, go check out that channel's videos on the movements of the planets and be amazed.

One of the benefits of owning everything in the world means you get to run the narrative that is given to everyone. Think about it. Say you owned something and didn't want someone to know something particular about it, would you omit those details? Would you be tempted to tell a white lie or make up a half-truth about it, so the truth wouldn't be known? It would be so easy for you to make up a story about it that people would believe it.

Stories of gentle giants?
There's a crazy, crazy narrative from a book that is basically taken out of the Christian Bible and it's called *The King of Og*. Now, if you watch my videos, you'll notice I say "Oggy Oggy Oggy" and "Og!" quite a bit. That's because Og is a Taffy, a Welshman. I learned about this in school, not that I went much. The narrative about this is really weird and creepy.

One Love in Ireland sent me the following from *The Lost Book of Kit*. The first part of it deals with the Roman Catholics who erased this section. It's a God-off between a Giant and Moses. The poem *'Fe Fi Fo Fum, I smell the blood of an Englishman'* came out of this book. This is the narrative and how it starts:

> *How will I, Og, murder corrupt one? I murder you, as Dog, torn by the bull at the slaughter. Should I lift an entire mountain of earth over my head? Is not Ba'al the God? Is this fertile earth that is Og, living? The Kingdom, supreme*

MARTIN LIEDTKE

Ba'al of a thousand answers to the pathetic excreta smeared insect-sized God?

So, a shit-covered, insect-sized God? But he's a giant. And everyone is puny human to him. Weird.

Israel, come here, that I Og, might bind you with bracelets and chords empowered by Ba'al of earth outside our Temple in high places. How many castaways have you killed since your insect-sized God told you not to kill? You were condemned, you faecal minded hypocrite. The spirits of the slain complain about and cry out, Moses, you drunk blood fester. Like a cowardly virgin with gift toys, you run before your mother. That we may do battle, I Og, will grind your bones to make dung.

He goes on with the vile threats that show him to have a real attitude, but the point here is that Og, though he's depicted as the bad guy, eating humans and so forth, he seems like the good guy. The reason why is that in the poem, he's accusing the puny humans of being the most murderous of all, even though they follow an 'insect-sized God that tells them not to kill. See what I mean? Weird.

The poem talks of 'men of old ruling with one mind and one heart' and talks about strange weapons being used when Moses was around. The giant threatens to tear Moses apart because of the people's murderous ways. It sounds like he's a bit of a peaceful dude who doesn't like the killing. This book was buried by the Catholic church, along with a lot of other insightful books. Not surprisingly, it's in the Vatican archives now.

Giants seem to be against murder, corruption and puny Gods, and the land of Syria seems to be the focus. What do you think it's all about? I'm guessing it's like a Phoenician death cult, but I'm open to ideas.

Why destroy history?
When you look at what are supposed to be Roman buildings and aqueducts (mentioned in my previous book), you see how massive and beautiful they are. Yet, there are a couple of puzzling things about them. One is that they can't seem to use the water for energy. The other is the size of them.

I always ask why did the people, 2,000 years ago, build these massive double-story aqueducts and never use them as energy devices? What are we not supposed to know about these buildings? What is their true history? Why have buildings that have supposedly stood for thousands of years been destroyed?

The Lion Gate, which is the main entrance of the Bronze Age citadel of Mycenae, seems to have something wrong with it. It seems as though it doesn't belong in the place where the images say it should be placed. As with what goes on with ISIS in this day and age, all the old buildings are destroyed. Ancient antiquity always appears to be rubbed out with the excuse of war, and it's either deliberately destroyed in plain view of everyone with eyes to see, or it's moved to another place. Do you think that's what happened to this gate?

The other thing I'm puzzled by is the size of these buildings. The Greeks and the Romans seem to have used advanced technology. Think of the equipment and the machinery we have today and what we can move with it. In an earlier chapter about the buildings in Cardiff, I mentioned those two massive cranes that came in to build the dome. As big as they were, those cranes would not be able to move some of the stone blocks that the ancients were supposed to have built with.

The buildings we are told come from ancient Greece and Rome, but they don't appear to come from the era at all. One thing I keep asking is, where are the depictions of the buildings being constructed? If you know or have some, please send them to me, I'd be very interested in adding them to the Flat Earth British Think Tank library.

The Phoenician Death Cult
When I came across the book *The Cult of Priapus – His relationships with the Mystic Theology of the Ancients,* I thought it was a weird book. The first of its images show male sexual organs in wax presented in, of all places, a church. They also show instruments of torture and weird ornaments relating to sexual organs

and bestiality (men having sex with rams).

There are lots of depictions of serpents on coils and resonance devices. In amongst them are images of the Statue of Liberty. Some of the images relate to the Hindu religion and show many-headed Gods with serpents.

The Cult of Priapus is ancient and yet it seems like they hadn't learned anything. In the book, they depict adults sacrificing children like they're still doing today. There are a lot of witches with frogs in the cauldrons. One of the pictures was *The Witches' Sabbath of 1630*.

These were the same people who were ruling the world in a past reset. The Egyptians are depicted too. They appear to be anti-Creator and seem to spit in His face with their weird behaviour and depictions of male sexual organs in their artwork and statues. It seems to have endless penis deities. You are welcome to view them in my videos or on the Flat Earth Think Tank.

Other evidence of a Great Reset
Radio-halos in tree trunks prove the earth cannot be as old as we are led to believe. There are also buildings being unearthed underground, buildings that are half-buried in the mud. It looks like there is so much evidence for a mud flood that covered whole towns and civilisations.

Photographs from the i800s show empty streets and it seems to me as though people are only just being introduced to the 'system' again. There were hundreds of magnificent old buildings that were demolished. There is also evidence of a comet destruction all over the earth.

HISTORY REPEATING ITSELF

History is what we are into on the Flat Earth British Think Tank. We attempt to expose the bullshit narrative that we're fed so that people can be empowered to take back their sovereignty as human beings in this God-forsaken realm, which is basically not a very good place to be.

Today, people are suffering from massive Stockholm Syndrome and playing right into the Controllers' hands. I've discussed this kind of thing with a relative of mine who is very much 'in' the Matrix. They know the situation, but they cannot unplug themselves from it, unfortunately. Many can't. But, I'm a great believer in things being able to change.

History repeats itself, but to what level? It's been obvious in the last fifty or so years how fashion and clothing styles have repeated themselves. If you haven't seen that, then you really are snoring happily away in sleepyby-land.

The whole thing is about technology being repeated over and over again. As the old saying goes, 'There's nothing new under the sun', but to what extent? Are we just seeing replicated styles from further back and they're just resetting every 200 years or so, playing us over and over again? How would we know? What is the meaning of having to reset the population of humanity? To what end? I'd like to know what the purpose is to of all this.

We can say that all of the buildings we see around us are attributed to the Victorian era of the 1800s. We're told that they arrived during that period yet, we have no evidence whatsoever this was so. In my mind, they're earlier and they are Tartarian with Phoenician alterations.

Technology from another era?
Another clue to technology being brought in from another era is an instrument that arrived in the 1800s, which recorded voices. *The Phonoscope,* published in 1897, has information in it that you wouldn't expect to see in the late Victorian era. I hold my hands up to the fact that I can't understand some of it, but it's there for you on the Flat Earth Think Tank if you want to take a look for yourself and do your own research.

The catalogue that I got hold of said that the phonoscope was to record not voices but human emotions and memories. This is massively mind-blowing. The Phonoscope was billed as a 'thoughts machine which recorded mental emotion'. A thought machine that records mental emotion? I can't really get my head around that. How can you record a mental emotion?

Apparently, it was a bio-scope created by Lumiere and was really expensive - $150,000 to be exact. In the late Victorian era, only the Elite would be able to buy that kind of thing and do anything with it.

What I can't understand is the photographs produced during that period were perfect. They had moving images and the first sci-fi film in history, clear colour HD moving images in the late Victorian era. So, if they have them that good then, my question is, how far back does that technology go? To get the answer to that, look up the Camera Obscura.

In the book, they're saying that in 1898, there were many films, or movies, being produced. I don't understand this. Why? Because, according to the official narrative, the 'talkie' films came out a lot later.

You may be wondering why I want to look at this subject. Because when you dig a little deeper than the bullshit narrative we're fed, you begin to understand how the Phoenicians (who created the phono-scope) were speaking in phonetics. We've worked out that 'spells' mean something too. Amplifying spells in the late 1800s.

There have been dictatorships in the past, in Cambodia, for example, that had the entire country rigged up with speakers. They would play party music to keep the population working with brainwashing narratives. Communist regimes have used this technology as well - music and words through loudspeakers.

The phonoscope instrument was called a 'talking machines' – were they Dictaphones? They had graphic phones and scopes back then and, according to the adverts of the day, the gramophone cost around $100. The first discs were made of a heavy ceramic material, not vinyl and it was considered the ghetto blaster of the day.

Did you know that electric lamps were being used in i899? I thought everything was gas-powered during that era, but if there were things like phonoscope instruments around, I guess they had to be run on electricity rather than gas. There was even a library of voices – so did they have audiobooks during that time?

Clues to our past in films?
The Lumiere Brothers made films in the early i900s in France. The one I saw was made in i903 and it was a sci-fi. The first thing that becomes apparent is that they are in a church and there are two pillars - one either side. The pillars look like they are bundled pipes bound together with copper. Does that ring a bell for you? Remember the fasces mentioned in my previous book?

This film was produced a mere four years after the patent of the shit hot camera that they had. In the film, the scientists had happy hats on and they looked like witches. What I find unusual for the age is that the women are dressed in gowns that seem to come from the i960s.

Wizardry is evident in the film. The story is that they basically plan to go to the moon. If you're wondering where NASA got its ideas from for orbiting around the moon, or sling-shotting it back to earth, they probably got it from this film.

All the evil magicians get a bit excited in that film. The rocket made an appearance, they got together as a group, and they organised a trip to the moon. Then in came the moon-craft which, looked more solid than the 1960s version they say they went to the moon. That 'modern' one looked like you could poke a hole in the bacofoil walls with your finger. The film goes on to show you how, after they smelted the metal for making the rocket, they got to the moon. It shows the stars and the planets, but the most important thing to note is that the quality of the film is epic.

Many films have colour in them and one of them is of the Eifel Tower. You can see the aerials that were up there, but they have been removed today. What is odd is that there are films of Paris from the early 1900s, in full colour.

If you look at photographs and films of soldiers during the First World War, you might see how brilliantly they are presented. There are some photographs in existence of the Great Expositions of the day as well and there are some available depicting Egypt. I think the photographs taken in Egypt look as though they're setting up the scenes to sell tourists goodies and boast that they built those things.

The odd thing about all these photographs and films is that they knew just what to depict. People travelled the world and showed images that would become popular during the next century.

I think wars are created to get rid of the age before, to hide the antiquitech and architecture under the rubble.

A common theme in these photographs is that there are so few people in them, the buildings stand in mud streets and the skies are blanked out.

Reverse-engineered technology?
Have you heard of EM Tech or plasma tech? The people who produce this type of stuff are not us. Their mentality is sceptic as it looks as though something went seriously wrong in the i800s.

Apparently, magnetism has beneficial effects on the human body and other organism. So, plants were electro stimulated for massive growth and there are some permeations that you've never even heard of before, which can all be linked to technasmia.

Technasmia is the decoded, or reverse-engineered, technology of Kirshsta, a known Jesuit, and it was developed between the late i600s through to the i700s. In survivor times, this technasmia was used through church machines. Church machines, which use the harmonics coming from massive organs, have been proved beneficial for the organs in your body.

The church organs put out a vibrational sound through the window. The window was made of a specific lead crystal, so the vibrations from the church organs through them would create a somatic pattern. Crystal has the ability to vibrate or resonate out into the ether for the benefit of humanity, plants and animal life. Couple this with antiquitech and you get the idea that this place, this earth, was bloody special. So, where has all this technology gone now? Sadly, the technasmia has been dismantled and the evidence destroyed. However, humans are clever. It is here, people have decoded it and they have taken it apart so it can be understood. Have faith.

Many Tartarian-styled buildings have technasmia in or attached to them, like portholes in rooves. But the mechanisms were dismantled in the i900s. Personally, I think angels and demons are electrical forces. Electric is impossible to define, it's bright, white, hot, it can kill you and evidence that has come from research into thunderbolts show that they are 'aware', which could mean electricity is possibly conscious too. With technasmia, I think we're dealing with electrical forces.

On the cover of my first book, *The Holy Grail of the Flat Earth*, there's a dude who haunts me. I refer to him as the faceless knight. You might have seen it, as it's the emblem for Napoleon and it was also used by Mussolini. All these logos you see about you are metaphors used to refer to EM (electro-magnetic) tech. Basically, when all these tools, the fasces, the rods, the labrys and a drum are put together, they can cause devastation for humanity.

- Bow = one of the four horsemen of the apocalypse holds a bow
- Drum = banged with an oscillating sound so loud that it can cause earthquakes
- Fasces = electromagnetic plasma charge

Note that there's also a bow which is no accident.

The reason why I call it the 'faceless' knight is because I think he's basically been evaporated by some kind of electrical force of energy. These statues and images are everywhere, they are all over Phoenician art and architecture and there always seem to be demonic faces nearby too.

Now, EM technology was more powerful in the past. Either after the comet had passed through, or as it was passing through, a large charge was left in the air. As it passed through, the comet agitated the atmosphere and caused the volcanoes to erupt, started massive earthquakes and tsunamis and maybe even took out a third of humanity in a short period. I don't think it's an overnight process, but it is apocalyptic. Thunderbolts were frequently mentioned in the last century, but they're not so frequent now though.

Technasmia can be transported on a ship, on a barge, in a balloon, and it is used in churches. It all works on electromagnetic technology. The Phoenician ships are very ornate, they look as though they have technology that they're not supposed to have during the time frame of the 1800s. There are even drawings that show they used electricity to decorate their buildings.

The forts in the shape of Stars, Star Forts, seem to have been used for geoengineering and terraforming after the floods to get the grass back onto the earth. Have you noticed that the only place people seem to have been able to grow stuff was on the roof or in a type of hanging garden, like the gardens in Babylon?

Or, they are for acoustic sound, which is a technasmia sound that emanates out into the environment.

All those star forts were found in the i700s and were obviously not built then. The technology that was found inside has been reverse-engineered. After the mud floods, people moved in, dug it all up, found what they needed, put down plans and used them for defensive purposes. But that doesn't appear to have been the technology's original intent. The original intent was probably to defend against the EM attack. When you look at some old German wood-cuts of star forts, you can see that they have some sort of stack that could make a sound.

Many of the depictions in the books I look at (available on the Flat Earth Think Tank) show a ruined world. You don't build those beautiful buildings and then just leave them to rot in the mud and become ruins. There's a lot of detail available about EM tech and this sort of weaponry and the Germans invested a lot of money in it as they seemed to want to understand how the vibrations from church organs and bells were used to kill humanity. Much of this is explained in my first book *The Holy Grail of Our Flat Earth*. It's a real science using architectural quality based on an EM model.

Unfortunately, humanity is missing out on a science that has gone before us. The magnetism seems to work on a double torus of our flat plane. We have the North Pole, which is Mount Meru, and a South Pole, which is twelve kilometres below Mount Meru, where the inertia plane is.

Here, I'm referring to *Magnetism and its Effects on the Living System (1974)*, written by A. Davis and Walter C. Rawls. The beginning is my favourite, 'Understanding Magnetism, Legends and Recorded History' and, in it, they discuss the use of EM in the past. The magnetic computer, uses and applications, bio magnetics, earth's magnetic fields and the pole flips.

Experiments have been done on seeds and worms. They have used a process referred to as electrostimulation of plants or soil. They have used it to find out the nutrients needed to make tomatoes and melons grow very big. It affects animals, snakes and birds and there have been some experiments on mice and rats.

The authors of *Magnetism and its Effects on the Living System* are aware of the Torus model, they even show you a picture of it in the book. They depict humans as electromagnetic animals living in an electromagnetic environment. They even discuss the forces on man and the effects of the electromagnetic field on cancers and give evidence of the amazing benefits.

Gravity is electromagnetic acceleration. The human aura is visible on special photographs as an electromagnetic field. Personally, I see them intensely, they shine brightly at me and, soon, I want to look deeper into this to see how people can be healed with it. Anything to help. The authors say the following:

> *Biomagnetism is used to aid and treat human and animal life and is far older than ancient science and Chinese acupuncture.*

What they're saying is that electromagnetic therapy is older than Chinese acupuncture and that it was brought to the attention of the American public in 1973 - after economic and political relationships with China had been established. It's because of this that the effects of acupuncture are being investigated.

The book says that there are many secrets in this science and it is a shame that Big Pharma wants to keep with its drug-based model. Electromagnetic therapy doesn't make any money for big business corporations.

The parchments and research were destroyed to prevent them from falling into the wrong hands. I agree that this shouldn't happen, but it should be possible to hide some of this for ordinary people. Ancient Greeks, who were Phoenicians, knew about the use of magnetism. The legend goes that a shepherd, called Magnus, had a staff or rod, and it was pulled towards a rock which was eventually called the 'magnus stone'. Yeah, and they had chroniclers following them around.

What I find most interesting is the exposure of magnetism to seeds. Apparently, it increases the protein, sugars and oils in them, and it especially happens when they are exposed to South magnetic pole energies. There's a lot of linkage between the North and South polarities.

Polar Flipping
If you've watched *The Greatest Secret Never Told* on my Martin Liedtke YouTube channel (about 30+ thousand people watched the synopsis of it, so I guess the chances are that you, reading this book, have watched it too) or, if you've read my first book *The Holy Grail of the Flat Earth*, you'll know that the model for this place, the electromagnetic model, the double-torus model, has been encoded into all our realities. Once you know this, you don't have any more psyche arguments. You just know that this is the case. You can't miss it.

All of this reality is a torus field. From the atom, remember the Russian doll comparison (going into or out of each other, bigger and bigger or smaller and smaller), and us. Atoms, if they are real, are the only magnets with a north and south polarity. The torus fields all around us, we emanate ourselves out into this consciousness soup. Motion and love are big players as well.

The benefits for magnetism, the benefits for Technasmia, are benefits for humanity. Technasmia and antiquitech are real things, but they need expanding upon. All is electromagnetic and vibration and you can tap into it. It's been done by the Elite for, well, ever, and it's available for you. They know the score, they have the free energy yet, humanity, the great population of the world, knows nothing of this because these Elites are keeping it all for themselves. That is, until recently, when people got their heads together and started thinking about it all. Go to Flat Earth British Think Tank and you'll find out more about this kind of stuff.

Fashions and products we buy
As well as technologies that have been re-engineered and recycled over the years, the history of fashion appears to be no different. Have you ever wondered why the fashions keep repeating on a cycle? It seems people have run out of ideas as they keep bringing out clothes that were in style only a few decades earlier. They also do it to music and products too, with reboots and copies.

The repeat mode is done with everything use, although some are not so 'in your face'. For instance, a skateboard will be brought out as a product in the 1970s and they'll say something like, "This is a brand new concept – never been thought of before!" But when you look back, they had skateboards and what we call 'bogies' in Wales, but you probably call them go-karts, and they had them in the Victorian era in the 1800s.

They weren't new, they were just rolled out to the masses as new.

You might be surprised at what types of products were in people's homes a hundred years ago.

Think of the clothes we wear, the flairs and platforms of the 1970s, will they be back soon? Your kids will be wearing them believing they're something new. Give it another decade or so and 1940s fashion will be all the rage.

It's all socially engineered out of a handbook so, how long has it been going on? Thankfully, the game is up. We know what is happening. It is over. We know the lies and those lies are coming to the light. The power is with the people, always has been.

***

When you start decoding the sciences, you begin to see how they might have had all of this before the era that we live in today. Technology seems to be replicated through the resets and each reset seems to be achieved with water and/or plasma - not necessarily flood, fire, flood, fire. It's indiscriminate as they have probably got to keep people on their toes. It could be two floods and a fire. Or a fire with a flood.

Is it a God or a Controller that does all of this? Is it that this place is a Creation of the Controllers? The worst thing about being confused with all this, is that the more willingly we move away from the idea of a Creator, and who we really are, the more we are set in the Controllers path of destruction.

11. IS THERE AN ANSWER?

I hope, by now, you are beginning to realise I have an idea as to the reason for these 'Great Resets' and I believe I know why they want to hide the truth from us. The whole thing may be all sinister and filled with horrific crimes against humanity on an industrial scale but, trust me, I can put a positive spin on it.

If you knew there was a better way, would you follow it? Would you choose it? Would you be brave enough to make the changes needed for it?

OUR AWAKENING
Everyone needs to turn their back on the evil deeds that are going on. I know it's difficult. It's like I said at the beginning of this book when I quoted that Timothy Leary said, "Tune In and Drop Out!" There's danger in doing that. Once you drop out, you end up on the streets, probably at a prostitute's doorstep. It's not a good idea, nor was it ever good advice.

What I'm saying is that you must collect the knowledge. You must gather the wisdom to prepare yourself for what's to come. Think about it, if you had no water, you'd be dead in a week. You can go three days without food, but with the way we're all addicted to these additives, I think we'll all be going a bit looney before that happens. You need medicines too. Plus, you need to be able to sort out your body frequencies.

You need to tap into what makes you well and find out what is missing – and know how to get it.

The knowledge is there and it's all available in the Flat Earth community. The Truther community will tell you about everything and unlock your human potential. This community is filled with love and kindness. If that's the case, then what's bringing out this ugliness and hatred that we see in the world today?

Before I was a Flat Earther, I always said this awakening would make good people really good and bad people really bad. When you look about you today, does it feel a bit like that? Whenever I interact with these globe believers, they tend to get nasty, as though I'm shaking their paradigm or the whole thing they are living for. I don't get nasty about the flat plane because it's a reality.

We must spread more love and truth. There is plenty of it around. I don't like turbulent times. I would like everyone to be like brother and sister, we don't need to pick on each other. We're up against nothing less than the Beast, who is almost fully grown by now.

Brave Truthers
I think to myself, are there any good guys in the background? Any good British, American, Russian, French, Italian, German… you know, all the nations of the world, are there any good spirits that are keeping their eye on what the Controllers are playing at? Of course, there are.

There's a game that's being played out before our eyes. It's called 'flood the country full of foreigners, make them hate each other through brainwashing and false flag events', yet our esteemed leaders are bringing the fight to the country. What's that all about? Do they want to get rid of the Arian or Caucasian races? What do you think? Who would want to do that? Why?

I don't like what has happened throughout our known history. It's a history that has been created by the hands of these evil people and, what is coming next, I like even less. But, I'm not one of these fearmongering types, as I do see a happy ending. My only is hope is that I'm here to witness it. I think, somehow, we will be there to witness something in our lifetime. If not, I'm quite happy being an Indigo Child in the meantime. I'm a Vanguard, as many of us are.

If you are a Truther, you are a brave person and you are not alone. Being a Truther is like doing your time in the trenches of World War One. So, hats off to you if you are giving it a go. It is brave to use your own name in your social media channels when you stand for truth. You have to learn to stand strong, stand proud and stand true to your convictions. There are plenty of these people around and the movement is growing ever bigger - which is Effing Awesome!

Martin's Mindset
To answer many of the questions I have asked, this is what I think: You have to be aware of all that is going on around you.

You can have a moan and be miserable, after all that is what makes you a human. But, mostly, you have to get up and get out there and rattle a few cages. This is why I have worked hard at putting these books together - to reach a wider audience and for you to keep or to give to someone who you know needs a gentle wake-up call.

This work is for everyone to know and it's also to keep my thoughts alive, even after the internet dies. The word in a book can't be changed by the flick of a switch by someone else. They are in this form for you to hold and read, either on your digital or physical hand. If you have the digital version, make sure you have downloaded it onto your own device as we can't guarantee that Kindle or Apple iBook and the like, will never be turned off.

You must admit, these days are interesting times to be living in. Even with this virus thing that's going around, I'm loving what's happening. Why? Because this plandemic has one good thing going for it - it's waking everyone up – and really fast. The government and big business have actually done humanity a favour by rushing this through. It's been a lot quicker than if

I had gone out there and spouted off my machine-gun mouth about it all. My thinking is this:

> *You just got to live your life and do the best you can with what you have. Just get out into the big wide space you see about you and question everything. You'll soon see the house of cards falling down around the constructs they've put up around them.*

Spread the Healing
We must step back into our human roots, as in going out there and caring for our brothers and sisters and doing what you can to help. I've been doing a lot of healing during the creation of this book. Changing the environment around us has had a big effect. Years ago, people were like this generally, you may have heard of it - it's called just 'being nice'.

It's not anyone's fault that there are ignorant people around us. We've all been socially engineered, the mechanism is deep and we're all locked into it. I often wonder where or how we got to the state of being when you see a homeless person sitting desperately hungry on the street. At the same time, someone walks past them, eating MacDonald's burger, ignorant of the desperation of another human being's situation.

The bigger picture is that positive vibes and a positive mental attitude spreads like no one believes. If they knew how good it was, people would feel it and say,

"Give me some of that!"

If everywhere looked like shit when you woke up in the morning and you stepped outside your door and all you saw about you was nasty rubbish bins, you would come out with "Urgh, it looks like shit!" or "The weather's crap!" But, if it was all cleaned up, and beautiful trees and flowers were everywhere, there and there were no bins to be seen, when you woke up, you would say, "This is a joy!" and you would be happy with your day. If every street was like that – WOW!

But are the Controllers are not going to let us have that. This is just the state of the nations now.

It's up to us to change it.

We must work at getting back to Tartarian values when we never had that evil Phoenician language hanging around and hypnotising us. We might not even have had a language at all for all I know. We might have been communicating with one another through our minds.

The dumbing down of humanity is bad, we're probably minuscule versions of what we possibly once were. But, as always, we will rise from the ashes again.

RESET SCENARIOS
Two reset scenarios are:

- Water and

- Fire

Both of these are perfect cleansers for this place. But they do leave evidence after the resets. We are beginning to see that this has happened over and over again. I've Red Pilled many people over the past couple of years with my work. I Red Pill most human beings with all of this, though you've got to gauge the way people are thinking first. Once I know they have a bit of an open mind, I just go in deep, which is what I urge you to do. If you can't do it, then just hand them a copy of this book.

The truth seems to be suppressed these days, and we're being corralled into one thought or another. I'm not sure about this, because there's more than one way to get the truth out. We seek remedies for truthing.

STATION OF CREATION
Going off track for a moment, I don't watch many films as a rule, but I did watch the new film, *Alien – The Covenant*. In the first five minutes of the opening scene, there's a character called Bishop Android. There's a bit of preaching about reality, the station of creation, and consciousness. It is an incredible thing, and reality is actually blown apart.

I've said it many times before and I'll say it again; I believe we are a species in amnesia. I believe we keep our memories from lifetime to lifetime. Sadly, we must have been deeply shocked by what has gone before us and, as a result, we must have morphed it way back in our psyche. But, all of it is coming out now, and we need to learn how to protect ourselves from it. How do you protect yourself from it?

Intent. You intend what you want in your life. The Creator is here.

SO, WHAT'S THE TRUTH?

Witnesses have proven there are too many holes in the stories the media tell. You can see this by the narratives on the tel-lie-vision, they've shown before the actual events happen. People see it happening in one part of the world before it happens in another part of the world. Sometimes the media eff up the time difference, 9/11 was a case to remember.

Everything is there to show you if you have eyes to see and ears to hear. If you follow the codes, if you follow the patterns, you'll find there's always more to come. Before elections, before sports matches, before big televised events, you are being prepared to get ready for what's going to happen. It's like when they put armed police all over the place, this is to get you used to seeing them.

We've only ever had one terrorist attack in Wales, it was in 1991. The Welsh Nationalists, apparently, put a bomb in the City Temple. If you go there today, you'll see the cracks in the building. It's good that we don't really have that kind of trouble here. It's a nice place to live and I think it's because we tend not to do all the bad shit that is done in the rest of the world.

I do believe this Agenda 21 is a real thing - and everyone can see that it is moving very fast now. I believe that the weather modification, the geoengineering of the social paradigm, are definite players. I believe that the drought and fires in California are a deliberate attempt to clear the East Coast of America for the Controllers purposes. I believe they will want to keep us all in mega-cities – the West Coasts of countries will clear while the East Coasts will be the populated areas.

I also believe the Wall is not to keep Mexicans out but to keep Americans in. Why? Because, if civil war broke out, people would want to go North to Canada or South to Mexico. The plain and simple reason for my thinking this is that tunnels could easily be dug. The British government did with the Channel Tunnel. You can get a train that goes from central London all the way to Paris.

Because of the rate of acceleration with these events, I can only presume that another Great Reset is in the very near future. What their end game is, I'm not sure. Obviously, it's evil. Evil is about destroying things – us and our spirits. Bill Gates has openly said he wants a de-population going on. The Controllers have had humanity as slaves - from the moment we are born our birth certificates registers us on their 'Berthing' system. It's all based on commodities that are shipped via ports all over the world – it's called Maritime Law.

Do the Controllers feel they are casting pearls of wisdom before swine? That's up to them. We should know better. If you want to look at this whole scenario of resets and annihilation, population destruction then, a positive approach would be to read it like this:

> *The truth is, we are living on a flat earth that has been created as an experiment for us to have an experience in a physical body.*

Over the years, what I think has happened is that the Freemasons found the frequencies needed to heal but used it to harm instead - and they used it against the people for their own benefit. These organisations were under the ultimate rule of the Jesuits, and they were following orders from the Phoenician overlords with their science and their religion.

These people could have caused lots of bad things to go wrong - things like mud-floods and fires so intense that nothing was left after it. The Controllers seem to set up scenarios where they beam down plasma charges upon the population, which kills us all. After that, a Great Reset is created for the next phase – and they cover all the evidence in mud.

I believe the abundance of electro-static charge was collected from the atmos-flat using antiquitech devices that can be stored in what you might think of as batteries to be used later when needed.

It seems we are helpless and cannot do anything about it, but there is a lot of blindfolding going on and that's for a reason. The reason is that they know we have a higher power and they're scared of it. Those in the know are taught to keep quiet to whatever they want to keep secret. All of this secrecy is so that these Controllers can continue having their gold toys and shiny things – and ultimate power.

I'm often reminded that all of this world is a stage, as Shakespeare mentioned, and it's much like the *Wizard of Oz*. The curtains are hiding what's really going on and many of us don't get to see it – but those who do, are beginning to pull back those curtains.

This all goes to smash the reality that has been made up for us. The narrative that has been pulled over our eyes. All this secrecy, the poisoning of us, the bad education we have received have all been done to keep us asleep and keep the truth from us. But, the good thing is, the awakening is taking a great hold and is accelerating. Whatever has happened in 2020 has lifted the hypnotism a bit. Sadly, I believe there's more to come.

These Great Resets are designed to confuse humanity. I know many people are happy to live in ignorance and be complacent to all of that but, at the end of it all, you have got to live your life and you've got to, well, die. When you die, you've got to meet your Maker. You have to think about that.

Freedom, peace, love and gratitude for Mother Earth. .

THE HOLY GRAIL OF THE GREAT RESET

APPENDIX

APPENDIX

ARE YOU AWAKENING YOUR DIVINITY?
There is a guidebook on the subject of spiritual awakening, when you start off down this road, you don't realise what you're getting yourself into. When you go down the rabbit hole, it's not a temporary thing, it's for life.

Everything in my mind is dedicated to love - I'm a sucker for it. Basically, what's happened is that I can see where I've been a bit selfish in my life and, just like most people, I have moaned about my own spiritual head effs. It is difficult, and basically, when you realise you're going through the steps towards spiritual awakening, you wonder where you go from there.

I've found there are twelve steps to awakening and, once you begin to recognise it, you begin to see the signs that you are opening up your consciousness. It's called a Krishna consciousness. It's the reality. It's the 'now' - as it is.

These signs are extraordinary, and their power is affecting more and more people throughout time. I get a lot of emails from people who are experiencing it. Just to give you a bit of guidance, here are the twelve steps, or signs, as I've experienced them.

Body aches and pains
Body aches and pains, I've had them, especially in my shoulders and in my back. It's the result of the changes that are taking place at the DNA level. The explanation for it is that the Christ seed is awakening within and, as it does, you tend to get tension in these areas.

Feelings of deep inner sadness.
You get this for no apparent reason and it has often applied to me. For a while, I kept crying for no reason, for something that wasn't even real. What went through my mind was that I was beginning to realise and understand the past - mine and others.

I'm a massive believer in reincarnation as I have memories of them. I've even brought aches and pains back from my previous lives. During one lifetime, when I was a soldier in World War One, I had my leg blown off. I brought that pain over from that time to this. I have lots of memories of that.

When you remember these past lives, you will feel sad because it's like moving from an old house to a new one. The house is a metaphor for your body. The old house has memories and emotions and you will be leaving them behind so you can fit in with your new house.

Crying for no apparent reason.
This is similar to the feelings of deep sadness. You must never forget that it's healthy to release your tears. Allowing your tears to fall is like releasing old energy and allowing the stronger energy to come through. Think of a pressure cooker when you open the valve to let out the steam. That's what it is like.

Sudden change of career.
As you change other things will change around you at the same time. This is why you should never worry about finding the perfect career from the start. It is called a transitional period and you'll have lots of changes in employment - until the one that is a good fit comes along.

I loved archaeology, basically because I was in love with an American bird. But that wasn't reason enough to get into that trade and my consciousness possibly fought against it. However, it gave me a great grounding for what I'm doing now though, so there was a benefit to it.

My other favourite job was working for the Merchant Navy. I loved it so much because I was able to travel all over the world. I arrived at the best ports you can imagine - and I was being paid for it. It was experiencing the new adventures and meeting all those different people that made it great for me.

Withdrawal from family
I don't know if you are aware of this but you are connected to your biological family through your old

karma – on a spiritual level. Your relatives are energetically connected to you through souls of different lifetimes. I'll give you an example, I used to go out with a girl who had a mother called Tessa. God love her. Tessa's granddaughter came up to her one day (6 or 7-year-old), and she said, "Nana, I was your mum in my last life." Her mother asked, "Whatever do you mean?" She didn't believe her until her granddaughter gave her details that could only have been her.

For me, that was 100% proof that reincarnation happens. When you manage to get off that karmic cycle, the bonds will be broken. When that happens, it can feel as though you're being cast away. After a while though, a new energy comes along, and you are able to form new bonds with new souls.

Unusual sleep patterns
Oh my good God, if I could only tell you what it's been like for me. It's likely that you can't sleep between 2am and 4 am and this is because there is a lot of work going on in your mind at that time. The way to deal with it is to wake up, get a breather and deal with it if you are able to. You can take my word as sanctum on this subject, as I've had fifty years of experience in these things.

Intense dreams
Dreams might include obstacle dreams like taking part in a war or a battle or you get chased in your dreams. A few months ago, I had these. They were vivid. I was being chased by someone and hid behind this big

tree, I stuck my head out and this guy shot me between the eyes with a hand crossbow and said, "Wake up!" Really weird.

When you have these types of dreams, what is happening is that you are releasing the old energy of the past that was in you, those old energies are played out as wars and battles, it's like your soul is battling to be free of them.

Physical disorientation
I've felt ungrounded and not part of the world on occasions. I have felt as though I was walking between two worlds if that makes any sense. This is something that I've discussed with a friend of mine. My friend told me to take my shoes off and stand on the grass to get a grounding. I recommend you do that, as it works.

You get this disorientation because your consciousness moves into another reality and your body is getting left behind. What I recommend you do is just spend some time in nature to feel grounded again.

Increased self-talk
I've found myself talking to myself. Time has gone by and I've suddenly realised I had been talking to myself for the past hour or so. This 'inner chatter' is something I discussed with another friend who said that, almost a decade ago, he went through a kundalini experience and, as a result, he doesn't have the chatter anymore and his mind is completely calm.

I know Eckhardt Tolle is a globalist and a capitalist but teaches the same thing. Listen to him, as he's very wise and interesting. That man's teaching will help you in your life journey. He and others explain it as though there's another level of communication inside you and you're starting to become aware of the soul level. Your self-talk will get more understandable and insightful. You're not going crazy. You're just moving into a new energy.

Feelings of loneliness
Even when I've been surrounded by people, I've felt lonely. I've also felt the need to run away. This is because when you're are walking a sacred path, it can be a lonely experience.

The loneliness does make me feel a bit anxious, and it is difficult to talk with other people about it. The explanation for why you're feeling this way is that your spirit guides have left you. Although they've been with you on your journey through life, they've left you so you can fill the empty space with your own divine connection.

Naturally, you feel the void, the emptiness when this happens. But that emptiness now has the opportunity to be filled with love and energy of your own Christ consciousness.

Loss of passion
At times I have felt unenthusiastic about projects, but this is a natural progression on the path towards being a whole person. I've started things and had no desire

to finish them. However, I've learned it is ok to not feel interested, as it's just a part of the process. When I knew that, I allowed myself to take the time to do nothing. Or, instead of doing nothing, I worked on my own mind and emotions. I've learned I am here to guide us all away from what this world has been presented to us as.

A deep longing to go home
As part of the spiritual awakening journey, this is the most difficult part. I've felt a deep yearning to go home. Don't get me wrong, it's not a suicidal feeling, I don't want to kill myself or anything like that. That wouldn't be right. It's not based on anger or frustration either.

When you stop and look back at the emotions you've experienced, it gets easier to understand them. What you've done is given yourself time to think about your karmic cycles. It's a bit like signing and completing a contract for your lifetime. When you understand this, you're ready to start a new lifetime.

Goose pimples!

ARE YOU READY?
Are you ready to move into the new energy? Do you remember home? I do. I stay here because I know that Spirit needs me on this plane to help others to move into the new energy. I'm one of those human guides who are needed to help others who are taking the journey from the old energy into the new.

When you recognise and understand these experiences and emotions, they help you become a divine teacher. Even though you might feel you are alone, you're not.

I hope you get the point of this. If it made any sense to you, let me know. We have to get many more to wake up, to realise what's going on. We need a new way of thinking.

God bless you.

WAKE UP PEOPLE!
The reason why I'm trying to wake people up as fast as I possibly can is - we haven't got a lot of time left.

I've got brothers and sisters that are doing the same thing as me and if you want to take part in the venture, and get your voice out there on YouTube, then get talking. Numbers are what we need. We need many, many people to start talking about this.

Another idea is to roll back to the time when we had 'chat raves'. The way YouTube works is that when you get thumbs-up, instead of raiding our fellow Flat Earthers, when they are live, raid their chat, thumbs them up and they get their channel up. If we did this to any content provider who held a LIVE session, then they would get more views. Everyone could co-ordinate something like that, support the Flat Earthers, get their channels up there, so they can be supported and get more views. If you think this is a good idea, then get back to me.

REFERENCES & LINKS

Each chapter has been transcribed from videos sourced from Martin's *The Celtic Tartarian Channel*. The titles of these videos have been listed in Numerical/Alpha order to encourage you to do your own research and come to your own opinions and form your own views.

You can find out more about Martin Liedtke and his work by visiting the following links:

Website http://www.flatearthbritish.info

Martin Liedtke:
https://www.youtube.com/channel/UClZhAJlC-oUFtsI6X1nUOiA

The Celtic Tartarian Channel:
https://www.youtube.com/channel/UClYM6KT4R8yMCYPCh8GwbgA

Flat Earth British Think Tank:
https://www.youtube.com/channel/UClYM6KT4R8yMCYPCh8GwbgA/videos

Patreon https://www.patreon.com/user?u=8515818

VIDEOS TRANSCRIBED:
1812! The London Blood Brick! & The Book.
https://www.youtube.com/watch?v=3H-3zFnSNhw

40.000 Tartars & Reset Signs With Strange Atmospheric Phenomena.
https://www.youtube.com/watch?v=BlF83VN3hCg

A Real Game Changer! 'Starforts' The Devils In The Details.
https://www.youtube.com/watch?v=w9x6rilpmig

Andirons! Knowledge Receivers! Phoney Art! & Incredible Church Yard Mud Floods!
https://www.youtube.com/watch?v=4tAYne1F3ic

Betwix The Devil & The Deep Blue Sea!
https://www.youtube.com/watch?v=brNSQRCeOV4

FLAT EARTH BRITISH, 1666 The Great Fire of London & Sabbatai Messiah.
https://www.youtube.com/watch?v=acrxu3IL38U

FLAT EARTH BRITISH. 5G - Fasces Resets! To Bedlam.
https://www.youtube.com/watch?v=Y53kO3dQUGA

FLAT EARTH BRITISH, Ancient Civilization, is it Recent?
https://www.youtube.com/watch?v=P8EK1sTvUgw

FLAT EARTH BRITISH. Anti/NWO Protests Ahead of G20 Hamburg, Erupt!
https://www.youtube.com/watch?v=FGKo6BU2Ebk

FLAT EARTH BRITISH. Channel Down! Odd Devices & Satirical Victorians & Radiation Experiment #1
https://www.youtube.com/watch?v=XBemzEEQF2s

FLAT EARTH BRITISH, Did Jesuits Play Both Sides In the American Civil War?
https://www.youtube.com/watch?v=a0sI3jiiczc

FLAT EARTH BRITISH, Early Mapping ,"The Theatre of Sky and Earth" (1602)
https://www.youtube.com/watch?v=laVww2dUfw0

FLAT EARTH BRITISH. Evidence of High Culture. "Hyperborean Miners"?
https://www.youtube.com/watch?v=gBwJmV3VgiM

FLAT EARTH BRITISH Flags, Boarders, Nationalism, Its all to divide US.
https://www.youtube.com/watch?v=EyaZMi0vNkE

FLAT EARTH BRITISH. Ghost Castle City - Reset Ready! https://www.youtube.com/watch?v=mKhh-Vm53SI

FLAT EARTH BRITISH. Hells Bells! Antiquidead! What If We Re-Animate?
https://www.youtube.com/watch?v=HhHP5uoier0

FLAT EARTH BRITISH. History Repeating! & The

Phonoscope Technasma!
https://www.youtube.com/watch?v=miYul3yxUXs

FLAT EARTH BRITISH Lest We Forget
https://www.youtube.com/watch?v=dHJz2flQaf8

FLAT EARTH BRITISH. Live! AntiquiTech Realities 1841 & Nottingham Castle, Caves, & Mud Flood!
https://www.youtube.com/watch?v=dA5DP0Zqom4

FLAT EARTH BRITISH. Live! Tartarian Magic! Flying Carpets! & Parabolic Mirrors!
https://www.youtube.com/watch?v=XNY0EsJ8bfE

FLAT EARTH BRITISH, Looking at Local "Cold War" Hoax Bunkers
https://www.youtube.com/watch?v=-YwuH4myAwA

FLAT EARTH BRITISH. Lost Civilizations?
https://www.youtube.com/watch?v=93J7VF3L0I8

FLAT EARTH BRITISH, Massive Anti/N.W.O. Protests in London. "Media Blackout".
https://www.youtube.com/watch?v=70FpnLy9ZK4

FLAT EARTH BRITISH, New Flat Earth Book. "The Global Deception" Has Unique A.E MAP.
https://www.youtube.com/watch?v=lzhUGtwwLFE

FLAT EARTH BRITISH, Nostradamus and the Flat Earth .Live Vlog # 17
https://www.youtube.com/watch?v=PC3s0O8E7hE

FLAT EARTH BRITISH, Paris, champs Elysees"

Terror" Attack? 19/06.2017
https://www.youtube.com/watch?v=IWYZ3s-Z28k

FLAT EARTH BRITISH. Petra The Phoenician Reset HQ!
https://www.youtube.com/watch?v=G2r2B3gPioc

FLAT EARTH BRITISH, "Piecing Together the Past"! LIVE Vlog
https://www.youtube.com/watch?v=D8-lsISJi0k

FLAT EARTH BRITISH, Ritual Magic & Changes in Consciousness
https://www.youtube.com/watch?v=dlq-WlkeJ3g

FLAT EARTH BRITISH, Sabbatai The 17th Century Anti/Christ
https://www.youtube.com/watch?v=lu61bXV5Ags

FLAT EARTH BRITISH, Satanist dates and British disasters. (Aberfan).
https://www.youtube.com/watch?v=KNbZUAv0Tkw

FLAT EARTH BRITISH So Whats The Real Age Of The Great Wall Of China?
https://www.youtube.com/watch?v=VQLQqS5gjpE

FLAT EARTH BRITISH. The "World Population" Could It Be Lower?
https://www.youtube.com/watch?v=28x5zaYZhQI

FLAT EARTH BRITISH, The 1500s Mindset "Hieronymus Bosch"

https://www.youtube.com/watch?v=QNPjMszgtas

FLAT EARTH BRITISH, The Anomalous Architecture Of St Petersburg #1
https://www.youtube.com/watch?v=YUZd5zXxlD4

FLAT EARTH BRITISH, The Anomalous Architecture Of St Petersburg # 2
https://www.youtube.com/watch?v=-vMq0b6Douo

FLAT EARTH BRITISH, The Anomalous Architecture Of St Petersburg # 3
https://www.youtube.com/watch?v=LElA1-UPlWk

FLAT EARTH BRITISH, The Censorship Of Flat Earth British ."YouTube Copyright
https://www.youtube.com/watch?v=2TbL4cbFWRU

FLAT EARTH BRITISH, "The Crystal Palace" & "The Expositions" Was It Arson?
https://www.youtube.com/watch?v=bRooWwVs-Q8

FLAT EARTH BRITISH, The Dresden War crime
https://www.youtube.com/watch?v=aVYdxaKpU1s

FLAT EARTH BRITISH, The Eradication Of The Past.
https://www.youtube.com/watch?v=NUihFrmDLeM

FLAT EARTH BRITISH. The Hidden Secrets Of The Mary Rose (Henry VIII Flag Ship).
https://www.youtube.com/watch?v=o2UmIeOB1pk

FLAT EARTH BRITISH The Missing Expositions of

the 1800s LIVE Vlog #19
https://www.youtube.com/watch?v=1QLUgKcwDxQ

FLAT EARTH BRITISH The Peter Loo Massacre Manchester 1819
https://www.youtube.com/watch?v=lD4U1nyrKTQ

FLAT EARTH BRITISH The Tale Of Three Cousins King George Part 1:
https://www.youtube.com/watch?v=F0rqYfxBGKc

FLAT EARTH BRITISH The Tale Of Three Cousins Kaiser Wilhelm Part 2:
https://www.youtube.com/watch?v=inMaztNaUMk

FLAT EARTH BRITISH The Tale Of Three Cousins Tsar Nicholas II Part 3:
https://www.youtube.com/watch?v=2YGAGdPJf30

FLAT EARTH BRITISH, The 'Tartaria Question' & Post Mud Flood Reconstruction & Off On A Comet.
https://www.youtube.com/watch?v=Io-TOq52BWk

FLAT EARTH BRITISH, The Vatican Archives. Live Vlog # 28
https://www.youtube.com/watch?v=bxFu7qs1D-Q

FLAT EARTH BRITISH, They Can Never Stop the Truth and the Truth is "ITS FLAT!"
https://www.youtube.com/watch?v=sTpLbJVcjnk

FLAT EARTH BRITISH, Was The Black Death a Hoax?

https://www.youtube.com/watch?v=TfB9y8kV2Ss

FLAT EARTH BRITISH What happened to Indus Valley Civilization?
https://www.youtube.com/watch?v=b8l8ColX0pw

FLAT EARTH BRITISH Whats The Real Age Of Photography?#6
https://www.youtube.com/watch?v=7nxwnFSCkM0

FLAT EARTH BRITISH, "Whats The Real Age Of Photography" #6 Just for Laughs!
https://www.youtube.com/watch?v=gIYF71QwFN0

FLAT EARTH BRITISH, Whats the Real Age of Photography? pt 3 Leonardo Da Vinci.
https://www.youtube.com/watch?v=IRVC--GvWFE

Flat Earth Theory - How Was It Debunked 2,000 Years Ago?
https://www.youtube.com/watch?v=313icHT2XF8

Flatterday! Splat! Antiqui'dead!
https://www.youtube.com/watch?v=-anGPcHaUI4

Holy Cow! 'The Congo' Africa. A Tar'nished Peoples From Riches To Rags.
https://www.youtube.com/watch?v=522K5DXfw7s

Making Tartaria Great Again! & The Anti-Utopia!
https://www.youtube.com/watch?v=1vbisCyKu1s

Mindblow! America! i671 (Phoenicia/Tartary) & The Horn Of Plenty!

https://www.youtube.com/watch?v=okbgw9Jx0s8

Mud Flood Mania! & Draining The Swamps.
https://www.youtube.com/watch?v=0RO04qNEda4

Phoenicia Rising! A Not So Divine Comedy.
https://www.youtube.com/watch?v=xnGt6TeLo_Y

Qiblah Walls & Starfort Clues.
https://www.youtube.com/watch?v=LrGg492OXlQ

Starfort Cartagena i667! The America's Hidden History & Who Are The Others?
https://www.youtube.com/watch?v=aLq-xJ5Qx-4

Starforts Secrets Found! Built By Phoney's, But For What?
https://www.youtube.com/watch?v=fFzx61d94K8

The Day Vancouver Exploded 'Wiped Out Of Existence' 1886.
https://www.youtube.com/watch?v=6UW8ely3do0

The Emerald Tablet & Thoth The Phoenician. Fasces Blue Prints Found?
https://www.youtube.com/watch?v=0Rzjac1DbW4

The Franco-Prussian War Cover Story 1871 Paris Reset.
https://www.youtube.com/watch?v=i4BVSDl07v0

The "Nilometer" & The Lost Canals Of Venice America.
https://www.youtube.com/watch?v=AWZZD36S970

The Phoenician Death Cult & Their Fake Moon Missions!
https://www.youtube.com/watch?v=bqVcOyS9RsI

The Phoenician Evil Entities & How It All Went Down!
https://www.youtube.com/watch?v=Io8KOmwT5rs

The Phoenician Submarines!
https://www.youtube.com/watch?v=cpgK7t3J4dY

'The Reset' Before, During & After. & Circuit Board Cities.
https://www.youtube.com/watch?v=vlKQU4hxxLA

The Sinking Of Tartaria & The Rising Of The Phoenicians From The Sea.
https://www.youtube.com/watch?v=LY2QqmbbJEw

The Twentieth Century Reset & Raising Chicago Out Of The Mud.
https://www.youtube.com/watch?v=5lCMKMVATh4

Time Bandit's & Crystal Palaces With FEB & Auto Didactic.
https://www.youtube.com/watch?v=i1qt1KS4XZk

Tuning Forks Of Healing! Or Destruction & 14th Century 'Punishment.
https://www.youtube.com/watch?v=NsBmTO98id8

With The Bacchusites Ball & Vatican Archive Releases
https://www.youtube.com/watch?v=OJknc4g7ixo

MARTIN LIEDTKE

ABOUT THE AUTHOR

Martin Liedtke is a proud Welshman who lives in Cardiff. An avid advocate for living at one with this realm, Martin, had a fascination for the way humans used to live and found himself working on a variety of archaeological digs. There, after too many questions raised their heads, he preferred not to stick with the narrative being presented and found a way to go about unearthing more of the real history of the world.

His work on YouTube demonstrates he is a persistent researcher and disciplined advocate for getting to the root cause of the issues at hand with a tenacity to get to the truth.

Martin presents some highly popular YouTube channels, which you can view on Martin's official website. There you will find thousands of images linked to this book, is on the following site:

http://www.flatearthbritish.info/

FLAT EARTH BRITISH
Crushing The Shackles of Thousands of Years of Lies

FROM THE PUBLISHER

Every effort has been made to ensure this book is quality piece of work. However, as in every industry, mistakes are made and it is for this reason we are unable to guarantee 100% accuracy. If you do come across any errors, we would appreciate if you could inform us about them directly. Please do help us to present good quality books by contributing your knowledge, email us at admin@bewleybooks.com

Thank you.

www.BewleyBooks.com

Made in the USA
Monee, IL
17 July 2021